PUBLIC POLICY MAKING
IN A FEDERAL SYSTEM

SAGE YEARBOOKS IN POLITICS AND PUBLIC POLICY
Sponsored by the
Policy Studies Organization

Series Editor:

Stuart S. Nagel, *University of Illinois, Urbana*

PUBLIC POLICY MAKING IN A FEDERAL SYSTEM

CHARLES O. JONES
and
ROBERT D. THOMAS
Editors

 **SAGE Publications**   Beverly Hills / London

Copyright © 1976 by Sage Publications, Inc.

For information address:

SAGE PUBLICATIONS, INC.
275 South Beverly Drive
Beverly Hills, California 90212

SAGE PUBLICATIONS LTD
St George's House / 44 Hatton Garden
London EC1N 8ER

Printed in the United States of America

ISBN No. 0-8039-0349-9 (cloth)
ISBN No. 0-8039-0678-1 (paper)

Library of Congress Catalog Card No. 75-42755

THIRD PRINTING

CONTENTS

SERIES EDITOR'S INTRODUCTION

This is the third volume in the series of *Yearbooks in Politics and Public Policy* published by Sage Publications in cooperation with the Policy Studies Organization. The first volume, edited by Matthew Holden, Jr., and Dennis L. Dresang, was devoted to a variety of substantive policy problems from a political science perspective. The second volume, edited by Kenneth Dolbeare, was devoted to a variety of methodological problems involved in analyzing public policy issues. This third volume, edited by Charles O. Jones and Robert D. Thomas, emphasizes the role of the federal system as a type of laboratory for applying various methodological techniques to various substantive problems.

The federal system, consisting of 50 semisovereign states and thousands of local governments with varying home rule and autonomy, has often been praised as a useful system at least from the perspective of facilitating the evaluation of alternative public policies. Under such a system, it was possible for the state of Wisconsin in the early 1900s to adopt the principle of workman's compensation to provide strict liability in the payment of damages for on-the-job injuries, and for other states and researchers to observe the effects before deciding whether to follow the Wisconsin lead. Numerous other examples can be given of legislation or judicial precedents that have been likewise incrementally adopted or rejected while policy analysis research has determined the effects of the policies using the adopting states as an experimental group and the nonadopting states as a control group. These policies have included the abolition of capital punishment, antidiscrimination legislation, gun control regulations, divorce laws, rules of evidence, and various codes relating to commercial transactions.

Policy research across states or cities often tries to account for the variation in legal rules in terms of differences between political systems while trying to control the socioeconomic variables that may be responsible for the variation. Policy research within political science has also been increasingly trying to use differences in legal rules as a causal variable rather than an effect variable. In doing so, the object is to determine how much, if any, of the variation in certain goal indicators like crime-occurrence or discrimination-reduction can be accounted for by differences in the legal rules. One special difficulty in either perspective involves the complexity of the relations between legal rules, political structures, and socioeconomic variables. That difficulty is compounded by the fact that legal rules are not randomly adopted; rather, those states which adopt new legislation may be disproportionately on one side of some important intervening variables that are difficult to control statistically with a sample of only 50 states. Nevertheless, political science researchers are developing more meaningful techniques for coping with such problems through the use of time-series analysis, causal path analysis, and a willingness to work with a large sample of cities where intrastate legal variation exists.

Although the federal system may be useful for evaluating alternative public policies, it creates numerous complications when it comes to implementing national policy on a more uniform basis. Those complications are also considered in this volume. The semisovereign nature of the 50 states, for example, often makes for intergovernmental conflict as in the regulation of the trucking industry, where the requirements of one state may be substantially greater than another. It also often makes for intergovernmental vacuums as in union-management relations, where the national government has chosen to regulate only certain industries or large firms, and many states have chosen only to regulate a portion of the remainder. In addition, the states and cities sometimes operate federal programs contrary to national regulations or even contrary to the Constitution, as in the welfare and public housing fields.

This volume deals with the problems of evaluation and implementation in a variety of subject matter areas. Those subject matter areas especially include revenue sharing, air and water pollution, and a variety of social welfare policies. Revenue sharing is an example of a governmental policy emphasizing decentralization of the federal system. It largely stems from the desire of the Nixon administration to place more power in the hands of more conservative local governments, although it may also be justifiable in terms of stimulating and utilizing local initiative and awareness. Environmental protection is an example of a governmental policy field moving toward greater centralization. That trend stems from the increased recognition that pollution readily moves across state lines, that states which are dependent on polluting industries are not so capable of regulating them, and that the public health matters at stake may be too great to be left to state and local governments given their relatively poor prior records in the field. The social welfare field seems to be moving in both directions, as indicated by an increased concern not only for more uniform national standards in welfare payments and procedures, but also by an increased concern for decentralized neighborhood schools and tenant-managed public housing.

In the continuing tradition of the Sage-PSO *Yearbooks in Politics and Public Policy*, the forthcoming fourth volume in the series will also be edited by the political scientist who was responsible for coordinating the previous year's set of public policy panels at the American Political Science Association. That fourth volume will tentatively be edited by Theodore J. Lowi, the 1976-1977 president of the Policy Studies Organization, and Alan Stone. The theme of that volume will tentatively be *Shaping Future Policy Change in America*. Like the previous volumes in the series, its contents will deal with a variety of policy problems, but its emphasis will be on the alternative possibilities for new policies in America. The papers included will stem mainly from the bicentennial APSA program which Ted Lowi is involved in coordinating. That volume and the present one should be welcome additions to the Sage Yearbooks in Politics and Public Policy.

Stuart S. Nagel
Urbana, Illinois

VOLUME EDITORS' INTRODUCTION

James Madison sounded an interesting theme in responding to the concerns of the Federalists that the Constitutional Convention had "framed a *national* government." Bearing in mind that "federal" then referred to a confederation, Madison strove to demonstrate the reasonableness of the compromise reached in Philadelphia. Writing in "The Federalist" No. 39, he argued that:

> The proposed Constitution, therefore, is, in strictness, neither a national nor a federal Constitution, but a composition of both. In its foundation it is federal, not national; in the sources from which the ordinary powers of government are drawn, it is partly federal and partly national; in the operation of these powers, it is national, not federal; in the extent of them, again, it is federal, not national; and, finally, in the authoritative mode of introducing amendments, it is neither wholly federal nor wholly national.

This new form, which we call "federal," was referred to by Hamilton or Madison as a "compound republic." Ever attentive to the importance of guarding against centralized power, Hamilton or Madison, in No. 51, found great advantages in this unique arrangement:

> In the compound republic of America, the power surrendered by the people is first divided between two distinct governments, and then the portion allotted to each subdivided among distinct and separate departments. Hence a double security arises to the rights of the people. The different governments will control each other, at the same time that each will be controlled by itself.

And so we continue to govern within the constraints set forth in this remarkable Constitution. With the growth of government in Washington, we never escape the hard realities of the compound republic. As the scholars of federalism have instructed us, national programs are seldom successfully administered solely from Washington. No amount of national-level planning can ever foresee all the state-local contingencies—just as Madison and his colleagues suspected. Thus, variable partnerships develop, with flexibility required whether or not routine-conscious bureaucrats acknowledge it.

It was with this understanding and the awareness of incredible growth in the national domestic agenda during the 1960s, that a theme was developed for the public policy panels at the 1974 annual meeting of the American Political Science Association in Chicago. Papers were invited on the general topic: "Intergovernmental Policy Development and Implementation." Three panels were organized as a result of the response to this call, one each on revenue sharing, environmental and energy policies, and social policies. The present volume contains several of the papers from these panels, plus two others which were related to the theoretical and methodological problems associated with the central topic.

We have organized the papers into four sections. The first includes two papers of a more theoretical nature. In "The Experimental Evaluation of Public Policy," Charles N. Brownstein, Lehigh University, clearly outlines "the logic of experimental design . . . the meaning of policy and impact in the context of experimentation, and . . . the utility of the method." He also lists the political, organizational, technical, and social problems in experimental policy impact research—realistically acknowledging the limits of this tool for evaluating real policies. While Brownstein is not specifically directing this paper to intergovernmental problems and policies, we had no doubt that our readers could make the adaptations necessary to profit from this most useful essay.

Carl E. Van Horn and Donald S. Van Meter, Ohio State University, contribute to our understanding of policy implementation in a federal system and to our research capacities for further analysis of this important function. "The Implementation of Intergovernmental Policy" offers a framework for sorting out the significant elements in a policy delivery system. It deserves a careful reading by students of federalism since Van Horn and Van Meter draw upon the wisdom of others who have thought about these problems as well as their own research on federal education policy.

The second section includes three papers on revenue-sharing—yet another process demonstrating the flexibility of our "compound republic." Richard P. Nathan is directing a study of revenue sharing for the Brookings Institution which began in December 1972 and is to continue over the five-year life of the legislation. We are fortunate to have a paper from Dr. Nathan which describes the problems studied and the methods employed in that project. This paper should be an invitation to read the first report of the Brookings research team entitled "Monitoring Revenue Sharing" (1975).

In the second paper, David O. Porter, University of California, Riverside, takes a very broad view of revenue-sharing in the intergovernmental system. He is particularly interested in how this mechanism might bring "local governments more fully into a system of intergovernmental administration." He proposes a conceptual scheme and offers specific strategies as aids to accomplishing this goal. Here then is a paper which sets revenue-sharing in the broader context and proposes means by which it might contribute to solving the complex problems of managing a federal system.

Sarah F. Liebschutz has served as one of the field research associates for the Brookings revenue-sharing project. In her contribution to this volume she examines revenue-sharing from the perspective of local politics, assessing the proposition that the funds "represent a political resource used in various ways by the chief elected officials." It seems that local politics is sufficiently stable to incorporate national funds into the ongoing decision-making apparatus, a finding predicted by Dr. Liebschutz (and, no doubt, by other careful students of local government) but quite at odds with the promise and expectation of some revenue-sharing rhetoric.

The third section of the book draws from the several fine papers given at the 1974 annual meeting of the American Political Science Association on environmental policy development and implementation in a federal system. Robert D. Thomas, coeditor of this volume, treats both air and water pollution policies in a paper that well illustrates the problems and dilemmas facing national administrators in their effort to achieve "national program objectives through diverse state and local processes." Madison's proposition that the Constitution "is, in strictness, neither a national nor a federal Constitution, but a composition of both," is soundly demonstrated in this paper. But there is much more. Thomas shows how it is that national, state, and local officials make the necessary adjustments for meeting the diverse policy and political needs of a federal network.

Sheldon M. Edner, Eastern Michigan University, focuses on the manner in which conflicting problem definitions affect intergovernmental relations in water pollution control. Working from a most interesting and useful conceptualization of "policy substance" and "legitimacy," Edner proposes four interactive styles, illustrating the utility of his theory with data drawn from the Arizona and California water pollution control programs.

In the third of these highly complementary papers, Bruce P. Ball, Angelo State University, San Angelo, Texas, traces the development of federal authority in water pollution control and then provides detail on local compliance activities (drawing from his study of Omaha, Nebraska). To order his analysis, Ball conceptualizes compliance as involving three interactive components: the legitimating decision itself (the law—what it means initially and how it comes to be clarified), enforcement, and public response. Taken together, these papers provide an unusually rich combination of theory and data, each highly supportive of the findings of the other. They should be welcome indeed to scholars of federalism and public policy.

While less reciprocal, the four papers in the final section individually contribute special knowledge to our understanding of this complex undertaking called the American federal system. Rufus Browning, San Francisco State University, and Dale Rogers Marshall, University of California, Davis, report on the first findings of a large-scale and highly innovative study of the social effects of implementing federal programs. The programs to be studied in the larger project are Model Cities and general revenue-sharing. While the plans for analyzing both are outlined in this paper, the findings are reported only for Model Cities. At this stage, the authors are appropriately tentative in their conclusions. Though they have found differences between Model and non-Model Cities in the responsiveness to the needs of disadvantaged groups, they are as yet uncertain as to whether these differences can be attributed to the Model Cities program.

The second paper in this section deals with the effect of a national health program on state policy formation and implementation or delivery. Christa Altenstetter, City University of New York, and James Warner Bjorkman, Yale University, have studied the impact of the child health programs included in the Social Security Act of 1935. Their conclusions are anything but satisfying: "In direct effects, federal intervention increased money supply but fewer children were served." Federal money was not without effect, however. If the children were not served, the state bureaucracy apparently was: "Program monies were spent on supplementary functions to establish and enlarge the state bureaucracy." Altenstetter and Bjorkman also provide interesting analysis of the effects of this program on the private sphere—a topic deserving of much more attention by social scientists.

The authors of the last two papers in this section tackle a topic which well deserves the increased attention it is receiving among political scientists. "Evaluation" is the new imperative for government programs. But requiring evaluation and actually accomplishing it are not at all the same. In his paper, Bruce A. Rocheleau, Northern Illinois University, offers an excursion through the dynamics of evaluation as they are evidenced in 14 mental health organizations in Florida. Relying heavily on interviews, observations, and questionnaires, the author explores how various officials react to evaluation and the effect of various organizational elements on evaluation. The results provide us with insights both about the evaluation process under varying conditions and the nature of organizational self-preservation.

It is appropriate that we close not only this section but the readings as well with "Follow Ups, Let Downs, and Sleepers: The Time Dimension in Evaluation Research," by Lester M. Salamon of Duke University. Salamon breaks fertile ground by putting in theoretical perspective when "program impacts can decrease, increase, or remain the same with the passage of time." He then examines his theoretical constructs in a case analysis evaluation of a New Deal resettlement program for black tenant farmers. Salamon's case analysis illustrates the sleeper effects of the resettlement program. He found that blacks who became land owners through the resettlement program later became more politically active, more efficacious, and better educated and achieved higher socioeconomic status. Through this case, Salamon demonstrates the complexity of program evaluation in the American federal system; however, he does not leave the policy evaluator wondering about how to deal with this complexity. He concludes his highly innovative analysis by offering policy evaluators guidelines for the appropriate time frame for conducting evaluations of different types of programs.

Here then is a sampling of the contemporary problems, policies, and processes characterizing the "compound republic of America." It is our fond hope that teachers, scholars, and students will find these papers as contributory and stimulating as we have.

Charles O. Jones
University of Pittsburgh

Robert D. Thomas
Florida Atlantic University

PART I

THEORETICAL MODELS OF
EVALUATION AND IMPLEMENTATION

1

THE EXPERIMENTAL EVALUATION
OF PUBLIC POLICY

CHARLES N. BROWNSTEIN

National Science Foundation

One area of major importance in contemporary policy research is the need for refinement in methods of determining the effects of policy decisions. Interest in the area has increased with governmental concern about the general efficacy of policy in dealing with social needs and the efficiency of particular programs of policy implementation. One indication of concern is that Congress has directed federal agencies to devote a portion of their budgets to program evaluation. An expected result is that evaluations will provide estimates for general review purposes and will serve as additions to other "rational" accounting and budgeting procedures. An immediate effect of this legislative policy has been to make funds available for evaluation research (Roos, 1972: 281). Moreover, research organizations in government have begun substantial programs of research into areas of national policy concern. A focal point of this research interest has developed in the Research Applied to National Needs (RANN) division of the National Science Foundation.[1]

Social scientists with an orientation toward applied research have long been interested in evaluation. A "traditional" topic of evaluative

AUTHOR'S NOTE: *This essay is a revised version of a paper delivered at the annual meeting of the American Political Science Association, Chicago, Illinois, September 1974.*

research was the analysis of innovations in the delivery of education and social services; much of the early literature reflects the fairly narrow interests of researchers in these fields. More recently, however, there has been an expansion of concern about evaluative research in "social action" programs in general and ameliorative programs in particular.[2]

Although purely academic interest (or "disciplinary" research) in policy impact research varies widely in scope, and despite the broad parameters of most policy questions, many evaluators are interested only in those impacts which fit into the traditional molds of their fields. As a result, impact research has taken on a generally interdisciplinary patina as teams of individuals, with both strong personal perspectives and an appreciation of the need for the contribution of other areas of expertise, have joined in searching for policy solutions to social problems. Others have expressed interest from the general perspective of discovering the relationships between governmental action and the state of social and environmental conditions.[3]

As a result of the atomization of "disciplinary" interest in evaluative research and the problem of bridging the gap between the needs and desires of "applied" and "basic" researchers, a systematic body of methods has been slow to develop for policy impact research (Coleman, 1972). It appears, however, that experimental design techniques and procedures, modified to deal with the realities of field research settings, can provide a vehicle for assessing policy impacts. Today there is a growing body of literature on methods for policy impact research in general. There is also some debate, of widely varying quality, about the applicability of experimental designs to policy impact analyses.[4]

The purpose of this paper is to review the logic and research requirements of experimental policy impact analyses, particularly as they differ from other policy analysis strategies in political research. An inventory of priority problems in the utilization of experimental techniques in policy impact research is also presented.

THE PURPOSE OF
EXPERIMENTAL EVALUATION RESEARCH

According to Boruch (1973), "the major function of a controlled randomized experiment is to obtain data in a way which is conducive to making a judgement about the efficacy of a treatment program." Nevertheless, the general notion of "experimentation" has both common language and highly technical meanings, and both are relevant to understanding and using policy experimentation. In common usage, "experiment" implies a temporary or trial activity, undertaken in order to gain experience, which in turn is used to decide if the activity is worthy of continuation. This aspect of experimentation figures strongly in policy experimentation. Experiments are conducted to test policy prototypes for the purpose of generating information to assist policy makers in their deliberations or to explore the effects of the introduction of innovation into existing policy programs. When used for decision-making purposes, the information competes with all of the other factors which enter policy deliberations and contributes to the determination of policy "outputs."[5] Also in the context of common language, "experimentation" implies the interruption of the normal mode of doing things or the intrusion into a "natural" process of some manipulated event or "experimental treatment." Policy or program alternatives being tested for their effect in a policy experiment are very much an interruption and an alteration in the existing course of action. They are presumed to have consequences for the "normal" flow of events.

There are also multiple meanings for the term "experiment" in the technical language of research design.[6] In a broad sense, "experiment" suggests the process of analyzing the effects of a causal factor in an interrelated system of variables. For example, the analysis of sudden discontinuities in time series data, attributable to a given causal factor with other factors held constant or accounted for, is often conceived of as a type of experimental analysis, a quasi-experiment. Such analyses have proven useful for descriptive and exploratory policy impact research probes. They have also been useful when research situations do not lend themselves to actual experimentation[7] or when only historical data are available. There are, however, limits to the usefulness of quasi-experimental designs. In particular, the "force fit" of data, ex post facto, into quasi-experimental designs is hazardous. The mistaken impressions which common statistical procedures can lead to have occasioned cautionary warnings even by former proponents of quasi-experimental research. Donald Campbell (1972: 25), for one, has recommended that, "the methodological community rule out all ex post facto studies (or policy impact), that is, studies lacking either a pretest similar in factorial structure to the post test or random assignments to treatments."

The reason for Campbell's rejection of ex post facto research designs relates directly to strict definitions of experimentation. There are a large number of strict definitions available, but the common feature among them is that experiments are observational arrangements which permit the determination of causality, uninterrupted by either the system of observation or by extraneous biasing factors.[8] The conditions for concise specifications of certain effects, and the effective elimination of others, can be achieved in many ways. It is thus appropriate to think of experimentation as a combination of research design properties, research procedures, and data analysis strategies.

PUBLIC POLICY IN IMPACT EXPERIMENTATION

One of the key elements of experimental design is the concise specification of the causal factors (independent variables) of primary interest to the researchers prior to the experiment. In the context of policy experimentation such factors are the policy alternatives whose effects are to be explored. As a result, a precondition for impact research is the definition of "policy."

Public policy is often broadly conceived. "American foreign policy" and "the administration's policy on the Watergate cover-up," are typical examples of commonly used expressions of general courses of governmental action. However, for experimental analysis, more exact definition is required for two reasons. First, policy is the thing that the policy maker can manipulate. To the extent that the impact research is undertaken for the purpose of assisting decision makers, the policy variable must be defined in terms which correspond with the exact alternative courses of action for achieving policy goals which are potentially possible in the policy maker's world. Equally as important, if the intent of the researcher is to develop or test theory about the effect of government action upon societal conditions (or any other substantive aspect of the impact process which interests him), careful distinctions are required about precisely which aspects of policy produce what effects. For this reason, policy must be defined in terms of content and include all related factors which may influence impacts.

The need to carefully define policy content has caused occasional confusion among those concerned with the "disciplinary" uses of policy impact research. If the aim of the research is to make theoretical statements, such as if X is done in situation Y, Z will occur, then failure to specify X in a way that it can be distinguished from any variation of X goes against the rules of scientific procedure. As a result, the content of policy, in terms of legislative or statutory rules of action and in terms of the actual activities of policy implementation, must be specified. This is a potential problem in evaluation studies, even those which concentrate upon the effects of modifications in ongoing program activities. In some cases it is easy to make distinctions between experimental treatment variations: for example, in terms of who receives a specified amount of some good, such as hours of counseling, amount of money payment, or even rate of taxation. However, not all policy alternatives are definable in the discrete terms of the "amount" of something which government provides. Some policies create qualitative distinctions by their course of action. For example, "open public meetings" or "public access to records" are certainly policy alternatives to secret legislative sessions or the use of "private" or "secret" classifications for documents. In these situations policy experimentation will be made more difficult, but so long as the different policies can be identified and the treatments given operational integrity, experimentation will be possible.

The same situation exists for the specification of impacts (measures of dependent variables). In policy experimentation, the primary dependent variables generally correspond to the conditions which the policy is intended to change: they are closely related to the goals of policy. The determination of policy goals may be a complex problem, but some degree of specification is needed in order to focus observations upon the impacts or policy consequences.

The requirements of goal specification vary according to the research design, expectations about impacts, and the assumptions which are made. It will be an absolute necessity in situations where before-after measurements are taken, for it is from goals that determinations are made about what to measure. In most cases, criteria of policy efficacy will involve the degree to which goals are accomplished by the specific course of action which constitutes the policy.

However, not all policy is made with narrow or easily measurable goals which can be translated into criterion measures. Some policy is simply directed broadly at ameliorating a pressing or obvious problem. In such cases experimentation will be difficult or even inappropriate. If the researcher or policy maker cannot define even the expected results of policy, there is some doubt about whether it can be evaluated in any scientific fashion, let alone by using the precise logic of experimental design techniques. Such policies are quite unlikely to become candidates for evaluation in any case. Still, the problem of operationalizing criterion measures of impacts should not be confused with the inability to specify policy goals or the expected effects of policy. It may be the case that impact measures are easily quantifiable things: dollars spent, time on the job, parts per million of air pollutants, levels of participation. Or qualitative measures may be used: "policy target group preferred treatment A to B"; "quality of existence appeared to change." How to measure and what to measure deserve a proper degree of analytical distinction.[9] It is fair to say that policy which has no specifiable goal is not amenable to policy impact experimentation; to the degree that goals are unspecific or broad rather than discretely identifiable, the task of the researcher will be complicated, but hardly precluded.

Useful distinctions in impact experiments can be made according to the level of government in which the policy under study is made. Broad constitutional powers defined for legislatures have given them responsibility for the general shaping of policy direction, while the execution of policy depends upon activities in regulatory agencies, "action" agencies in the bureaucracy, and the field offices where programs are implemented. There is thus a "level of analysis" component to policy impact research. As far as this researcher knows, most policy experimentation has taken place at the action agency level. It has consisted of testing alternative means (programs) for their efficacy in reaching the agreed-upon goals of a given broad policy. These policy alternatives are actually program variations or versions of a generalized policy goal relating to the solution to a problem. For example, various treatment strategies using community based delinquency programs are compared to traditional institutional methods in their effect on recidivism. Or, military and collegiate training atmospheres in a police academy are contrasted in terms of their impact on subsequent police performance.[10] The general policy goals of reducing recidivism and improving police performance are probably expressed in the budgetary decisions at the national and state levels as well as at the local agency level of government. Policy alternatives are also considered at the "higher" (above local agency) levels of government. Experimentation can be conducted from these levels as well. Examples include the currently operating experiments on income maintenance which are supported by HEW and OEO but are conducted by external research organizations.[11]

Some types of policy impact experimentation have no particular agency as client and no legislatively predetermined program variations at the initiation of the experiment. For example, NSF is currently supporting field experiments to test the feasibility and utility of two-way cable television technology for delivering medical and social services. The very borad policy questions (such as "should the FCC require two-way capability or how should its use be regulated") cannot be answered directly because the possible impacts of the policy on society are unknown. One purpose of the research is to generate basic knowlege about the effects of the new communication technology. The experiment is to produce evidence for regulatory-policy decision making as well, but only indirectly.

The key point here is that although policy experimentation has tended in the past to be limited to the evaluation of social action programs at the agency level, it appears that its use can be extended to other levels of policy deliberation. As a practical matter, no matter what the level of government involved, several preconditions are necessary in order to justify experimentation. From his review of experiments which have been conducted, Boruch (1973: 60-61) has determined that there must be: "acknowledgement of the arguability of existing solutions to a problem," a problem serious enough "to warrant the investment(s)" demanded by experimentation, and "a capacity to resolve a complex of problems that can be anticipated prior to the experiment."

THE LOGIC OF EXPERIMENTAL POLICY RESEARCH

Although every policy research endeavor has idiosyncratic needs, certain common features exist in terms of approaches to data collection and the logic of data analysis. In this section the general approach of experimental policy evaluation is described. Data collection and analysis approaches common in nonexperimental social research and program evaluation in government are contrasted with the experimental approach.

The basic logic of experimental impact research is generally some variant of an input-output approach. The input-output approach views public policy as a goal-directed interruption by government upon the existing environment. Policy in this view is an interference in the ongoing sequence of events and pattern of relationships which identify a process in any particular policy area. In contrast with the study of policy outputs (i.e., the determination of the causal factors leading to a policy promulgation), where variations in policy variables are conceived as dependent variables, policy variations are viewed as independent variables, and their effects are the dependent variables. The distinction is basic, and it necessitates analytical, philosophical, and methodological departures from more familiar policy research endeavors.

One departure, of special relevance for political scientists, is the analytical direction of impact research. As external observers of "real world" political events, political researchers have generally conducted "naturalistic" studies. Nature has been taken "as it came" and researchers have done their best to untangle its complexities. Compared to this unsystematic activity of "merely observing," the systematic scientific procedures of naturalistic social science have yielded substantial knowledge and theory about worldly political events. The analytic approach has traditionally been to take a single dependent variable and search among plausible alternative independent variables for likely (most likely) causes, competing causes having been selected by theory, intuition, prior knowledge, or in some instances, the degree of observed statistical relationship. In policy impact research, the problem is somewhat different. Policy is presumed to be a cause, and the purpose of the research is to determine its efficacy among other (nonpolicy) causes. In turn, the determination of policy efficacy is made by demonstrating that policy is related to changes or variations in environmental variables. To this end it might seem as though the appropriate analytic outlook might be merely to reorient data collection procedures to pick out the relevant prepolicy environmental conditions, document the presence of policy in action, remeasure the environment, and compare prepolicy and postpolicy measures to determine policy impacts. However, in naturalistic data, severe interpretive problems may be caused by the immeasurable biases which result from the fact that units are self-selected to treatments. Statistical control techniques and ex-post-facto matching procedures may lead to incorrect interpretations of data. At the least, the results are open to severe differences of interpretation.[12] Equivocal data are not of great use to decision makers. The alternative to ex post facto research is prepolicy research activity. This suggests an approach in which the researcher is more of an active participant in the event under study than is normally the case in social science research. In turn, this raises questions about the conduct of policy impact research.

Addressing the question of the conduct of policy research, James Coleman (1972) has suggested that policy research is different from disciplinary research in that it cannot be exclusively oriented toward a theory. Policy research, he states, focuses upon problems which originate "outside the discipline, in the world of action," and the results of policy research are destined "for the world of action, outside the discipline" (Coleman, 1972: 3). In defining policy research, of course, Coleman suggested that its primary purpose is to assist in the making of decisions rather than (only) the construction and testing of theory. One might argue, according to one's values, that the advancement of scientific knowledge is more "relevant" or less "relevant" than improving policy making. Although I see clear distinctions in the intentional differences between applied and pure research and appreciate the differing needs of the two types of research, I have not found any convincing arguments that the logical necessities of well-conducted research differ in kind where the quality of the final product is concerned. But what of the world of applied evaluation research?

According to Light (1973), three "techniques" currently dominate the evaluation of policy programs in the field: the use of anecdotal evidence, managerial records, and the sample survey. The use of impressionistic information by program operators, clients, and external observers is a very common evaluation technique. It is informal, easy to accomplish, and monetarily inexpensive to undertake. Its principal shortcoming is that it is generally unsystematic and likely to produce equivocal results. Personal views are typically idiosyncratic and subject to biases which are not relevant to the effects of policy variables. As a result, the information must be considered equivocal even when it is in fact accurate. As such, it is too uncertain a basis for decision making except when an obvious disaster has consensual identification. Unfortunately, even then, unsystematically gathered impressions are seldom satisfactory in suggesting specific ways to alter policy. Moreover, decision makers who rely on unsystematic impressions have considerable freedom to rely on their own impressions (which, since they are responsible in the final instance, they must do at some point) and may prefer less and more equivocal, rather than more and less equivocal, information. As Campbell (1967) has cautioned, this is particularly true of "trapped" administrators in situations where there is political vulnerability from knowing outcomes.

Since experimentation requires substantial probing into program activities, a considerable change in organizational values away from internalization and from the guarding of bureaucratic integrity is required of program administrators. This can be accomplished in a variety of ways. The most global mechanism for change to facilitate experimental evaluation might be to establish an ethic, among officials and society in general, which promotes the notion that policy offers instrumental benefits to society and that it is in the public interest for it to be both efficacious and open to scrutiny.[13] Less idealistically, and more realistically, policy evaluation might be routinized, so that the results are not used for absolute judgments of worth, but are used to continually reshape policies to better accomplish their goals. In this way, the desirability of continuous systematic feedback-gathering procedures can be made to replace or add to the collection of impressionistic evidence.

Managerial records, which are often legally required for administrative purposes, constitute another type of evaluative data. Light (1973) indicates that these records are normally used for monitoring administrative performance rather than program performance. Since administrative performance may be itself a primary determinant of program performance, such records should be conceived as part of the overall evaluation mechanism and be routinely operationalized as an independent variable.

Sample surveys, gathering both impressions and objective measures of policy performance, are the third typically used evaluation technique. Even sophisticated longitudinal survey designs suffer from the serious limitation that "they must accept a population of persons (or experimental units) assigned to different program versions, 'as is' " (Light, 1973: 57). Thus the problem of sample self-selection arises constantly and results cannot be generalized to larger populations. Equally as important, the bias in impact measures resulting from differential recruitment of comparison groups cannot be determined (Campbell and Earlbacher, 1970). The result is that bias may be systematically present in impact measures. Thus, at a minimum, the results of surveys are often equivocal or, worse, misleading. This is not to imply that surveys are inappropriate or necessarily defective means of assessing impacts. They are, however, clearly second best to experiments. The ideal situation is that the technical requirements for sound evaluation be included as part of the policy implementation plan.

In order to undertake research which can produce unequivocal results, a change in policy toward public policy analysis is required of decision makers. They must come to view policy not necessarily as the solution to pressing demands, but as a step toward the solution, requiring continual tinkering and readjustment. Moreover, it may be necessary to reconsider goals according to changing social conditions apart from those caused by policy and in light of actual positive or negative policy impacts.

Equally as important, policy makers must become convinced that evaluation is useful. This can only happen with experience. Evaluation must be made useful to policy makers. Research, thus, must seek answers to policy makers' questions and be presented in normal language and understandable terms. Thus, questions about whether a program is working and meeting its goals and what it is costing must remain primary questions for policy makers; but an understanding of why it is or is not working, and what can be done to make it work, must serve as the basis for the answers which analysts give to decision makers.

APPROACHES TO ANALYSIS

A key analytical distinction between experimental and correlational analysis procedures for impact research is in the statistical model employed. Political scientists, in particular, typically analyze a single event or outcome (the dependent variable) in terms of a search for plausible causes of the event (independent variables). Thus, for example, variation in policy output (expenditure) is examined in terms of many possible causes suggested by theory, plausibility, and the degree of statistical covariation. Competing causes are subjected to scrutiny to remove (by statistical control) spurious or substantively inconsequential sources of variation. The analysis procedure is to consider competing causes for an observed (measured) event. This procedure is well established in terms of multivariate regression and related causal modeling techniques. Some have suggested that problems of multicoliniarity and incomplete model specification may render the results of such research equivocal at best and misleading at worst. However, the "normal" operating condition of social researchers is that they depend upon correlational data. Social researchers traditionally have been unwilling or unable to physically manipulate independent variables or to assign units of analysis (or respondents) to conditions. This has made the logic of correlation seem to be the only possible approach to the determination of causality.

In policy experimentation, however, the researcher begins with an independent variable, the policy, in the form of conditions created by a program or set of program alternatives, and then attempts to discover both what is affected and how much pre-specified dependent variables, selected because of their probable relation to the policy goals, are affected. The policy or program alternatives are the causal factors of primary interest, and they can be created and manipulated by the researcher. Untangling their impact from the other possible causal variables over which policy makers, program managers, and the analyst have no control is accomplished by the techniques of experimental design. Post hoc adjustments, by statistical analysis techniques similar to those used in nonexperimental research, are available for additional elaboration of experimental data.

The difference is basic, for despite not being able to exhaust in the preexperimental treatment phase of the design effects which can occur, attention is focused in the direction where they do occur, so that there is a greater opportunity to notice unanticipated impacts. Moreover, the intention of the research is to discover the efficacy of the policy-relevant variables—the program or policy implementation activities which are subject to alteration by the policy decision maker or program manager. The resulting information permits the decision maker to decide that, given a set of social conditions, a policy or program is or is not the most effective way to accomplish policy goals.

The stress is thus upon the impact; the question is the efficacy of the cause under direct control given other conditions. Moreover, to the extent that the other conditions are described, there is a specification of the necessary noncontrollable conditions in which policy can be expected to operate effectively. Clearly, this type of information is more useful for policy makers than results which focus upon global environmental causes. Policy makers are unable to influence background or extraneous variables, but are able to influence policy and program operations.

Theoreticians will welcome this sort of information as well, for only by an assessment of both manipulable and unmanipulable independent variables, in a setting which permits the unequivocal assignment of variation in dependent variables to both sets of causal factors, can the unique impact of the workings of government upon social conditions be assessed. The reworking of the orientation of theorists from that of passive external monitor to that of active participant and manipulator of causal factors, represents perhaps the most substantial philosophical shift for traditionally trained social researchers.

Another important intellectual divergence which arises for political scientists is that of seeking information beyond the traditionally recognizable bounds of political institutions. For those who have come to interpret social and environmental conditions as the consequences of politics, or have attempted to understand the process of political behavior in terms of institutional reactions to the larger social or physical environment, the shift will be very easy to make. It will involve an appreciation of the intellectual contributions and research foci of other fields, especially economics, sociology, and social psychology and the physical sciences as well (for example, where physical conditions such as air pollution or energy are involved).

To participate in and contribute to policy impact research, political scientists will have to venture beyond the comfortable confines of familiar models of the political and policy process. The "systems" model of David Easton (1965), with its inputs of demands and supports, its conversion processes, and resulting outputs of authoritative decisions, has served for many years as an organizing framework for policy research. Every aspect of it, except for the post-output, "feedback" loops which presumably lead to modifications of inputs, has been elaborated in policy research. The experimental analysis of policy impact is a self-conscious attempt to expand the range of knowledge into this area of the model. Whether the stress of political research is upon the impacts of policy which are directly consequential to political phenomena or upon the relationship of political activity to society in general, the goal of analysis should be to produce the surest possible conclusions.

CURRENT CONSTRAINTS TO THE USE OF EXPERIMENTATION:
PRIORITY TOPICS FOR METHODOLOGICAL RESEARCH
IN POLICY IMPACT ANALYSES

The purpose of this brief paper was to outline the logic of experimental design, to explore the meaning of policy and impact in the context of experimentation, and to suggest the utility of the method. Any such review would be remiss in avoiding the considerable difficulty encountered in transforming the logic of the experimental approach into implementable, useful, and valid research. Indeed, one of the most persistent topics encountered in the literature is the problem of implementing experimental research designs. It is fair to say that until very recently, more research into the specification of problems than their resolution has been published. It seems to me that this research ought to be regarded as an inventory of research tasks for those interested in producing solutions, rather than a litany of reasons for prematurely giving up on what is generally recognized to be the ideal approach to impact research. Four broad and occasionally overlapping categories of difficulties dominate the policy impact literature. They are political, organizational, technical, and social in nature.

The political problems in experimental impact research derive from the political nature of all public policy choices. Policy making involves the aggregation of competing notions of social values; it is imbedded in ongoing social and political contexts. Among the problems are:

—the time constraints on decision makers to take some (any) sort of action;

—the ramifications of knowing the outcomes of impact research;[14]

—competing notions of what a policy should attempt to maximize, who should benefit, who should bear the costs of policy;

—the question of defining benefits and computing ratios of benefit to cost;

—the difficulty of separating economic from social criteria of policy benefits;[15]

—the problem of getting agreement that answers for dealing with policy problems do not exist;

—the need for prior (prepolicy implementation research and planning) research as opposed to "catch up" review to generate the answers to policy questions;

—the lack of ways to use partial information and to continually readjust policies to maximize the chance for goal attainment;

—the conflict between using resources for research and using resources for policy purposes;

—the nature of the budgetary system and its limits as compared to the budgetary requirements of competent evaluation research.[16]

Organizational problems in impact research generally stem from the requirements and conditions of intrusive field research. Included are:

—fitting designs to feasible courses of action;

—solving role conflicts between evaluators, program personnel, and decision makers (who are the clients of research and may be the topic of study);[17]

—removing threats or the perception of threat to individual competence among diverse personnel involved in the research task;

—generating and maintaining cohesion among scientific researchers with varying backgrounds and interests;

—maintaining the research activity over the lengthy period of time necessary to initiate and conduct the research;

—finding ways not to disrupt the research setting (particularly where ongoing organizations are involved).[18]

Methodological problems have mainly to do with measurement and control in experimental policy research. These problems include:

—determining impact criteria and ways to measure them;[19]

—defining and making operational the policy alternatives;

—establishing and maintaining the integrity of treatments;[20]

—specifying and maintaining experimental samples; accomplishing randomization;[21]

—developing models which are capable of handling multiple treatments (each with multiple levels), multiple impacts, and multiple controls;[22]

—dealing with the intrusion of external events including changing policy goals;

—selecting "representative" sites for experimentation and maximizing replication opportunities via multiple experiments;

—developing and learning to use complex multistage designs which produce partial results as they work toward final conclusions;

—producing or aggregating theory for future experimentation;[23]

—maintaining the verisimilitude needed to generalize from the experiment to other situations.

Social constraints to experimentation have to do with morality, ethics, values, and patterns of human interaction. Major problems in this area include:

—deciding who should benefit, or not benefit, by inclusion in an experiment;

—getting the cooperation of subjects without biasing their "performance" in the experiment;

—maintaining the privacy of data collected from individuals;[24]

—fitting experiments into the social milieu.

CONCLUSIONS

The principal reason for applying experimental design techniques to the study of public policy is to produce the least equivocal information about the impact or effect of the policy on the policy target. Public policy, in its many forms, is assumed to be goal directed activity by government explicitly designed to effect the modification of social or physical conditions. Experimental policy research is undertaken to evaluate policy according to various criteria which someone finds relevant.

In a normative sense, the determination of the effects of public policy is a pressing but complex problem. Legislative policy makers presumably could use information about policy impacts to determine the extent to which their actions are consequential to society. The executors of policy, especially those charged with the daily operation of policy programs, might use the information about impacts to increase the efficacy and efficiency of their activities in implementing policy and attaining performance levels consistent with policy goals. Society, and in particular the immediate beneficiaries of policy, should welcome information which reviews the progress of policy in meeting policy goals. The polity, to play a rational part in the selection of policy makers, should welcome impact information for reviewing governmental performance. And last, but not least of all, social scientists ought to regard impact data as useful for formulating and testing theory, especially that which relates government action to social and political process in the general social environment.

NOTES

1. An elaboration of recent RANN concerns and a useful statement of the logic underlying the RANN program is found in Holmes (1971).

2. See Caro (1971), Fairweather (1967), Suchman (1967), Weiss (1972), and Rossi and Williams (1972) for both a general introduction and discussions of specific issues in evaluative research.

3. Both substantive examples and philosophical discussions of this perspective are in Campbell (1969, 1972).

4. The contending ideas are well illustrated in Weiss and Rein (1970) and Campbell (1970).

5. "Outputs" and "impacts" are distinguished in Scioli (1972).

6. Cattell (1966) provides an elaboration of various dimensions of experimental design.

7. For a review of the logic of quasi-experimental design and examples of applications see Caporaso and Roos (1973).

8. Campbell and Stanley (1966) and Meehl (1970) provide excellent discussions of this logic.

9. The difficulties of defining and measuring impact criteria are of course not limited to experimental studies. For relevant discussions of the problem see Ackoff (1962: Chapter 6) and Bauer (1966).

10. These examples are taken from abstracts of over 40 experimental program evaluations compiled by Boruch and Davis (1973).

11. An example is reviewed in Watts (1971).

12. A lively debate on these issues is presented in Hellmuth (1970: 185-220).

13. Campbell (1972) discusses this issue at length.

14. See Campbell (1969: 429).

15. See Wildavsky (1968).

16. Light (1973) and Lewis and Zarb (1974) discuss this problem.

17. This problem is of sufficient scope to be treated in detail by many evaluation specialists. See especially Aronson and Sherwood (1972), Suchman (1972), Wholey (1972), Rodman and Kolodny (1972).

18. See, for example, Mann (1972).

19. This is discussed by Campbell (1972), Suchman (1972), Hyman and Wright (1972), Horst, Nay, and Scanlon (1974).

20. See especially Hyman and Wright (1972).

21. In particular see Campbell (1972: 16-19) and Conlisk and Watts (1969).

22. See, for example, Scioli and Cook (1973).

23. This problem is considered by Wilson (1974) and Portland (1974).

24. See Boruch (1972, 1972) and Westin (1967).

REFERENCES

ACKOFF, R. L. (1962). Scientific Method: Optimizing Applied Research Decisions. New York: John Wiley.

ARONSON, S. H., and SHERWOOD, C. C. (1972). "Researcher versus practitioner: problems in social action research." Pp. 282-293 in C. H. Weiss (ed.), Evaluating Action Programs: Readings in Social Action and Education. Boston: Allyn and Bacon.

BAUER, R. M. (1966). Social Indicators. Cambridge, Mass.: MIT Press.

BLALOCK, H. M., Jr. (1970). An Introduction to Social Research. Englewood Cliffs, N.J.: Prentice-Hall.

BORUCH, R. F. (1971). "Maintaining confidentiality in educational research: a systematic analysis." American Psychologist, 26: 412-420.

--- (1972). "Strategies for eliciting and merging confidential social science research data." Policy Science, 3: 275-297.

--- (1973). "Problems in research utilization: use of social experiments, experimental results and auxiliary data in experiments." Annals of the New York Academy of Sciences 218: 56-77.

BORUCH, R. F., and DAVIS, S. (1973). Abstracts of Controlled Experiments for Planning and Evaluating Social Programs. Unpublished manuscript, Department of Psychology, Northwestern University.

CAMPBELL, D. T. (1969). "Reforms as experiments." American Psychologist, 24(April): 409-429.

––– (1970). "Considering the case against experimental evaluations of social innovations." Administrative Science Quarterly, 15: 110-113.

––– (1972). Methods for the Experimenting Society. Unpublished manuscript, Department of Psychology, Northwestern University.

CAMPBELL, D. T., and EARLBACKER, A. (1970). "How regression artifacts in quasi-experimental evaluations can mistakenly make compensatory education look harmful." Pp. 185-210 in J. Hellmoth (ed.), Compensatory Education: A National Debate (vol. 3 of The Disadvantaged Child). New York: Brunner, Mazel.

CAMPBELL, D. T., and STANLEY, J. C. (1966). Experimental and Quasi-Experimental Designs for Research. Chicago: Rand McNally.

CAPORASO, J. A., and ROOS, L. L. (eds., 1973). Quasi-Experimental Approaches: Testing Theory and Evaluating Policy. Evanston, Ill.: Northwestern University Press.

CARO, F. G. (ed., 1971). Readings on Evaluation Research. New York: Russell Sage Foundation.

CATTELL, R. B. (1966). "The principles of experimental design and analysis in relation to theory building." Pp. 19-66 in R. B. Cattell (ed.), Handbook of Multivariate Experimental Psychology. Chicago: Rand McNally.

COLEMAN, J. S. (1972). Policy Research in the Social Sciences. Morristown, N.J.: General Learning Press.

CONLISK, J., and WATTS, H. (1969). "A model for optimizing experimental designs for estimating response surfaces." Social Statistics Section. American Statistical Association Proceedings.

EASTON, D. (1965). A Framework for Political Analysis. Englewood Cliffs, N.J.: Prentice-Hall.

FAIRWEATHER, G. (1967). Methods for Experimental Social Innovation. New York: John Wiley.

HARRIS, C. W. (ed., 1963). Problems in Measuring Change. Madison: University of Wisconsin Press.

HELLMOTH, J. (ed., 1970). Compensatory Education: A National Debate (vol. 3 of The Disadvantaged Child). New York: Brunner, Mazel.

HOLMES, J. (ed., 1974). Energy, Environment, Productivity––Proceedings of the First Symposium on RANN: Research Applied to National Needs. Washington, D.C.: U.S. Government Printing Office.

HORST, P.; NAY, J. N.; SCANLON, J.; and WHOLEY, J. (1974). "Program management and the federal evaluator." Public Administration Review, 34(July/August): 300-308.

LEWIS, F. L., and ZARB, F. (1974). "Federal program evaluation from the O.M.B. perspective." Public Administration Review, 34(July/August): 315-317.

LIGHT, R. J. (1973). "Experimental design issues in the evaluation of large scale social programs." Experimental Study of Politics, 2: 53-75.

MANN, J. (1971). "Technical and social difficulties in the conduct of evaluation research." Pp. 175-184 in F. G. Caro (ed.), Readings on Evaluation Research. New York: Russell Sage Foundation.

MEEHL, R. E. (1970). "Nuisance variables and the ex post facto design." Pp. 373-401 in M. Radnor and S. Winokur (eds.), Analysis of Theories and Methods of Physics and Psychology (vol. 4 of the Minnesota Studies in the Philosophy of Science). Minneapolis: University of Minnesota Press.

PORTLAND, O. F. (1974). "Program evaluations and administrative theory." Public Administration Review, 34(July/August): 333-338.

RODMAN, H., and KOLODNY, R. (1971). "Organizational strains in the researcher-practitioner relationship." Pp. 117-135 in F. G. Caro (ed.), Readings on Evaluation Research. New York: Russell Sage Foundation.

ROOS, N. P. (1973). "Evaluation, quasi-experimentation, and public policy." Pp. 281-304 in J. A. Capraso and L. L. Roos, Jr. (eds.), Quasi-Experimental Approaches: Testing Theory and Evaluating Policy. Evanston, Ill.: Northwestern University Press.

ROSSI, P. H., and WILLIAMS, W. (eds., 1972). Evaluating Social Programs. New York: Seminar Press.

SCIOLI, F. P., Jr. (1972). "Policy impact research in political science." Paper delivered at the Midwest Political Science Association meeting, Chicago, Illinois.

SCIOLI, F. P., Jr. and COOK, T. J. (1973). "Experimental design in policy impact analysis." Social Science Quarterly, 55(September): 271-281.

SUCHMAN, E. A. (1967). Evaluative Research: Principles and Practice in Public Service and Social Action Programs. New York: Russell Sage Foundation.

――― (1972). "Action for What?" In C. H. Weiss (ed.), Evaluating Action Programs: Readings in Social Action and Education. Boston: Allyn and Bacon.

WEISS, C. H. (ed., 1972). Evaluating Action Programs: Readings in Social Action and Education. Boston: Allyn and Bacon.

――― (1973). "Where politics and evaluation research meet." Evaluation, 1: 37-45.

WEISS, R. S., and REIN, M. (1970). "The evaluation of broad-aim programs: experimental design, its difficulties, and an alternative." Administrative Science Quarterly, 15: 97-109.

WESTIN, A. F. (1967). Privacy and Freedom. New York: Atheneum.

WHOLEY, J. S.; DUFFY, H. G.; FUKUMOTO, J. S.; SCANLON, J. W.; BERLIN, M. A.; COPELAND, W. C.; and ZELINSKY, J. G. (1972). "Proper organizational relationships." Pp. 119-122 in C. H. Weiss (ed.), Evaluating Action Programs: Readings in Social Action and Education. Boston: Allyn and Bacon.

WILDAVSKY, A. (1968). "The political economy of efficiency." Pp. 55-82 in A. Ranney (ed.), Political Science and Public Policy. Chicago: Markham.

WILSON, J. Q. (1974). "Crime and the criminologists." Commentary, 58(July): 47-53.

2

THE IMPLEMENTATION OF
INTERGOVERNMENTAL POLICY

CARL E. VAN HORN
DONALD S. VAN METER

The Ohio State University

The 1970s have been marked by a revival of the study of intergovernmental relations in the United States. Recent policy developments in the areas of manpower, transportation, housing, and environmental pollution—and, of course, the advent of general revenue sharing—have encouraged social scientists to turn their attention to the character of contemporary federalism. In particular, scholars have focused on grants-in-aid programs and the intergovernmental policy delivery system that the national government has relied upon to achieve many of the broad social policies that emerged in the 1960s and continue in the 1970s.

The principal foci of the existing literature have been on the formulation of policy at all levels of government and the characteristics of the intergovernmental system: researchers have been interested in describing and prescribing the distribution of power

AUTHORS' NOTE: *This article is a revision of a paper delivered at the 1974 Annual Meeting of the American Political Science Association, Palmer House, Chicago, Illinois, August 29-September 2, 1974. Research support provided by the Graduate School of the Ohio State University greatly facilitated the completion of this paper. The authors are indebted to Aage Clausen, William Gormley, Judson James, Michael Reagan, and Randall Ripley for their helpful comments on an earlier version of this article.*

among different governmental jurisdictions and the degree of autonomy or interdependence of participating levels of government. We wish to shift the emphasis of study to the "policy implementation process."

We are proposing that the central focus of intergovernmental relations research should be the policy implementation process. Studying policy implementation suggests an effort to describe and explain the process by which policies are transformed into public services, directs attention to the process of delivering public services (which is at the heart of the intergovernmental system), and provides explanations for the realization or nonrealization of program objectives. Finally, it offers an analytic focus that moves beyond descriptive maps of intergovernmental relations not adequately linked to an examination of policy outcomes.

The purpose of this paper is to explore several approaches to the study of intergovernmental relations and to offer a conceptual framework for analyzing the delivery of policies that require the participation of various governmental units. In addition, we shall demonstrate the utility of this framework by reference to the existing literature and to our research on federal education policy.

THE STUDY OF INTERGOVERNMENTAL RELATIONS

Speculation about the consequences of American federalism dates back nearly two centuries, most notably to the *Federalist* papers. The prevailing concern of much of the early and contemporary literature is the constitutional and normative foundations of federalism. Numerous writers (for example, Wheare, 1964; Publius, 1972) have debated the issue of which powers and functions are reserved —or should be reserved—for each governmental jurisdiction within the federal system. This constitutional-normative perspective viewed federalism in static terms; it also treated each unit of government as a relatively autonomous entity with separate sources of legitimacy and authority—thus spawning the concept of "dual federalism."[1]

During the last two decades a number of social scientists (Grodzins, 1965, 1966; Elazar, 1962, 1972; Break, 1967; Maxwell, 1969; Weidner, 1967; Wright, 1972) have moved the discussion of federalism beyond the hortatory, legalistic, and constitutional arguments (at least in part) to a more dispassionate *description* and *analysis* of the distribution of power, which they view as apportioned among partners in a cooperative federal system. Impressed by the dynamic nature of the intergovernmental system, these writers are less interested in prescribing the proper allocation of responsibilities than with charting existing relationships where the assignment of responsibilities is shared by various governmental units. The primary task of these works has been to provide a description of the intergovernmental system with emphasis on such concerns as the distribution of power, the sources of leverage held by each governmental jurisdiction, and the consequences of administrative centralization and decentralization.

While this body of literature has alerted us to a number of important considerations, it has failed to provide an analytic framework promoting either tests of the significance of particular variable clusters (e.g., the characteristics of administrative personnel), an examination of the importance of the degree of cooperation and conflict between governmental units, or the policy implications of a particular administrative arrangement (e.g., general or special revenue sharing). Since most of these works lack a coherent theoretical perspective, the results of the analysis lack generality, and they tell us little about how public policy is implemented in the intergovernmental system.

The relative lack of knowledge about the process of intergovernmental policy implementation is a deficiency in our understanding of the policy process because it is likely to lead to ill-advised conclusions by policy makers. For example, when faced with an unsuccessful program, many observers will attribute its failure to poor planning or inadequate funding. This attribution of blame is often unjustified. Viewing the Great Society's social policies generally, Robert A. Levine (1968: 86) has concluded that most of the trouble with the War on Poverty resulted "not so much from the nature of the programs as from difficulties of administration." Pointing to the possible gap between the intentions and statements of public officials on the one hand and the delivery of public services on the other, Kenneth Dolbeare and Philip Hammond (1971: 149) have argued that:

> ... very little may really be decided by the words of a decision or a statute: the enunciation of such national policy may be just the beginning of the decisive process of determining what will happen to whom, and understanding this further stage is essential to a full understanding of politics.

The focus on implementation adds a new dimension to the study of intergovernmental relations. It gives the student of politics and the policy maker a new understanding of how the intergovernmental system succeeds or fails in translating general policy objectives into concrete and meaningful public services.

THE STUDY OF POLICY IMPLEMENTATION

In their study of the Economic Development Administration's Oakland Project, Jeffrey Pressman and Aaron Wildavsky (1973: 166) write:

> There is (or there must be) a large literature about implementation in the social sciences—or so we have been told by numerous people. . . . It must be there; it should be there; but in fact it is not. There is a kind of semantic illusion at work here because virtually everything ever done in public administration must, in the nature of things, have some bearing on implementation. . . . Nevertheless, except for a few pieces mentioned in the body of this book, we have been unable to find any significant analytic work dealing with implementation.

While we share Pressman and Wildavsky's concern that far too little attention has been paid to the question of policy implementation, we believe that there is substantial literature that can assist us in developing a better understanding of the process by which general policy decisions are translated into public services. This literature can be divided into two types. First, a growing number of policy analysts have turned their attention to the problems of implementation. Among the most important published studies of policy implementation are Herbert Kaufman's study (1960) of the U.S. Forest Service, Stephen Bailey and Edith Mosher's examination (1968) of the administration of the Elementary and Secondary Education Act of 1965, Martha Derthick's analysis (1970) of federal grants-in-aid programs, Neal Gross and associates' examination (1971) of planned organizational innovation, Joel Berke and Michael Kirst's study (1972) of federal aid to education programs, Derthick's analysis (1972) of the Johnson Administration's effort to create new communities on federally owned land in metropolitan areas, Pressman and Wildavsky's study (1973) of Oakland's community development program, Jerome Murphy's analysis (1974) of the implementation of Title V of the Elementary and Secondary Education Act, and Charles Jones's investigation (1975) of air pollution policy. While these and other studies have helped identify factors that contribute to an understanding of the process of policy implementation, there is still no coherent conceptual framework for guiding the analysis of intergovernmental policy implementation. Instead, where the literature does attempt to provide explanations, it has tended to focus—perhaps inevitably—on the set of variables that emerged in particular case studies. The aim of the conceptual framework presented here is to assist those seeking to derive generalizations from the findings of seemingly disparate case studies, and to provide a general blueprint for scholars wishing to embark on the study of implementation.

Second, there is a rich heritage from the social sciences that is often overlooked by those purporting to discuss the policy implementation process. This literature includes theoretical and empirical work in several disciplines, including sociology, public administration, social psychology, and political science. While most of these studies do not specifically examine the implementation of intergovernmental policy, close inspection reveals their significance.

In developing the conceptual framework that is advanced in this paper, we were guided primarily by the organization theory literature; and more specifically, by the work in the area of organizational change (innovation) and control. Since the contributions of this literature are presented in considerable detail elsewhere (Van Meter and Van Horn, 1975), we shall limit ourselves to a brief overview of the major ideas which have relevance to policy implementation.

Students of organizational theory and practice have dealt extensively with the topic of change (for example, Downs, 1967; Gross et al., 1971). In an analysis of organizational change, Herbert Kaufman (1971) explores a variety of impediments to innovation in organizational structure and action. He examines such factors as resource limitations and the accumulation of official and unofficial constraints on behavior that "tend to keep organizations doing the things they have been doing in the recent past, and doing them in just the way they have been doing them" (Kaufman, 1971: 39). Kaufman recognizes the many advantages of stability, and makes a serious effort to identify those forces conducive to organizational change—those that occur involuntarily and by design. Yet he concludes that most organizations "are imprisoned in the present and often cannot change, even when the future threatens them unless they do" (Kaufman, 1971: 40).

Organizational control has also been a frequent research topic. Harold Wilensky (1967: 3) defines control as the "problem of getting work done and securing compliance with organizational rules." Amitai Etzioni (1961) utilizes the concept of compliance—which can be useful in the study of implementation—as a basis for comparing complex organizations. He argues that different types of organizations will require different kinds of compliance systems. For example, where participants in an organization are alienated and have an intense negative orientation toward the organization, *coercive* power—the application, or the threat of punitive sanctions—may be required to achieve adherence to the organization's rules and objectives. Where most participants have intense positive orientations and are highly committed to the organization's goals and objectives, compliance can usually be achieved through the use of *normative* power—the allocation and manipulation of symbolic rewards and deprivations. And where participants do not have intense orientations toward the organization and their involvement is a function of perceived costs and benefits, *remunerative* power—the allocation of material resources such as salaries, commissions, and fringe benefits —is likely to be the most effective means of achieving compliance.

Integral to Etzioni's thinking, and to all discussions of control, is the relationship between superiors and subordinates in complex organizations. The classic Weberian interpretation of this relationship holds that the ideal role of subordinates is one of implementing faithfully the decisions made by their superiors. Policies are made at the highest levels; they are then carried out by lower participants whose discretion is acutely limited. While this interpretation is widely accepted, most organizations deviate considerably from it. Numerous studies have shown that such "lower participant" groups as attendants in mental hospitals (Scheff, 1961), maintenance workers in factories (Crozier, 1964), and prison inmates (Sykes, 1961) exercise power and affect the performance of complex organizations.

Not infrequently these instances are dismissed as exceptions to the rule. David Mechanic (1962) suggests, however, that they are manifestations of a general pattern. By acquiring control over persons, information, and instrumentalities, lower participants can wield considerable power that is not normally associated with their formally defined positions within the organizations. He (1962: 351) argues that "organizations, in a sense, are continuously at the mercy of their lower participants. . . ." In developing an analytic model of the judicial implementation process. Lawrence Baum (1976: 91) suggests that lower-court judges be viewed as independent actors "who will not follow the lead of higher courts unless conditions are favorable for their doing so." This perspective requires that we seek to identify those factors which determine the autonomy of lower participants.[2]

DEFINING POLICY IMPLEMENTATION

Several often-conflicting uses of the concept of implementation are found in the existing literature.[3] Our definition is quite explicit: *policy implementation encompasses those actions by public and private individuals (or groups) that affect the achievement of objectives set forth in prior policy decisions.* This includes factors affecting one time efforts to transform decisions into operational terms, as well as continuing efforts to achieve the changes mandated by policy decisions. As Walter Williams (1971: 144) observes: "In its most general form, an inquiry about implementation . . . seeks to determine whether an organization can bring together men and material in a cohesive organizational unit and motivate them in such a way as to carry out the organization's stated objectives."

It is important to make clear the distinction between policy *implementation,* policy *performance* and what is generally referred to as policy *impact.* These are distinct albeit related concepts. Policy impact studies examine the linkage between specific program approaches and observed consequences (e.g., What impact do compensatory education programs have on the reading or math skills of disadvantaged children?). The study of policy implementation, on the other hand, highlights one of the forces that determines policy impact by focusing on those activities that affect the rendering of public services. As Dolbeare observes (1974), impact studies typically ask "What happened?" whereas implementation studies also ask "Why did it happen this way?"

The difference between the dependent variables of policy impact and policy implementation research parallels the distinction drawn by Levine (1969: 1190) between a program's proximate and ultimate effects. An implementation study investigates the proximate effects —the *delivery* of services to educationally deprived children in schools having high concentrations of children from low-income families. Policy impact studies typically address questions of ultimate effect—the upgrading of the educational opportunities of educationally deprived children.

The model utilized here is not designed to measure the ultimate impact of intergovernmental programs, rather it seeks to measure and explain program performance—the degree to which anticipated services are actually delivered to intended beneficiaries. Policies may be fully implemented but fail to have positive effects because they were poorly conceived or because there were numerous other circumstances beyond the scope of the specific remedy. Adequate program performance is a necessary, but not sufficient, condition for the production of positive ultimate impacts.

A MODEL OF INTERGOVERNMENTAL POLICY IMPLEMENTATION

The policy implementation model directs attention to a set of variables and their interrelations that determine policy performance within a particular jurisdiction. Therefore, the selection of criteria for assessing performance is a crucial stage in the analysis: the performance measures are the dependent variables that are employed to determine whether or not federal policy objectives are realized. The ability of the policy analyst to make statements about the adequacy of implementation actions and to propose specific remedies that might be undertaken to correct deficiencies depends upon the development of performance measures that are precise and meaningful (to policy makers).

In selecting performance indicators one can rely on a number of alternative sources—the statements of policy makers in the legislative history of the act and amendments, the program's regulations, criteria suggested by client groups or by specialists in the field. Ultimately the measures deduced by the researcher should be based on the purpose for which the research is conducted (Rossi and Williams, 1972).

An analysis of policy implementation requires more than the measurement of program performance: the principal goal is to derive explanations from the events and factors that intervene between the articulation of a national policy and the results that occur within the states and localities. The research involves two stages: one must first establish that the measured program performance is indeed related to the introduction of the legislation; then one must attempt to explain the patterns of effects. The remainder of this paper discusses the set of variables that would be utilized in the second phase of the research.

The model outlined in Figure 1 posits eight variable clusters —policy resources, policy standards, communications, enforcement, dispositions of implementors, characteristics of the implementing agencies, the political conditions, and economic and social conditions—that influence implementation efforts to achieve local program performance. The model delineates several factors that shape the linkage between policy and performance, and it specifies the relationships among these independent variables. It aids in the description of the policy implementation process and serves as a guide in research by generating suggestive hypotheses. The model's utility can be illustrated by reference to three general explanations for unsuccessful implementation which are similar to Kaufman's explanations (1973: 2) for noncompliance in organizational settings.

—*The Communications Process.* Effective implementation requires that implementors know what they are supposed to do. As messages pass through any communications network, distortions are likely to occur —producing contradictory directives, ambiguities, inconsistencies in instructions, and incompatable requirements. Even when directives and requirements are clear, problems may arise as implementors fail to comprehend fully what is expected of them.

—*The Capability Problem.* Successful implementation is also a function of the implementing organization's capacity to do what it is expected to do. The ability to implement policies may be hindered by such factors as overworked and incompetent staffs; insufficient information, political support and financial resources; and impossible time constraints.

—*Dispositional Conflicts.* Implementation efforts may fail because implementors refuse to do what they are supposed to do.

Most of the studies that we have identified rely primarily upon one of these three general explanations for unsuccessful implementation. Few investigators have sought to integrate each of these explanations into their analyses. Our conceptual framework utilizes these partial and insufficient explanations in an effort to provide the basis for a comprehensive understanding of the implementation process. We will now turn to a definition and brief elaboration of each variable cluster in our model.[4]

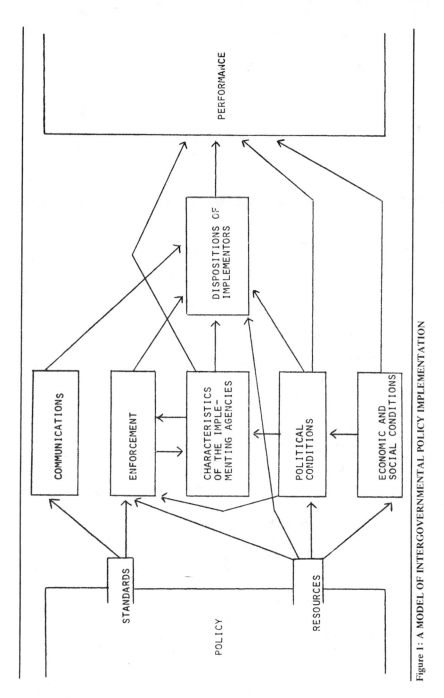

Figure 1: A MODEL OF INTERGOVERNMENTAL POLICY IMPLEMENTATION

[48]

THE POLICY: RESOURCES AND STANDARDS

Two components of the policy decision influence the implementation process: policy resources and policy standards. Policies provide financial and other resources for programs and their administration and enforcement. Funds and incentives are usually not adequate—a cause often cited for the failure of implementation efforts (Derthick, 1972: 87; Murphy, 1971). In addition, the timing of the release of funding information to the agency can have important consequences for the success of the program: administrators forced to plan with insufficient knowledge about the amount of funds available for the school year will experience serious difficulties (Berke and Kirst, 1972: 44). The amount of funding in any given year relative to previous levels will influence decisions made by program administrators. Agencies that are faced with severe budgetary cutbacks will perceive and carry out their tasks quite differently from those that enjoy expanding budgets. Finally, policy resources may influence the environment where implementation occurs, stimulating interested individuals and groups to press for full implementation and successful policy performance.

The other significant component of the policy decision is its standards. Policy standards move beyond the general legislative goals and preamble rhetoric and establish requirements, in varying degrees of specificity, for how those goals shall be implemented. Standards are commonly contained in the legislation and program regulations, but they may also be elaborated upon in such diverse sources as technical assistance guides, statements by policy makers, and news releases and brochures from the agency responsible for obtaining compliance.

A detailed profile of the standards relating to the performance measures should be constructed, and the changes over time charted. A longitudinal approach will enable analysts to examine the changing nature of the standards and to relate them to alterations in implementation actions and program performance. This profile of policy standards can be utilized to assess the quality, clarity, consistency, and accuracy of national level direction. It should also be compared with the interpretations of federal, state, and local implementors and with policy standards (if any) developed at state and local levels. If the policy standards when viewed longitudinally are inconsistent, confusing, unclear, and inaccurate, then they will create problems that will seep into the policy delivery system.

Likewise, the actions of federal, state, and local actors must be compared with the standards, however imperfect, at the national level.

Policy standards tell federal, state, and local implementors what is expected of them and indicate the amount of discretion left open to them. Policy standards also provide overseers with the tools of influence and enforcement, since they set limits on the types of activities that are tolerable, and on the sanctions that can be imposed for deviations.

Ambiguities in policy standards may be fostered deliberately by policy makers in order to insure positive responses by implementors. National program regulations must accommodate diverse settings. Moreover, standards may remain vague because policy makers are unwilling or unable to reach a consensus on the directives that should be promulgated (Bailey and Mosher, 1968; Murphy, 1971).

COMMUNICATIONS

Policy standards represent no more than exhortations: they are inanimate messages that must be communicated to those in charge of executing the policy. Judicial impact studies (Milner, 1971; Dolbeare and Hammond, 1971; Wasby, 1973) have frequently reported that the failure of lower court judges to show compliance with higher court decisions can be attributed to their ignorance of those rulings. Policy standards cannot be complied with unless they are communicated with sufficient clarity so that the implementors will know what is required of them.

Communication between levels of the federal system is a complex and difficult task. In transmitting messages, communicators inevitably distort them either intentionally or unintentionally, placing their own emphases and interpretations on what often begins as a uniform statement by the federal government (Downs, 1967; Wilensky, 1967). Moreover, different sources within the federal government are not always uniform in providing directives and interpretations, and the same source may serve up conflicting policy positions over time, diluting the impact of the message even further. While good communications will not necessarily contribute to a positive disposition on the part of implementors, variations in their support for the policy may often be explained partially in terms of their understanding and interpretations of the policy standards and the manner by which they are communicated.

It will therefore be important to investigate the nature and content of the specific advice, orders, and clarifications communicated by federal implementors to state and local implementing agencies. Several questions should be raised: What is the accuracy, clarity, consistency, and timeliness of the communication compared with the national policy standards and of the information going to a particular state or locality over time? What interpretations do the field representatives bring to their understanding of the program, and what are their definitions of acceptable local performance? What policy standards do they *emphasize* in their reviews of state and local activities and in their consultations with state and local officials?

Poor communications may be caused by a variety of factors, not the least of which is the original ambiguity contained in the national policy standards. Added to these inherent problems are the selective perceptions and concerns of federal implementors. Examining the record of standards and the process of communicating them to state and local actors will help isolate the areas where corrective action is most needed.

The problems inherent in the communication process are reflected in the case of Title I of the Elementary and Secondary Education Act of 1965 (ESEA).[5] State and local education officials had anticipated the passage of a "general aid" bill in 1965. Many state and local officials believed that the enacted program provided general aid—an impression that was reinforced by a widely distributed and erroneous document that listed programs which were "permissible under the law." However, this document left out many important requirements, including those that dealt with the "targetting" of aid for educationally deprived (or disadvantaged) children from low income areas.

While the Title I formula for the allocation of federal funds to the disadvantaged was precise, the types of programs which would qualify were not outlined in the original statute or the early regulations developed by the U.S. Office of Education (USOE): wide discretion was delegated to state and local education agencies to determine their own approaches for aiding educationally deprived children. According to one federal program officer, at least one state defined a "disadvantaged" student as one lacking art, music, and physical education skills. It tested students in the state's schools and found nearly all to be "disadvantaged," using these criteria of "needs assessment." Thus, whatever the merit of this action, the state provided general aid, contravening the legislative purpose of the program.

In large part, this early ambiguity and confusion was a consequence of statutory provisions written primarily to insure fiscal accountability; they addressed casually the matter of program standards. Moreover, as one area desk officer in the USOE's Title I unit observed, the USOE did virtually nothing between 1965 and 1969 to clarify the program's standards. Regulations and guidelines that were distributed lacked clarity and concreteness, were subject to frequent change, and were generally confusing and incoherent. He asserted that it was not uncommon for local education agencies (LEAs) and state education agencies (SEAs) to request further direction; they complained that the USOE never told them what they were supposed to do and that they frequently had no way of knowing whether their actions were consistent with Title I policy standards. In successive authorizations, Congress was able to provide greater specification and clarification of its intent. Eventually, the USOE rewrote its regulations, specifying that programs would have to be developed that contributed to the improvement of basic cognitive skills (for example, reading and math).

ENFORCEMENT

Successful implementation usually requires mechanisms and procedures whereby the federal government may increase the likelihood that state and local officials will act in a manner consistent with policy standards. There is no hierarchy of officials in the intergovernmental system that can be ordered toward a set of predetermined objectives: the careful specification of plans and standards, while important, will not suffice to guarantee effective program performance (Schultze, 1969: 202; Neustadt, 1960).

Federal officials have essentially three means of achieving compliance from agencies and individuals who implement the program: norms, incentives, and sanctions. These correspond to Etzioni's (1961: 5-8) distinction between normative, remunerative, and coercive forms of power. He argues that in different contexts, and with different organizations, one must employ different forms of power in order to achieve adherence to the organization's rules and objectives. Federal officials must be sensitive to the characteristics of the agencies they are dealing with when they make similar choices among the means of enforcement. State and local agencies with competent staffs and leadership require different enforcement approaches than those that are poorly staffed and led. And those with limited political resources may be more vulnerable to coercive power than those enjoying extensive support from public officials. Finally federal assessment should change with the evolution of the program within the state or locality. Early efforts may be directed toward gaining minimal compliance, while later actions will be devoted to developing more effective programs.

Norms and incentives are frequently used enforcement techniques. An important method of federal influence is the socialization, persuasion, and co-optation of state and local officials. Federal agency personnel attempt to build alliances with state and local implementors—cultivating allies who can be counted on to carry out federal policy willfully (Derthick, 1970; Bailey and Mosher, 1968; Etzioni, 1965; Kaufman, 1960). A fragmented federal system makes constant oversight impossible and thus requires heavy reliance on this approach.

It is equally important to examine the possibility of the co-optation of the federal enforcers by the state and local implementing agency (Lazin, 1973; Pressman and Wildavsky, 1973; Murphy, 1971). Federal officials may be so concerned with maintaining cooperative relationships that they soften demands for compliance, lose sight of the goals of the policy, and even assume advocacy roles for the local agencies.

Federal officials may also use incentives in order to influence the behavior of implementors.[6] Besides providing dollars for administration of the program, the federal government may render valuable services to them, such as technical assistance, research, and staff loans, or may assist them in obtaining physical and other resources.

One of the most important enforcement relationships is the provision of support by the federal government to state and local agencies when they face hostile forces within their environments. This is particularly true with respect to bolstering state agencies in their dealings with large cities within the state. Compliance with policy standards will be enhanced if the federal government is willing and able to back state and local agencies that adhere to its policies when these agencies receive pressure to deviate from prescribed paths of acceptable performance. For example, several U.S. Office of Education officials made the point that their task has largely been one of standing behind state education agencies when they take action against a local education agency for noncompliance.

Federal officials also have more compelling devices at their disposal, ranging from gentle to explicit forms of coercive power. A common practice is to require that states and localities draw up elaborate plans for the administration of federal programs. Once these assurances are made by the states and localities, the federal government will allocate funds on the condition that they may be withdrawn if the objectives set forth in the plans are not fulfilled. By concentrating on the initial stages of policy formulation and planning, the federal government seeks to employ "compliance in advance" (Derthick, 1970: 209).

A similar strategy is to specify conditions and procedural requirements, such as elaborate reporting and accounting systems, in the regulations that accompnay the acceptance of federal funds. There are, however, dangers in this procedure (Derthick, 1970: 200): "Specificity entails risks. . . . The more specific the language of the federal requirements, the lower the federal capacity to adapt to state peculiarities and the greater the danger that the limitations of federal capacity to compel conformance may be revealed." Moreover, stringent regulations and guidelines may induce a sort of goal displacement, wherein state and local officials strive to meet federal requirements in order to obtain funds and avoid sanctions, while ignoring the basic mission of the program.

Assurances do not guarantee that federal objectives will be fulfilled (nor that the federal government will be willing to impose sanctions), so more reliable forms of surveillance such as on-site visitations, state and local program reviews, program evaluations, and audits are usually conducted. And other feedback mechanisms, including reports by nongovernmental advisory committees (such as local manpower planning councils or parent advisory boards), can be used to keep the federal government informed about the performance of state and local agencies (Downs, 1967: 143-153; Blau and Scott, 1962: 170-172; Kaufman, 1973).

The most threatening form of potential federal power is the authority to withdraw or recover funds from a state or local agency for noncompliance. This ultimate weapon is rarely used. It may cause embarrassment to the federal agency and damage the only ally that it has within the area. Generally, the federal government negotiates with state and local officials in an effort to attain the greatest possible compliance without withholding funds. Federal officials will usually refrain from overt threats which could undermine cooperative relationships and generate congressional hostility at the expense of program goals. The more common practice short of withholding funds is the audit exception. State and local awareness of this regularized process of audit discovery often acts as a powerful deterrent to errant behavior (errant, that is, from a federal perspective).

DISPOSITIONS OF IMPLEMENTORS

The success or failure of many federal programs has often been attributed to the level of support enjoyed within the agency responsible for implementation. As Petrick (1968: 7) observes, this stems from the fact that "human groups find it difficult to carry out effectively acts for which they have no underlying beliefs." Three elements of the implementors' response may affect their ability or willingness to implement federal policy: their cognition (comprehension) of the policy's standards, the direction of their response toward them, and the intensity of their response.

Even when the policy standards are communicated with accuracy, clarity and consistency, successful implementation may be frustrated when officials are unaware that they are not in full compliance with the law and do not know what they must do to get there. The message transmission may operate correctly, but the receiver may malfunction due to ignorance or overload (Wasby, 1970: 98).

Implementors may not execute the policy's standards because they reject the objectives contained in them (Peltason, 1961; Dolbeare and Hammond, 1971; Etzioni, 1961; Wasby, 1970). The objectives may be rejected for a variety of reasons: they may offend the implementors' personal value systems, self-interest, organizational loyalties, or existing preferred relationships. Finally, the intensity of the implementors' response may affect the implementation process. Those holding intense negative orientations toward the policy may openly defy program objectives (Bailey and Mosher, 1968). Less intense attitudes may cause implementors to attempt surreptitious diversion and evasion (Lazin, 1973).

CHARACTERISTICS OF THE IMPLEMENTING AGENCIES

The formal and informal attributes of the organization responsible for implementation affect its ability to carry out the policy's standards (Ripley et al., 1973; Rourke, 1969; Downs, 1967; Kaufman, 1971). No matter what the attitudes of its personnel, certain features of the agency's staff, structure, and relations with other officials and units of government will tend to limit or enhance the prospects for effective implementation.

One important factor is the experience and competence of the staff to perform the tasks required of them. Obviously, a staff which lacks sufficient training and knowledge in the area of policy will have difficulty coping with the type of tasks they must perform. For example, Title I (ESEA) programs place heavy demands on federal, state, and local agencies, requiring new procedures and mechanisms for achieving the policy's goals. At the same time, these agencies are burdened with the requirement to keep the federal government informed of activities relating to the program. A poorly led and staffed organization will be unable to conduct effective programs since they will have their hands full surviving and meeting minimum federal criteria.

The status of the agency within either the parent organization of which it is a part or the local government structure also affects its administrative capacity. An organization without sufficient financial and political support and without the necessary independence to make decisions and hire qualified personnel will face severe problems in administering programs. For example, if the agency must implement several programs simultaneously its effectiveness will undoubtedly be reduced (Bailey and Mosher, 1968).

POLITICAL ENVIRONMENT

The political environment of the implementing agencies affects the nature of policy performance and the implementing actions of the agencies. The extent of support for or opposition to the policy objectives by organizational superiors and by public and private individuals and groups influences implementation efforts and results, regardless of the positions of the implementors or the quality of the agency executing the program. Several scholars have noted that public and elite opinion, and the salience of the program to them, are important determinants in the policy implementation process (Dolbeare and Hammond, 1971; Derthick, 1970; Lazin, 1973; Peltason, 1961; Wasby, 1970).

Where the problems to be remedied by a program are severe and private citizens and interest groups are mobilized in support of a program, it is more likely that implementors will accept the policy's goals and objectives. Officials are compelled to accede to program standards by political demands within their jurisdictions. As one Title I (ESEA) area desk officer asserted, officials in many southeastern states have conformed to program requirements not only in response to enforcement efforts, but also because they are anxious to get the badly needed federal aid for which there is substantial local support.

The impact of federal enforcement activities may be mitigated when state and local implementors are opposed to certain aspects of the program and can enlist the support of organizational superiors or their congressional delegations. For example, there is evidence of the USOE's reluctance to intervene in situations where Department of Health, Education, and Welfare audits uncovered gross misappropriations of Title I funds, including the construction of swimming pools in one state and the purchase of a $1.4 million church in another. This hesitancy derived in part from the desire to demonstrate success by avoiding embarrassing publicity. But more important, USOE was faced with pressure exerted by legislators and other public officials who did not wish to have reports of fund abuse in their districts disclosed.

ECONOMIC AND SOCIAL CONDITIONS

Economic conditions, both as needs and resources, influence the chances of successful program performance. Although specific indicators must be constructed around the types of policies in question, one would want to examine the needs of the jurisdiction for the service that the federal program is offering and the structure of those needs. Depending on the types of need within the community the implementor may be led to accept or reject certain goals of the policy or its approaches. Likewise, the extent of need may influence otherwise negatively oriented officials to embrace the policy in order to minimize public hostility or to respond to public wishes.

The resources of the community must also be considered. Some areas may have the capacity to carry out public services without federal assistance. If federal requirements are objectionable, they may refuse to participate in the program altogether. Also, the types of economic resources within the community will influence the kinds of services that can be offered and their importance. For example, in manpower programs, localities that enjoy extensive private industrial development and a high demand for skilled labor can structure their programs to take account of this potential.

Although our discussion has been presented in static terms, it is important to recognize the dynamic character of the policy implementation process. The implementation of intergovernmental policies may follow a developmental path: factors that affect the execution of a policy in its initial stages may be of little consequence at a later point in time. In its early stages policy may represent a radical departure from past practices and, therefore, engender great conflict over its goals and objectives. During this phase certain features of our model—particularly communications, enforcement, and the dispositions of implementors—may explain the success or failure of implementation efforts to achieve desired results. Later, individuals and organizations may adapt to the policy and consensus over goals may be achieved. At this point, other factors, such as the characteristics of the implementing agencies, may contribute more to the realization of program objectives. With this in mind, it is vital that the study of implementation be approached from a longitudinal perspective (as well as cross-sectionally); relationships identified at one point in time must not be extended casually to other time periods.

CONCLUSION

While far too little attention has been paid to how policy decisions are *transformed* into public services, we have succeeded in identifying a number of studies that look explicitly at the problems of policy implementation. Our conceptual framework draws upon this literature and directs attention to a set of attributes, processes, and behaviors that will help provide a more comprehensive understanding of the policy implementation process and the performance of intergovernmental policy.

In discussing the eight variable clusters that comprise our model of intergovernmental policy implementation, we have not attempted to describe and justify each of the hypothesized relationships posited in Figure 1. It should be noted, however, that this conceptual framework not only specifies the relationships between the independent variables and the ultimate dependent variable of interest but also identifies explicitly the linkages among the independent variables.

We would suggest that this framework be viewed as an heuristic model. It is designed for the purpose of discovering facts about the policy implementation process and is useful for empirical research, but probably is not capable of definitive proof (and it is not intended for such purposes). It can be contrasted with the deductive-deterministic models which dominate political science and have been employed by many policy researchers—especially in *policy-making* studies. Both types of models have their place and purpose; however, the heuristic model is more appropriate for studying implementation and for deriving useful policy advice.

The policy implementation model aspires to discover how the law is implemented. It allows one to chart variations, and then to relate them to outcomes. The end product is no concise formula that can be employed to explain (in any strict sense) the observed results; rather it can be used to extract a better understanding of the process and of those factors that facilitate or hinder policy performance.

The deductive-deterministic model aspires to provide precise explanations that are neither temporally nor spatially bound. These explanations rely on the best available sets of empirical laws or, in the case of most political science, on hypotheses that have been regularly confirmed. The more abstract and generally applicable the variable, the more amenable it will be to replication and refinement in similar analyses at other times and in other settings. Ideographic variables are rejected because they move the researcher away from his primary goal.

The major weakness of the deductive-deterministic model is that it offers little or no information to the policy maker who wishes to make changes in implementation actions. By ignoring those immediate process-oriented factors that influence policy implementation, it forfeits the ability to make policy relevant advice. The parsimonious virtues of such a model are liabilities in most policy research enterprises, especially where administrative behavior is the subject of inquiry.

Therefore, it is our contention that this model offers a blueprint for the description and analysis of the policy implementation process, and that it proposes explanations for program achievements and failures. We maintain that studies of intergovernmental policy implementation—when approached in this manner—have much to offer policy analysts and policy makers alike. For the policy analyst, implementation studies offer the promise of systematic explanations of the complexities of intergovernmental relations, as well as a more thorough understanding of the policy consequences of the federal system. Implementation research may also lead the policy makers to explanations for observed impacts and point to variables that may be manipulated to improve the delivery of public services.

NOTES

1. For a more detailed discussion of "dual federalism" and of the concept of federalism in general, see Elazar (1972, 1962), Grodzins (1966, 1965), Leach (1970), Reagan (1972), and Sundquist (1969).

2. Other students of judicial politics have utilized the literature on organization theory to construct partial theories of judicial implementation or impact. See, for example, Krislov (1965), Wasby (1970), Johnson (1967), Petrick (1968), Brown and Stover (1974), and Dolbeare and Hammond (1971).

3. See, for example, the differing interpretations implied by Pressman and Wildavsky (1973), Smith (1973), Lazin (1973), Bunker (1972), Derthick (1972), Gross and associates (1971), and Dolbeare and Hammond (1971). See also the following studies in which a variety of concepts are employed to explore the implementation process: Jones (1970), Gergen (1968), and Gross (1966).

4. The framework will be elaborated in the context of a federal program that is implemented principally by state and local agencies. In the discussion, we assume the perspective of the federal government as it attempts to influence the actions of state and local officials. In selecting the "federal" perspective, one does not necessarily accept the federal government's position as more correct or desirable. Moreover, one cannot ignore the influence of state and local implementors on the federal government. The model could be applied to any combination of federal (national or regional), state, and local relationships and responsibilities.

5. Information about the implementation of Title I of the Elementary and Secondary Education Act of 1965 (ESEA) is drawn from the authors' research on the implementation of compensatory education programs.

6. For a more detailed discussion of the utility of incentives, see Porter (1973), Levine (1972), Derthick (1970), and Schultze (1969).

REFERENCES

BAILEY, S. K., and MOSHER, E. K. (1968). ESEA: The Office of Education Administers a Law. Syracuse: Syracuse University.

BAUM, L. (1976). "Implementation of judicial decisions: an organizational analysis." American Politics Quarterly, 4(January): 86-114.

BERKE, J. S., and KIRST, M. W. (1972). Federal Aid to Education: Who Benefits? Who Governs? Lexington, Mass.: Lexington.

BLAU, P. M., and SCOTT, W. R. (1962). Formal Organizations. San Francisco: Chandler.

BREAK, G. F. (1967). Intergovernmental Fiscal Relations in the United States. Washington, D.C.: Brookings.

BROWN, D. C., and STOVER, R. V. (1974). "An economic approach to compliance with court decisions." Paper delivered at the 1974 Annual Meeting of the American Political Science Association, Palmer House, Chicago, Illinois, August 29-September 2.

BUNKER, D. R. (1972). "Policy sciences perspectives on implementation processes." Policy Sciences, 3: 71-80.

CROZIER, M. (1964). The Bureaucratic Phenomenon. Chicago: University of Chicago Press.

DERTHICK, M. (1972). New Towns In-Town. Washington, D.C.: The Urban Institute.

――― (1970). The Influence of Federal Grants: Public Assistance in Massachusetts. Cambridge, Mass.: Harvard University Press.

DOLBEARE, K. M. (1974). "The impact of public policy." In C. P. Cotter (ed.), Political Science Annual: An International Review (vol. 5). Indianapolis: Bobbs-Merrill.

DOLBEARE, K. M., and HAMMOND, P. E. (1971). The School Prayer Decisions: From Court Policy to Local Practice. Chicago: University of Chicago Press.

DOWNS, A. (1967). Inside Bureaucracy. Boston: Little, Brown.

ELAZAR, D. J. (1972). American Federalism: A View from the States (2nd ed.). New York: Crowell.

——— (1962). The American Partnership. Chicago: University of Chicago Press.

ETZIONI, A. (1965). "Organizational control structure." In J. March (ed.), Handbook of Organizations. Chicago: Rand McNally.

——— (1961). A Comparative Analysis of Complex Organizations. New York: Free Press.

GERGEN, K. (1968). "Assessing the leverage points in the process of policy formation." In R. A. Bauer and K. H. Gergen (eds.), The Study of Policy Formation (chap. 5). New York: Free Press.

GRODZINS, M. (1966). The American System: A New View of Government in the United States D. J. Elazar, ed.). Chicago: Rand McNally.

——— (1965). "The Federal System." In Goals for Americans: The Report of the President's Commission on National Goals. Englewood Cliffs, N.J.: Prentice-Hall.

GROSS, B. (1966). "Activating national plans." In J. R. Lawrence (ed.), Operational Research and the Social Sciences. London: Tavistock.

GROSS, N.; GIACQUINTA, J. V.; and BERNSTEIN, M. (1971). Implementing Organizational Innovations. New York: Basic Books.

JOHNSON, R. M. (1967). The Dynamics of Compliance. Evanston, Ill.: Northwestern University Press.

JONES, C. O. (1975). Clean Air: The Policies and Politics of Pollution Control. Pittsburgh: University of Pittsburgh Press.

——— (1970). An Introduction to the Study of Public Policy. Belmont, Calif.: Wadsworth.

KAUFMAN, H. (1973). Administrative Feedback. Washington, D.C.: Brookings.

——— (1971). The Limits of Organizational Change. University: University of Alabama Press.

——— (1960). The Forest Ranger. Baltimore: Johns Hopkins.

KRISLOV, S. (1965). The Supreme Court in the Political Process. New York: Macmillan.

LAZIN, F. A. (1973). "The failure of federal enforcement of civil rights regulations in public housing, 1963-1971: The co-optation of a federal agency by its local constituency." Policy Sciences, 4: 263-273.

LEACH, R. (1970). American Federalism. New York: W. W. Norton.

LEVINE, R. A. (1972). Public Planning: Failure and Redirection. New York: Basic Books.

——— (1969). "Policy analysis and economic opportunity programs." In The Analysis and Evaluation of Public Expenditures (vol. 3), U.S. Congress, Joint Economic Committee, 90th Congress, 1st Session.

——— (1968). "Rethinking our social strategies." Public Interest, (Winter): 86-96.

MAXWELL, J. A. (1965). Financing State and Local Governments (2nd ed.). Washington, D.C.: Brookings.

MECHANIC, D. (1962). "Sources of power of lower participants in complex organizations." Administrative Science Quarterly, 7(December): 349-364.

MILNER, N. (1971). The Impact of Miranda in Four Wisconsin Cities. Beverly Hills, Calif.: Sage Publications.

MURPHY, J. T. (1974). State Education Agencies and Discretionary Funds: Grease the Squeaky Wheel. Lexington, Mass.: Lexington Books.

——— (1971). "Title I of ESEA: The politics of implementing federal education reform." Harvard Educational Review, 41(February): 35-63.

NEUSTADT, R. (1960). Presidential Power. New York: John Wiley.

PELTASON, J. W. (1961). Fifty-Eight Lonely Men: Southern Federal Judges and School Desegregation. New York: Harcourt, Brace and World.

PETRICK, M. J. (1968). "The Supreme Court and authority acceptance." Western Political Quarterly, 21(March): 5-19.

PORTER, D. O. (1973). The Politics of Budgeting Federal Aid: Resource Mobilization by Local School Districts (Sage Professional Papers in Administrative and Policy Studies 03-001). Beverly Hills, Calif.: Sage Publications.

PRESSMAN, J. L., and WILDAVSKY, A. (1973). Implementation. Berkeley: University of California Press.

Publius (1972). "The Publius symposium on the future of American federalism." (Spring): 95-146.

REAGAN, M. D. (1972). The New Federalism. New York: Oxford University Press.

RIPLEY, R. B.; FRANKLIN, G. A.; HOLMES, W. M.; and MORELAND, W. M. (1973). Structure, Environment, and Policy Actions: Exploring a Model of Policy-Making (Sage Professional Papers in American Politics, 04-006). Beverly Hills, Calif.: Sage Publications.

ROSSI, P. H., and WILLIAMS, W. (eds., 1972). Evaluating Social Programs. New York: Seminar Press.

ROURKE, F. E. (1969). Bureaucracy, Politics, and Public Policy. Boston: Little, Brown.

SCHEFF, T. J. (1961). "Control over policy by attendants in a mental hospital." Journal of Health and Human Behavior, 2: 93-105.

SCHULTZE, C. L. (1969). "The role of incentives, penalties, and rewards in attaining effective policy." Pp. 201-225 in The Analysis and Evaluation of Public Expenditures: The PPB System, A compendium of Papers submitted to the Subcommittee on Economy in Government of the Joint Committee, 91st Congress, 1st Session.

SMITH, T. B. (1973). "The policy implementation process." Policy Sciences, 4: 197-209.

SUNDQUIST, J. L. (1969). Making Federalism Work. Washington, D.C.: Brookings.

SYKES, G. M. (1961). "The corruption of authority and rehabilitation." In A. Etzioni (ed.), Complex Organizations. New York: Free Press.

VAN METER, D. S., and VAN HORN, C. E. (1975). "The policy implementation process: A conceptual framework." Administration and Society (February).

WASBY, S. L. (1973). "The communication of the Supreme Court's criminal procedure decisions: A preliminary mapping." Villanova Law Review, 18(June): 1086-1118.

――― (1970). The Impact of the Supreme Court: Some Perspectives. Homewood, Ill.: Dorsey.

WEIDNER, E. W. (1967). "Decision-making in the federal system." In A. Wildavsky (ed.), American Federalism in Perspective. Boston: Little, Brown.

WHEARE, K. C. (1964). Federal Government (4th ed.). New York: Oxford University Press.

WILENSKY, H. L. (1967). Organizational Intelligence. New York: Basic Books.

WILLIAMS, W. (1971). Social Policy Research and Analysis: The Experience in the Federal Social Agencies. New York: American Elsevier.

WRIGHT, D. S. (1972). "The states and intergovernmental relations." Publius, 1(Winter): 7-76.

PART II

REVENUE SHARING

3

METHODOLOGY FOR MONITORING REVENUE SHARING

RICHARD P. NATHAN

Brookings Institution

In December 1972, the Brookings Institution initiated a five-year monitoring study of the State and Local Fiscal Assistance Act of 1972. This study, financed by a grant from the Ford Foundation, will result in a series of Brookings reports. The first—*Monitoring Revenue Sharing* (Brookings)—was published January 26, 1975. It examines three major types of effects of revenue sharing on recipient state and local governments: (1) distributional, (2) fiscal, and (3) political.

THE IDEA OF MONITORING RESEARCH

For this research, the term "monitoring" has been used instead of the more typical term "evaluation." An evaluation study generally proceeds from the definition of a specific set of objectives of a given policy or policy change and measures the extent to which these

AUTHOR'S NOTE: *Mr. Nathan is a Senior Fellow at the Brookings Institution and director of the Brookings study of general revenue sharing. The views stated here are those of the author and do not represent the views of the trustees, officers, or other staff members of the Brookings Institution. The author acknowledges the assistance of Messrs. Allen D. Manvel and André Juneau of the Brookings staff in the preparation of this paper.*

objectives are fulfilled. A common problem in this kind of research is the inability to obtain a clear—even semimeasurable—definition of objectives. In many cases this problem reflects a deliberate decision. Charles E. Lindblom once noted that the best way to influence a legislative body to adopt a new policy is to be "vague" about one's purpose. Revenue sharing is an obvious case in point.

In the period during which the idea of revenue sharing was being debated, it attracted proponents of diverse philosophies. Among the most commonly cited objectives were:

—To decentralize government and strengthen American federalism;

—To help meet the needs of domestic programs at the state and local levels, especially fiscally hard-pressed central cities;

—To equalize fiscal conditions as between rich and poor states and localities;

—To stabilize or reduce state and local taxes, particularly the property tax;

—To alter the nation's overall tax system by placing greater reliance on income taxation, predominantly federal, as opposed to property and sales taxation.

Other reasons advanced for supporting revenue sharing were more subtle. Some opinion among conservatives held that revenue sharing would create a political climate in which specific categorical grants could be reduced or terminated more easily. Still other arguments pertained to specific provisions of various revenue-sharing bills. Several versions of such legislation contained provisions to stimulate the use of income taxes by state governments. Another group looked to revenue sharing as a means of encouraging governmental reform. Representative Henry S. Reuss introduced legislation in three successive sessions of Congress to tie revenue-sharing payments to broad reform programs on the part of state and local governments, although this idea in the final analysis failed to attract wide support.

In this setting of different and often contradictory ideas about the goals of revenue sharing, the Brookings study was designed as a longitudinal policy study. The aim has been to focus on the principal policy issues raised by the new program.

The first type of effect studied—distributional—involves the working of the formula contained in the 1972 act. How are different sizes and types of jurisdictions affected—central cities versus suburbs, large states versus small, rich versus poor? This is the most straightforward of the three types of effects studied. The analysis is based on U.S. Treasury and Census Bureau data; the focus is on the shared revenue received by eligible governments in relation to major demographic, structural, and financial characteristics of these governments.

The other two types of effects—fiscal and political—are harder to get at. Field research data has been heavily relied upon in these two areas, especially in the early phases of the research.

For the fiscal effects, we are interested not so much in what public officials *say* they are doing with revenue-sharing funds as in probing to determine what really was *different* because of them. A uniform set of definitions of the fiscal effects of revenue sharing, as described below, has been used by the field research associates (twenty-three in number) for a panel of 65 recipient governments of shared revenue. In addition, the fiscal effects of revenue sharing are being studied using national statistics on the finances of state and local governments, mainly from the Census Bureau.

The political effects of shared revenue get at its decentralization aims, described by proponents in terms such as "revitalizing" state and local governments and strengthening governments "closest to the people." These goals are the most amorphous of all and yet among the most important to the coalition of interests behind the 1972 act. To convert these objectives into reasonably researchable questions, the Brookings study concentrates on the budgetary process. How do revenue-sharing funds affect the decision-making processes of recipient governments? Who decides on their use? How? Are new and additional groups involved in the decision process? Is more public interest and attention focused on state and local budgetary processes as a result? Do states relate to localities differently because of revenue sharing? Are relationships between cities and counties affected?

The largest share of the research funds for the revenue-sharing study to date have been devoted to the establishment of the field research network. Three sets of reports (with supplementary materials) will be submitted by the associates for the planned Brookings volumes on revenue sharing.

Both the field research and work on the distributional effects of revenue sharing have been under way since the beginning of 1973. (A grant from the National Science Foundation in 1974 will permit an extension of the plans for the analysis of distributional effects in order to test alternative versions of the revenue-sharing formula contained in the 1972 act.)

THE FIELD RESEARCH SAMPLE

The field research sample includes 8 states, 29 municipalities, 21 counties, 6 townships, and 1 Indian tribe. (A list of these jurisdictions and the associates appears in the Appendix.) The jurisdictions selected were chosen to be representative in terms of: (1) type of government, (2) size, (3) geographical location, (4) economic conditions, and (5) for local governments, structure and scope of responsibility. Among the principal advantages of this approach, as compared to a mail survey, is the ability to obtain complete responses for the full sample and to be able to verify these responses and probe or resurvey for additional information.

Aside from New York City, for which the Center for New York City Affairs of the New School for Social Research is providing the field research reports, the 22 other field researchers (some covering three and four jurisdictions) are part-time Brookings associates. The group was chosen to obtain a cross section in types of experience and background. However, none are officials of governments in the sample; all reside in the areas they are studying. Half of the associates are political scientists (principally persons associated with university research bureaus), five are economists, two are journalists, one is a lawyer, and one was formerly a state fiscal officer who is now in private business. The associates were brought together for two conferences in Washington in April of 1973 and again in April of 1974.

The Brookings panel on revenue sharing includes from one to six jurisdictions in each of 19 states. The sample is generally skewed toward larger-sized (in population) jurisdictions. In all, these 65 jurisdictions received $1.1 billion of shared revenue for 1972, or 21 percent of the nationwide total. The 8 state governments received $645 million, or 36 percent of the aggregate for all 50 states. The 57 local jurisdictions received $470 million, or 13 percent of all locally shared revenue for 1972, distributed by type and size of government as shown in Table 1.

The local jurisdictions in the sample differ not only in size but in the scope of their responsibilities. At one extreme are two rural townships in Wisconsin, which have a very limited governmental role. At the other extreme is New York City, which (like four other municipalities in the panel) is a composite city-county government and is responsible for the provision of public schools as well as for the usual array of municipal services. Ten other surveyed local units

Table 1.

	Surveyed Panel of Jurisdictions		Surveyed Panel as Percent of U.S. Totals	
	Number	Shared Revenue for 1972	Number of Jurisdictions	Shared Revenue for 1972
State governments	8	$645,126	16.0	36.4
Municipalities	29	341,883	0.2	17.9
By 1970 population (000s):				
100-plus	12	331,893	7.8	31.6
50 to 100	9	8,345	3.9	4.2
10 to 50	4	1,188	0.3	0.3
Less than 10	4	458	(a)	0.2
County governments	21	126,882	0.7	9.4
By 1970 population (000s):				
100-plus	11	123,008	3.5	16.3
50 to 100	5	2,495	1.5	1.6
Less than 50	5	1,379	0.2	0.3
Townships	6	1,003	(a)	0.4
Indian tribe	1	134	0.3	2.1

(a) Less than one-twentieth of 1 percent.

(four counties, five municipalities, and one township) are also school-administering governments, while the remaining 45 reflect the more common arrangement whereby public education is a responsibility of independent school district governments.

Early in 1973 each associate was furnished a copy of the revenue-sharing law and regulations, a set of background data for his assigned jurisdictions, and two sets of report forms. (The subjects included on the forms involved both open- and closed-ended questions.) The main report form for the first period of the field research was an individual-jurisdiction report; a second consisted of an overall report on the associate's findings for all of the field sites assigned to that particular associate. As sources, associates interviewed officials of the assigned jurisdictions, examined budget and fiscal documents and related public records, and met with selected representatives of local interest groups. Each associate was instructed to record *his own considered judgment* on all questions calling for evaluation.

FOCUSING ON POLICY EFFECTS

As emphasized, the principal aim of this design has been to focus on the main policy issues raised by revenue sharing. How are the funds being used? What about "urban focus" as an objective of the distribution formula for revenue sharing? How are low-income rural areas affected? What are the decentralization effects of revenue sharing? What has been its impact on minority groups? What about its effects on the structure and intergovernmental relationships of state and local government?

It is often tempting—in fact, revenue sharing is a cardinal illustration of this problem—to study the most easily measured effects of policy changes, as opposed to trying to get at issues of principal concern to policy makers. The rest of this paper discusses preliminary data from the Brookings study from the point of view of this proposition: the need for analysis of the most important policy effects of the State and Local Fiscal Assistance Act of 1972. It is divided, as is the research, into three parts relating to the main types of revenue sharing: distributional, fiscal, and political.

PROBLEMS IN ANALYZING DISTRIBUTIONAL EFFECTS

The first example of the need to go beyond the most easily available data concerns the distributional effects of revenue sharing. Considerable publicity has been given to comparisons of the per capita amounts of shared revenue received by particular large cities. Various efforts have been made to examine such amounts in relation to economic and demographic characteristics of individual cities. Rarely however have presentations of such data taken specific account of the *layering* involved in the local distribution of shared revenue, which urgently needs to be recognized if meaningful comparisons are to be made.

For example, the first year's allocation to New York City was $27 per capita, or more than twice the $11 per capita that went to the city of Los Angeles. But Los Angeles County, which provides an extensive array of services countywide (including services in the central city) also received $12 per capita. With both allocations taken into account, the resulting $23 per capita for the area and residents of the city of Los Angeles is not much below the amount for New York City, where there is no overlying county government.

There is great variation in the extent to which shared revenue going to individual city governments is in effect supplemented by allocations to overlying counties. In the first report on the Brookings study, there are tabulations which show, for the nation's largest cities individually and for all municipalities by population size, not only the amount of shared revenue paid directly to municipal governments but also the sum of such allocations *plus* a population-based proration of the entitlements of overlying county governments.[1]

These composite figures provide a much better basis for comparative analysis than "municipal government" amounts standing alone, which disregard the varying degree of city-county layering in the distribution of funds. At the same time, the use of population as a basis for proration involves the arbitrary assumption that benefits form each county's shared revenue (whether through improved services or lower taxes) accrue uniformly to noncity and city residents of the county. There are bound to be instances of considerable urban or rural bias in the flow of benefits. In an effort to pin down and quantify these variations for future reports, we have asked the field research associates, in the nine cases where our field research panel includes both a metropolitan central city and an overlying county government, to make an assessment of the city's relative benefit from the county government's use of shared revenue. The resulting data will be presented in the second volume on the Brookings study of general revenue sharing.

FISCAL EFFECTS OF REVENUE SHARING

The need for intensive and probing analysis of the impact of revenue sharing is especially important when one considers the problem of trying to gauge the effects of revenue sharing upon the finances of recipient governments. The main problem in this area is that insufficient attention has been given to the difficulty of saying how shared revenue is actually used. The reporting system prescribed in the law for local units relates to eight so-called "priority-expenditure areas." Yet in many cases the resulting "attributions" of shared revenue by local public officials mask its real effects. Although a given recipient government may attribute shared revenue to police protection, if it does not spend any more for police than it would have anyway, then the real uses (or what we have called the net fiscal effects of revenue sharing) must be sought elsewhere.

As of the end of June 1973,[2] all the field-research associates for the Brookings panel reported their "best judgment" estimates as to the initial uses of revenue sharing funds for each unit in the sample in relation to the following categories of net fiscal effects:

A. **New Spending Effects**

   (1) *New capital expenditures:* Spending for capital projects or the purchase of equipment that, without shared revenue, would not have occurred at all or would have occurred at least one year later.

   (2) *New or expanded operations:* Operating expenditures begun or expanded with shared revenue (excluding pay and benefit increases).

   (3) *Increased pay and benefits:* Using shared revenue for pay and fringe benefit increases that otherwise would not have been authorized, either at all or at the levels approved.

B. **Substitution Effects**

   (1) *Tax cut:* Using shared revenue to finance ongoing programs with a consequent freeing of the jurisdiction's own resources to permit a reduction in tax rates.

   (2) *Tax stabilization:* Using shared revenue to finance ongoing programs with a consequent avoidance of an increase in tax rates that otherwise would have been approved.

   (3) *Program maintenance:* Allocating shared revenue to ongoing programs for which the alternative course, without revenue sharing, would have been to eliminate the programs or cut their scope.

   (4) *Avoidance of borrowing:* Substituting shared revenue for borrowing that otherwise would have been undertaken.

   (5) *Increased fund balances:* Allocating shared revenue to ongoing programs, with a consequent net effect of increasing fund balances.

   (6) *Restoration of federal aid:* Using shared revenue to offset actual or anticipated reductions in federal grants-in-aid.

The data from the field reports were analyzed both in the aggregate and by unweighted means. The latter measure (which compensates for the skewing effect that a few very large jurisdictions can have for the sample size used in this study) can be regarded as accounting for revenue-sharing decisions rather than revenue-sharing dollars. For example, if a city of 100,000 population used 20 percent of the shared revenue that it had allocated as of July 1, 1973, for what the field research associate classified as new capital purposes, and a city of 1 million used 10 percent in this way, the former counts twice as heavily in the unweighted mean even though the amount involved for the larger city is several times greater.

To provide an additional yardstick with which to assess revenue-sharing allocations, the field associates were asked to classify (also from a set of uniform definitions) the fiscal pressure on their jurisdictions as extreme, moderate, relatively little, or none.

On the average, local governments in the sample applied more than half of their shared revenue (57.5 percent) to *new* purposes and the rest (42.5 percent) in various different ways to *substitute* for funds that would have been raised from other sources or from program cuts. The average state government in the sample used 35.7 percent of its revenue-sharing allocations in this period for new spending and 64.3 percent for various substitution purposes. (See Table 2.)

This method of analysis (mean percentage basis) indicates an important fact about the fiscal effects of revenue sharing, which is that larger jurisdictions have tended to use less shared revenue for new purposes than smaller ones.

Since larger units receive significantly greater amounts of revenue-sharing funds in terms of total dollar amounts than do smaller units, when these same classifications are compiled on an aggregate basis, the relative amount of new spending goes down. On an aggregate basis, local units in the sample applied 31.4 percent of their shared revenue to new spending and the states 21.1 percent.

Table 2. USES OF REVENUE SHARING BY SAMPLE JURISDICTION
(Mean Percentage Basis by Net Effect through June 1973)

	Mean Percentages	
	Local	State
New Spending:	57.5	35.7
New capital	46.0	21.6
Expanded operations	10.8	11.6
Increased pay and benefits	.8	–
Unallocated	–	2.5
Substitutions:	42.5	64.3
Tax cut	3.5	13.2
Tax stabilization	13.8	–
Program maintenance	12.6	15.3
Borrowing avoidance	9.5	3.3
Federal aid restoration	.3	3.0
Increased fund balance	2.7	4.5
Other	.1	–
Unallocated	–	25.0
Total	100.0	100.0

NOTE: The table is based on responses for 8 state governments and 55 local units. Two local governments in the sample had not allocated shared revenue as of July 1, 1973, and therefore are not included in these tabulations.

This conclusion that a sizable proportion of shared revenue has been used to substitute for funds which would have been obtained from other sources rather than for new spending does not necessarily indict the revenue-sharing program. Many of the original proponents of revenue sharing said that these funds should be used to reduce tax pressures, particularly in the field of property taxation.

One of the cities in the Brookings sample is Newark, New Jersey, a city with very serious social and economic problems. It has the second highest residential property tax rate in the nation. According to the field-research associate, Newark used all of its shared revenue in the early period to reduce and hold down property taxes. This is what city officials felt was most urgently needed to improve the relative economic position of the city and enhance its ability to hold and attract residential and business property-owners. Because central cities in the nation receive relatively more shared revenue than their suburban hinterlands, official decisions to apply shared revenue to finance tax reductions can in the long run help deal with the stubborn fiscal problems of central cities like Newark.

POLITICAL EFFECTS

One of the main arguments on behalf of general revenue sharing was decentralization. As researchers, we have found this to be another case of data that are hard to get at—but very important. We have in our study examined the effects of revenue sharing on the budgetary processes of the 65 jurisdictions in our field research sample as a way of getting at the effects of the new program on basic political roles and relationships of recipient "general purpose" units of state and local government.

To generalize about experience to date, there are significant indications that revenue sharing has increased the competitiveness and prominence of local budgetary processes. This statement, however, needs to be made subject to three qualifications: *first,* such developments appear in some places but not others; there is no clear pattern yet to explain these variations; *second,* there is reason to believe that the changes may not have a sustained effect; *third* and most important of all, it would be wrong to characterize the observable effects to date of revenue sharing on state-local budgetary processes as deeply important where they have occurred or as pervasive in terms of their overall national impact.

We need to define what is meant here by "increasing the

competitiveness and prominence" of state-local budgetary processes. For purposes of analysis, we have identified three main types of "actors" in the budget process:

(1) *Generalist officials* (mayors, governors, city and county managers, legislators, budget officers and the staff aides of all of these officials);

(2) *Internal interests* (agencies of state and local government, e.g., highways, welfare, health, housing);

(3) *External interest groups* (groups in the community interested in having certain types of programs undertaken, or in the case of existing programs, expanded).

Important to the basic idea of revenue sharing was the belief of many of its original supporters that the role of *generalist officials* would be enhanced because there would be concern on the part of both *internal* and *external* interest groups to have such officials allocate shared revenue for their particular favored purposes. Shared revenue, unlike categorical grants (some of which are paid directly to functional agencies or special-purpose districts), must be allocated by the regular appropriation process involving these generalist officials.

In this connection, a very interesting thing happened on the way to revenue sharing. Whether by design or coincidence (a debatable point), the program went into effect at the same time that the Nixon Administration, in its proposed budget for fiscal 1974, announced significant and, in some cases, deep cuts in federal domestic spending. This created a "pincer effect," whereby revenue sharing and these proposed budget cuts coming together created much more interest in state and local budgeting than would have been the case with either of these two events alone. Not only were federal budget reductions threatened, but local governments now had supposedly "new" funds so that the affected internal and external interests could turn to generalist state and local officials and say, "You should save these programs by allocating revenue sharing to them."

This pincer effect of proposed budget cuts and the onset of revenue sharing occurring simultaneously appears to have been mitigated by several forces. One is the fact that the courts (in the case of impoundments) and the Congress (in the case of budget reductions) would not go along with the administration's budget plans for many domestic programs. In addition, we found cases where state and local agencies and interest groups favoring certain programs threatened by proposed federal budget cuts decided not to press for shared revenue as a replacement because they were concerned that this would undermine the case they were making in Washington that particular grant-in-aid funds should be resotred in the *federal* budget.

The basic issue in regard to the political effects of revenue sharing is whether or not the new program is churning up the budget-making processes of recipient state and local governments and providing more groups with access to the policy-making process. In about half of the 65 sample jurisdictions, those changes in the budgetary process which occurred because of revenue sharing tended to increase the overall competitiveness and public visibility of the budgetary process. These changes varied in nature and intensity. Some sample units set up special budget-review procedures to decide how to use shared revenue; in others, local interest groups pressed for funds in a manner that increased the competitiveness of state and local budgetary processes, although the processes themselves were not changed.

Other critical policy questions raised about the political effects of revenue sharing relate to its impact on the structure of state and local government. A major issue in this area is the extent to which revenue sharing props up small and limited-function local jurisdictions. The principal conclusion is that the revenue-sharing law is seriously inaccurate in designating all townships as general-purpose local governments. Again, the issue is a complex one and any remedies involved therefore must be carefully designed. A state-by-state distinction among such jurisdictions would overlook the graduation that can be found even within states in the scope of local units that bear the township label.

CONCLUSION

The Brookings experience with revenue-sharing research to date has been instructive. The process itself has been an iterative one, with important alterations being made in the overall plan as the work has proceeded. Interesting methodological issues have been raised from the outset. The idea of monitoring research, as opposed to evaluation, is one such issue already noted. Another involves auspices. Who should do monitoring research; can it be done inside the government, and (if not) should it be financed by government agencies? The process of compiling uniform judgmental assessments for a fairly large field research network (the approach used here) needs to be compared with other techniques—for example, a larger mail-questionnaire or opinion survey of local officials, both of which are being undertaken in related studies of revenue sharing sponsored by the National Science Foundation. Another alternative is simply to wait the necessary time to rely entirely on time-series analyses of census statistics on state and local finances and employment. The various approaches that could be used of course, are mutually reinforcing and the intention of the Brookings study is to draw on other data. But the question of priorities—that is, which techniques are to be preferred—is one that should be addressed by persons working with the emerging body of data on the impact of revenue sharing. The policy change involved here is a significant one. It needs to be noted that the social science research community has focused considerable (some critics say too much) attention on the question of what happens when such a policy change is adopted. In any event, the fraternity has responded on a basis which in my personal view is both appropriate and suitably broad-gauged.

It also needs to be borne in mind in thinking about research or revenue sharing that there are several different kinds of research being done. To summarize, there is research done: (1) by government (GAO, Treasury, and the various state and localities), (2) by academic researchers, as in the case of Brookings, and (3) by particular interest groups collecting data on whether, and the extent to which, shared revenue is being allocated to programs and purposes they particularly favor. By way of illustration, the latter includes social action, civil rights, library, environmental, and public health organizations, as well as public-employee unions.

All of these data provide rich insights into contemporary American federalism. They were developed to influence the national debate on the shape and characteristics of an extension of the current revenue-sharing legislation. Whether it will work out this way is anyone's guess. Once enacted, the political forces created to continue a revenue-sharing program in essentially its present form may be so strong as to preclude important changes. In the hearings on the 1975 federal budget, then Secretary of the Treasury George P. Shultz was asked by Chairman George H. Mahon of the House Appropriations Committee if the federal government would ever be able to get rid of revenue sharing. Shultz said he did not think so. Mahon agreed, responding, "We will stop the tides of the Passamoquoddy before we ever stop revenue sharing."

APPENDIX

FIELD RESEARCH ASSOCIATES FOR GOVERNMENTAL UNITS SURVEYED
(Affiliations are as of September 1974)

Arizona: Maricopa County, Phoenix, Scottsdale, Tempe
Arlyn J. Larson, Associate professor of economics, Arizona State University

Arkansas: Little Rock, North Little Rock, Pulaski County, Saline County
George E. Campbell, Attorney, Little Rock; former executive secretary, Arkansas Constitution Revision Study Commission

California: State of California
Leslie D. Howe, Vice president, California Retailers; former state and local financial officer

California: Carson, Los Angeles, Los Angeles County
Ronald W. Lopez, Consultant; former director, Mexican American Studies Center, Claremont Colleges

Colorado: State of Colorado, Longmont
R. D. Sloan, Jr., Associate professor of political science and director, Bureau of Governmental Research and Service, University of Colorado

Florida: Jacksonville-Duval, Orange County, Orlando, Seminole County
John DeGrove, Director, Joint Center for Environmental and Urban Problems, Florida Atlantic–Florida International University

Aileen Lotz, Staff consultant, Joint Center for Environment and Urban Problems

Illinois: State of Illinois
Leroy S. Wehrle, Professor of economics, Sangamon State University; former director, Illinois Institute for Social Policy

Assisted by

Robert Schoeplein, Associate professor of economics, University of Illinois

John N. Lattimer, Executive director, State of Illinois Commission on Intergovernmental Cooperation

Louisiana: State of Louisiana, Baton Rouge
Edward J. Steimel, Executive director, Public Affairs Research Council of Louisiana, Inc.
Arthur Thiel, Research director, Public Affairs Research Council of Louisiana, Inc.

Maine: State of Maine, Bangor
Kenneth T. Palmer, Associate professor of political science, University of Maine

Maryland: Baltimore, Baltimore County, Carroll County, Harford County
Clifton Vincent, Assistant professor of political science, Morgan State College

Massachusetts: Commonwealth of Massachusetts, Holden Town, Worcester
James A. Maxwell, Professor emeritus of economics, Clark University

Missouri: St. Louis
Robert Christman, City hall reporter, St. Louis *Post-Dispatch*

New Jersey: Essex County, Livingston Township, Newark, West Orange
Robert Curvin, Associate professor of political science, Brooklyn College

New York: State of New York
Charles Holcomb, New York manager, Gannett Newspapers, Albany

New York: New York City
Center for New York City Affairs, New School for Social Research

New York: Greece Town, Irondequoit Town, Monroe County, Rochester
Sarah F. Liebschutz, Assistant professor of political science, New York State University at Brockport

North Carolina: State of North Carolina, Orange County

Deil Wright, Professor of political science, University of North Carolina

Ohio: Butler County, Cincinnati, Hamilton, Hamilton County

Frederick D. Stocker, Professor of business research, Center for Business and Economic Research, Ohio State University

Oregon: Cottage Grove, Eugene, Lane County, Springfield

Herman Kehrli, Director emeritus, Bureau of Governmental Research and Service, University of Oregon

South Carolina: Camden, Fairfield County, Kershaw County, Winnsboro

C. Blease Graham, Assistant professor of government and research associate, Bureau of Governmental Research, University of South Carolina

South Dakota: Minnehaha County, Rosebud Indian Tribe, Sioux Falls, Tripp County, Turner County

W. O. Farber, Chairman, Department of Government, and director, Governmental Research Bureau, University of South Dakota

Assisted by

Dan Crippen, University of South Dakota

Wisconsin: Beaver Dam, Dodge County, Lowell Town, Mayville, Theresa Town

Clara Penniman, Director, Center for the Study of Public Policy and Administration, University of Wisconsin

NOTES

1. See chapter 5 of R. P. Nathan, A. D. Manuel, and S. E. Calkins, *Monitoring Revenue Sharing,* Washington, D.C.: Brookings Institution, 1975.

2. Recipient jurisdictions as of this date had received their entitlements for the first 15 months and were informed of their entitlement amount for the next three months. Altogether, we found a quite rapid rate of decision making on the use of these funds. All but two local governments in the sample as of June 30, 1973, had allocated some shared revenue. In total, the 65 jurisdictions in the sample had allocated 106 percent of the amount of shared revenue they were eligible to receive as their first 18 months' entitlements. Many had advance-funded. The term "allocate" is used to refer to decisions in the appropriations process, whereby the funds in the required separate accounts for shared revenue were officially assigned to a particular purpose. This does not mean that funds were actually expended, especially in the case of capital items where a considerable time lag can occur between allocation and expenditure.

4

FEDERALISM, REVENUE SHARING
AND LOCAL GOVERNMENT

DAVID O. PORTER

International Institute of Management, Berlin
University of California, Riverside

There is little dispute that the United States is becoming a national culture and economy. National (and international) patterns of business, communication, education, career development, recreation, and entertainment have given impetus to federal legislation which recognized a growing national interdependence. Stabilization of the economy, regulating business practices, civil rights, voting rights, and the poverty programs are among these laws. At the same time, trends such as increasing levels of education and income have encouraged citizens to be more quality-conscious and selective in their consumption of public goods and services. People are impatient with insensitive, unresponsive, or cumbersome bureaucracies.

These pressures to deal with national interests while at the same time being responsive to the diversity of local communities and individuals are straining our system of federalism. To deal with

AUTHOR'S NOTE: *An earlier version of this paper was presented at the 1974 annual meetings of the American Political Science Association in Chicago. The author thanks George H. McGeary, a fellow at the Joint Center for Urban Studies of the Massachusetts Institute of Technology and Harvard University, for his reading of the article in its first draft. His contribution is acknowledged, but responsibility for the final manuscript remains with the author.*

national interests, federal agencies and programs have been created; to respond to diversity among individuals and localities, vital state and local governments are necessary. If an administrative structure capable of simultaneously responding to national interests and local diversity is to be developed, each of the traditional levels of government—with some new ones added in—must be utilized and their activities coordinated. James L. Sundquist (1969: 268-269) focused repeatedly on this theme:

> As the federal government continues to establish national objectives that can be executed only through state and local initiative and participation, the stake of the country in the upgrading of state [and local] government . . . becomes ever greater.

(On this theme, see also Wright, 1974.)

The policies often associated with general revenue sharing deal with only a segment of the more general problem identified by Sundquist. Many early justifications for revenue sharing focused on the frustrations of citizens and officials within state and local governments as they related to the various federal agencies and programs. Relatively little attention was given to what Sundquist identifies as a need to guide "the evolution of the whole system of federal-state-local relations, viewed . . . as a *single* system" (Sundquist, 1969: 246). For instance, Richard Nixon, in a 1971 message urging the passage of the revenue-sharing bill, emphasized the complaints of state and local officials. He said there would be a reversal "of the flow of power and resources to Washington to states and communities." State and local officials could allocate these funds according to local priorities, not those of "distant bureaucrats in Washington."

It is not clear, however, that giving resources, and discretion, to state and local governments must reduce the ability of our intergovernmental system · to coordinate programs which have national objectives. A considerable body of writing in economics, political science, administrative theory, and industrial organization argues that effective local administrative and political jurisdictions are essential elements in multilevel organizational structures (for example, see Bish, 1971; Ostrom, 1973; Sundquist, 1969; Williamson, 1970). But for local governments to fulfill their potential as part of an intergovernmental administrative system, rather substantial changes in their jurisdictions and powers may be needed. Local governments, as presently constituted, have tremendous variations in their resources, size, and powers. Some cities are larger than states; others are smaller than neighborhoods. With such diversity, it is difficult to design an intergovernmental system which includes an active role for local governments.

This article looks at the potential of general revenue sharing as a vehicle for bringing local governments more fully into a system of intergovernmental administration. Through positive incentives and guidelines, federal policy makers can encourage the evolution of more capable local governments. Revenue sharing is particularly suited to this task for two reasons. First, the impetus for these reforms must come from the federal government. The federal government is the only jurisdiction which has a national perspective and therefore the ability to guide reforms of local governments in a consistent direction and to help it serve as an integral part of an intergovernmental system (Sundquist, 1969: 244-246). Second, general revenue-sharing funds pass, in the main, directly to general purpose jurisdictions.[1] Guidelines and incentives associated with revenue sharing would alter the capability or structure of general purpose governments rather than specify how a particular program is to be carried out, as is done with categorical grants-in-aid.

If the incentives and guidelines associated with a revenue-sharing program are to be effective, however, they must be tied to a conceptual framework for an intergovernmental administrative system. This article looks to some developments in economics, administrative theory, and industrial organization for concepts which may serve as building blocks of such a framework.

In the body of the article, we first examine some of the trends leading to a more intense expression of national interests, and the equally compelling expression of demands for responsiveness to local preferences and diversity. We then suggest how a policy of revenue sharing can be used in the development of an intergovernmental administrative system which has an increased capability to function effectively under conditions of national and local pressures. The role that local government can play is particularly explored, in that it is on local governments that the most intense pressures may be felt. Local governments have a "dual role." First, they articulate demand for local public goods and then supply many of them. Second, they function as the local element of an intergovernmental administrative system which provides public services in response to state or federal legislation. Sections five through seven discuss strategies for developing a body of theory with which to guide the reform of local governments so that they may function in their dual role. These strategies include a conceptual scheme for assigning functions to local governments, the use of vouchers, and the use of "multi-division" forms of organization. The final section summarizes the arguments of the article and relates them to revenue sharing.

A QUEST FOR GIANT ORGANIZATIONS WITH A GENTLE TOUCH

One of the major themes running through discussions of general revenue sharing has been the hope, or fear, that this method of financing would permit state and local governments to be more independent of the federal government; in other words, "give them their head" to choose priorities and programs.[2] The fragmentation of the American governmental system implied in some of these discussions runs counter to the trends in public and private organizations in the United States. In many respects, this yearning for smaller, non-federal governments parallels actions aimed at breaking up American industry into small competitive firms and regulating these firms completely through market mechanisms.

Both sets of suggestions (i.e., revenue sharing and trust-busting) envision a world of competitive organizations, supervised by a government whose primary functions are to provide for national defense and to discourage monopolies. Whether these conditions ever existed is seriously disputed, but clearly they do not exist in the 1970s. Both the public and private sectors are filled with large organizations. Over half of the manufactured goods in the United States are produced by fewer than 500 firms. Giant multinational firms and large state-owned industries account for an increasing proportion of the gross world product. In the public sector, the federal government raises close to half of all governmental revenues. The Department of Defense and the Department of Health, Education, and Welfare will spend over $200 billion next year. The state governments in New York and California or the cities of New York, Chicago, and Los Angeles have huge bureaucracies and spend billions of dollars yearly.

The dominant pattern in the United States, then, appears to be the presence of very large organizations. John Kenneth Galbraith (1973, 1972) argues that these organizations are a product of capital intensive technologies, modern marketing practices, and pervasive "externalities." However, neither Galbraith nor many other writers from a variety of orientations and disciplines are satisfied with the performance of these large public and private bureaucracies. Writers from the left, middle, and right in the political sprectrum are advocating that these large organizations be broken up or made more responsive and humane (Eldon, 1971). Radical economists in the United States look to self-governing worker cooperatives as models (Reich et al., 1972); the New Public Administration is exploring ways to coordinate social activities without using hierarchies (Thayer, 1973) or at least to help large organizations become more humane through techniques such as organizational development (Kirkhart and Gardner, 1974) or citizen participation (Frederickson, 1972); the New Political Economy, usually identified with conservative writers, has found a large and sympathetic audience for their suggestions that government organizations should be made smaller and more competitive so that they will take better account of individual preferences and be technically more efficient (Bish, 1971; Tullock, 1970).

It was from this broadly based ground swell of dissatisfaction with large, insensitive, and unresponsive organizations that much of the support for general revenue sharing was derived. But to adopt a policy aimed at simply breaking up large organizations into smaller, uncoordinated pieces runs into some of the very strong contrary pressures discussed earlier. In government there are an increasing number of national and regional interests on which action can only be initiated and coordinated by units with extensive geographic and political jurisdiction. In business, mass production and marketing techniques depend on the development of large organizations. Further, both public and private organizations are increasingly interdependent from region to region and from nation to nation for materials, labor, and clientele. The coordinative mechanisms of markets, by themselves, have not been able to handle these interdependencies and external effects. Regulatory institutions in large government and large private firms are relied on more and more to coordinate activities among smaller organizational units. To accept, without careful evaluation, a policy (implicit in general revenue sharing) which may further fragment our system of intergovernmental relations thus runs counter to many of the needs of our governing system. Instead of adopting a strategy aimed primarily at re-creating or perpetuating a series of semiautonomous state and local governments, perhaps we should consider a more comprehensive policy which will also improve the capability of state and local governments to function more effectively as part of an intergovernmental administrative system. Such a policy could build on the capabilities and strengths of each level—federal, state and local—to coordinate and guide in the performance of many governmental goods and services.

REVENUE SHARING:
A TOOL TO REFORM LOCAL GOVERNMENT?

Another theme in discussions of revenue sharing, but much less developed than the theme of state and local independence, suggests that revenue sharing can be used as a vehicle to encourage reforms in state and local governments. For instance, the Humphrey-Reuss version of a revenue-sharing bill stipulated, among other things, that receipt of revenue sharing funds be conditional upon the adoption of a state income tax. Wilbur Mills supported a similar proposal. These suggestions were not included in the bill that was finally enacted.

There have been, however, revenue-sharing plans which have required or induced substantial reforms in the receiving jurisdictions. The most notable example is in the field of education. In the 1930s, state governments began to provide large amounts of general aid to local school districts. These were essentially revenue-sharing programs—i.e., the greater capacity of state governments to raise money was shared with local school districts. The state legislatures required and encouraged many reforms for this money. The length of the school year was standardized; teacher certification moved to the state level; curricula were specified. Further, since many school districts were thought to be too small to provide quality education, legislatures often promised supplemental grants to "consolidated" school districts. This incentive, along with many other factors, contributed to an absolute decline in the number of school districts from 67,355 in 1952 to 21,782 in 1967 (Bish, 1971: 2). The dynamics of these programs of state aid in education should be studied further to see what guidance they may provide for federal revenue sharing to state and local governments.

Revenue sharing can become an effective instrument for encouraging and guiding reform in our intergovernmental administrative system. Presently, the administration of intergovernmental programs relies on an amalgam of jerry-built administrative structures, including federal, state, and local units, to carry the major burden in the ultimate delivery of services.[3] Such practices are increasingly unsatisfactory in the face of the tremendous growth in domestic programs at all levels of government. Developing administrative structures which integrate the capabilities of each level of government is becoming a critical need. Perhaps through revenue sharing, positive incentives can be developed to induce state and local governments to increase their capability to work effectively within an intergovernmental network.

Local governments, particularly, are not prepared to carry their weight in such an administrative system. This article concentrates on suggestions for improving the capacity of these governments to assume significant intergovernmental responsibilities. In fact, it is argued that the development of an effective intergovernmental administrative system must include a revamping of our theories, implicit and explicit, of local government. To this end, we review briefly the implicit theory of local government inherited from the common law and discuss the inadequacy of that theory in a modern setting.

A DUAL ROLE FOR LOCAL GOVERNMENTS

When the legal concepts behind municipal corporations (cities and towns) were being worked out in the eighteenth and early nineteenth centuries, the implicit administrative model was one which (1) permitted considerable local autonomy and (2) assumed that there was a bundle of services peculiar to that geographic area.[4] These two assumptions allowed the establishment of a local governmental unit which encompassed the urban development in an area and allowed that unit a good deal of discretion in the selection of functions it would undertake. If a community decided on a high (or low) level of services, the consequences of that decision rarely affected residents of other communities.

Modern conditions have made such a theory of local government inadequate and unrealistic. First, most municipal corporations do not encompass all of the urban development in an area. Benefits and costs of decisions frequently spill over the boundaries of a local jurisdiction. Urban sprawl, interdependence among governments, increasingly complicated patterns of social interaction, a national economic system, and modern technologies often make an expression of purely local demands parochial and disruptive to the interests of the larger community. Second, local governments have become, in addition to being vehicles for expressing local preferences for urban services and goods, an integral part of the intergovernmental administrative apparatus. As a result, many of their activities are either mandated or constrained by other governments.

Currently it cannot be said that local governments are suited for *any* single purpose. They are too varied. The populations they govern range in size from under 20 people to over 8,000,000. The bases for their financial resources range from ample and diverse to meager and narrow. Their jurisdictions and powers vary substantially. If local governments are to fulfill their potential roles in the expression of the preferences of local residents and as an integral component in an intergovernmental administrative system, perhaps there should be more uniformity among local governments with respect to size, resources, and powers. How can Congress delegate responsibilities in an intergovernmental program to "local government" if local governments are so diverse? Some local units are more like state governments than cities; others more like rural villages than urban centers. Further, how can local governments meet the demands of local citizens? They are either too large for citizens to relate to or too small to provide the services. A local citizen can empathize with Goldilocks in her quest for porridge that was "just right." Goldilocks found a bowl to her liking. Few citizens of local government are so lucky.

Suggestions for the reform of local governments have concentrated on one function, one level of government, or one type of problem. For instance, much of the impetus behind the movement for metropolitan governments was aimed at solving such area-wide problems as air pollution, water supply, sewage treatment, or land-use planning. Economies of scale in production or the pervasiveness of cost or benefit spillovers were stressed. A problem in this literature is that no two functions are optimally performed by the same jurisdiction. Some writers even came close to suggesting the creation of a separate jurisdiction to correspond to the optimum scale of operation for each function. (See Oates, 1972: 31-53, for a review of this point of view.) Focusing on a different set of problems, the literature on citizen participation and neighborhood government (Schmandt, 1972) emphasized the local government's role as an articulator of local demands and provider of local services. One element or the other of the dual role of local governments—i.e., the intergovernmental or the local articulation roles—is recognized in either literature, but these roles are seldom discussed together.

A brief summary statement may highlight the capabilities needed by local governments to meet their dual role. They must satisfy two broad and often conflicting requirements. First, they must be able to fit into an intergovernmental system in which several levels of government interact. The federal government will usually formulate objectives in areas of growing national interdependence, and state governments may adjust these objectives to satisfy regional interests and needs. Local governments should provide a capability for fine-grained coordination in the actual delivery of services or in the articulation of local demand for them. Second, local governments need to perform their traditional functions as articulators for and providers of local services and goods. In both roles, local political leadership encourages responsiveness to citizen-consumers.

Three strategies are suggested in this article for improving the performance of local government in our intergovernmental system. These are not necessarily competing strategies, but they are also not completely complementary. A good deal of analysis remains in sorting out how to fit these ideas together into a coherent policy for guiding the development of local government. Broad outlines are drawn for each approach, but their integration is left for a later effort.

We will first discuss some administrative theory which suggests the necessity of a "local presence" in the administration of activities which are characterized by complex technologies and/or complex social environments. Next, we examine some of the implications for intergovernmental administrative systems of using vouchers to distribute certain goods and services. Finally, we discuss the feasibility of adapting a "multidivision" form of organization for use in intergovernmental systems.

A NEED FOR A LOCAL PRESENCE

Developing the notion of a need for a local presence fits into some of the proposals made under the rubric of the New Federalism during the Nixon Administration. These proposals are founded on the idea that certain levels of government should perform particular functions. Richard P. Nathan, who was an early advocate of the New Federalism, summarized this position:

For two major functional areas, decentralization policies have been pursued: (1) human resources *services* and (2) *community services*. On the other hand, for (3) *natural resources* and (4) *income support* (both cash and in-kind), the Administration's initiatives emphasize further central action. [Nathan, 1973: 5]

Problems arise when this policy is made operational because there are aspects in each of these functional categories that require a local presence or, conversely, a central role. Natural resources policy, for instance, requires decisions at the central level on what standards are to be followed, but enforcement requires a rather extensive local presence.

Perhaps a more productive approach recognizes that functions will be shared among all levels of government but that each level will have greater proficiency in performing certain aspects of these functions. Tasks with highly interactive technologies or environments will be more effectively performed by smaller, localized administrative units. Conversely, tasks which rely on standardized techniques or affect large geographic areas will require state or federal action.

The logic of such an approach is rather straightforward. As has been convincingly stated by Herbert Simon (1965), people have a "bounded rationality." They cannot understand or perceive everything that is going on around them. Consequently, the more complex or variable an aspect of a function, the more need for either "satisficing" (i.e., making do without fully understanding or analyzing a problem) or dividing the activity into bundles, with each bundle being small enough to be understood.

James D. Thompson (1967), using the concept of bounded rationality, has suggested that organization structure will reflect the complexity of a task's technology and environment. The more demanding or interactive the technology, and/or the more heterogeneous and unstable the environment of the organization, the more the organization will need to subdivide its tasks to cope with the increasing complexity.

Thompson analyzed tasks according to the complexity of the interdependence among the variables within their production process. The simplest process was what he called "pooled" interdependence. The activities of the various subunits in an organization draw strength from each other, but are able to go about their activities quite independently. Their actions are coordinated, to the extent they need be, through the adoption of standardized procedures. The branches of a banking firm are good examples of pooled interdependence. Each branch adds to the assets and strength of the bank, but the activities in each branch can go on quite independently of each other. Standard forms for deposits and withdrawals coordinate most of their activities. Many governmental regulatory agencies operate in much the same fashion.

A more complicated type of interdependence is present if tasks must come in a particular order. Thompson called this "sequential" interdependence. Coordination is handled through plans. Administrative structures become somewhat more complicated. Relationships among the various units within the organization must be coordinated so that work can flow smoothly through the production process. A more active central direction is needed than when the technology of the task requires pooled interdependence.

Many important tasks are characterized by "reciprocal" interdependence. There is a constant interaction among key variables within the technology. Coordination is accomplished through mutual adjustment and feedback. Many government activities use technologies of this type. Teaching and social work involve a continual interaction between the student or client and the teacher or worker. Current actions of the teacher depend in part on the response of the student to a previous action by the teacher. Such mutual adjustment requires an organizational structure with a capacity for two-way communication. Central direction of a large organization using intensive technologies is difficult because of the volume of the interactions. Bounded rationality comes into play, and the directors must divide up their responsibilities or lose effective control.

The characteristics of the environment of an organization will have a similar effect. The more complicated the environment, the greater the impact of bounded rationality on its structure. If an environment is relatively stable and homogeneous, the structure of the organization can be simple and centrally directed. If the environment is shifting and heterogeneous, the organizational structure will need to be more complicated if it is to divide the complexities into bundles that can be understood.

As applied to local governments, this theory suggests that the effective performance of certain tasks requires a *local presence*. Tasks with technologies that require mutual adjustment and/or have environments which are shifting and heterogeneous require an organizational structure which includes small, localized units. To be effective, these units should be endowed with considerable discretion, for they must make judgments about appropriate responses to clients or decide how to cope with complicated environmental situations. If local governments were designed to accomplish those aspects of tasks requiring a local presence, they would be vigorous and important administrative units.

DELEGATIONS OF FUNCTIONS TO CITIZENS

Since Milton Friedman (1955) wrote about education vouchers in 1955, there has been a growing interest, on the right and left of the political spectrum, in the possibility of using this device as a method of making local governments more responsive and effective.[5] The main appeal of vouchers is that, for certain functions, they decentralize important tasks to citizen-consumers. Consumers are allowed to choose suppliers and to decide what mix of services they will receive. The suppliers need not even be in the public sector. Private suppliers are used in such programs as Medicare, Medicaid, and housing allowances. Because of political constraints, only public providers were allowed in the voucher experiment in Alum Rock School District, but both Jencks and Friedman argue that vouchers would work better if private suppliers were permitted.

Housing and education are policy areas thought to be particularly suited to voucher programs. The national objective in housing programs has been to help people who cannot afford standard housing. Up to now the policy has been to construct public housing. Under an allowance scheme, it is hoped that additional money to purchase housing will be sufficient to solve the problem. Participants can use their increased purchasing power to rent acceptable quarters in the private market. In public education, the problem was that individuals had no choice among suppliers. Parents or students either took what was offered in their neighborhood school or forfeited their education tax dollars. In both public education and housing, suppliers lose their monopoly power if vouchers are used. If the performance of a particular neighborhood school is unsatisfactory to parents, they may shift their child to another school without penalty. The same is true in housing. Instead of having to accept what is available in a public housing project, a participant can choose to live anywhere in the city where modest rentals are available. Public officials are relieved of the very complicated tasks of deciding what educational or housing services their constituents want. Citizen-consumers make those decisions through their own private calculus.

A model of administration appropriate to a voucher system has several features. First, there must be some standards set and funds provided. This is the responsibility of larger governments, on the state and federal levels. The federal government is usually thought to be the most proficient in income transfers (Oates, 1972: 3-20). The state and federal levels often share the responsibility to set the standards which constitute the "earmark" for the voucher, i.e., the restrictions placed on its use. Second, the administrative structure must be capable of enforcing the stipulations of the earmark. This administrative structure usually requires reciprocal interdependence and works within a dynamic environment. Thus, a local presence is needed. In the case of housing, for instance, this means that a local agency must be able to restrict the expenditures of the housing allowance to acceptable housing, with a minimum amount of the funds being diverted into substandard housing or nonhousing expenditures. In addition to the necessity for housing inspections, this implies that some minimum level of housing information may be necessary to assist participants in their search for acceptable housing. Finally, the local agency must determine who is eligible to receive the allowances. This process can be long and complicated, depending on the method used to determine eligibility and the variability of the income of participants.

In education, the tasks of the local agency would be similar. There is a need to have some kind of quality control to select the schools eligible to accept voucher students. Certain minimum standards in educational offerings, personnel, and health standards could reasonably be required by the federal and state governments. Further, not unlike the housing allowances, there may be certain families who are eligible for higher or lower payments. The local agency would need the capability to determine the entitlement of each family.

Several problems are inherent in voucher systems. Most obviously, this approach increases demand for a service, but does little to increase the supply. The market is expected to expand the supply as demand increases. In Medicare and Medicaid, demand was substantially increased by providing citizen-consumers with open-ended vouchers for physicians' services. Little has been done to regulate the fees charged by physicians or to increase the number of practitioners. Inflation in fees, not surprisingly, has resulted.

Education vouchers and housing allowances have not been widely used, but are both being experimented with by the federal government. The assumption, in both sets of these experiments, is that citizen-consumers will be able to exercise much more choice in the education and housing services they desire (Porter, 1975). But, for a variety of reasons, the voucher in itself may not empower the citizen-consumer to exercise his "sovereignty." "Producer sovereignty" (Galbraith, 1973: 111-112) may be the stronger force. Since in an intergovernmental system the production of goods or services is carried on at several levels of government, there are multiple points where citizen-consumers can be frustrated or closed out. Professionals at the local level, for instance, have an opportunity to exercise producer sovereignty if the voucher or allowance is given to the citizen-consumer by local agencies. The manner in which these professionals transfer the voucher will greatly influence the choices the consumer perceives as possible. In this situation, the professionals in the local agency, not the citizens, may gain power from the use of vouchers.

In summary, the administrative system needed to support a voucher system involves all three levels of government. The federal and state levels provide the funds, set levels of payment, and write standards of quality and eligibility. These earmarks set the parameters within which local agencies and participants make choices. Local governments determine the eligibility of each participant, apply the rules in the earmarks, and make adjustments for individual needs. These functions are consistent with the tasks that would be assigned to local governments through the rationale of a local presence. Problems of supply are handled somewhat uncertainly through the market. It is not clear what role local governments could play in guaranteeing to fill in for shortfalls in supply. Finally, producer sovereignty may be a significant factor. By restricting access or information, professionals may be able to control the exercise of consumer choice.

WHAT'S GOOD FOR GENERAL MOTORS . . .

As discussed earlier, one of the most persistent problems in an intergovernmental system is to design administrative units which can simultaneously pursue the goals of the national government and still give to local jurisdictions enough discretion to deal with the complexity inherent in the production processes of many functions and to deal with the diversity of the preferences of citizens. Very large private firms have dealt with a similar problem by breaking

their operations up into a number of "profit centers" or divisions.[6] In this way, firms delegate responsibility for day-to-day
operations to division managers. How a particular division functions
on a daily basis is not of primary interest to the central office. As
long as a division contributes a reasonable share to overall profits, the
central office is satisfied.

It may be useful to examine the multidivision form of organization to see if some of the ideas can be applied to the
administration of intergovernmental programs. On the surface, it
appears that the problem faced by large business firms and our
intergovernment system are similar. Both have a need for some
central direction, and the local agencies or operating divisions face
very diverse and complicated situations in which local managers need
to exercise considerable discretion.

There are three key elements in the design of a multidivision
organization. These elements, to be discussed in turn, are (1) the
divisibility of tasks into relatively independent bundles of activity,
(2) the availability of summary evaluative statistics such as profits or
growth, and (3) a central guidance cluster which is supported by an
elite analytical staff and which has the power to discipline the
actions of division managers. Obviously, not all public sector
operations will be able to meet these rather demanding prerequisites.

The basic idea behind the multidivision form is that the local
divisions should be given considerable discretion in carrying out the
tasks delegated to them by the central office. For this scheme to
work, local divisions must be relatively independent of each other. If
there is a substantial degree of interdependence among local
divisions, it is difficult to evaluate the performance of any one
division. Some interdependence can be dealt with through a
budgeting system which charges each division its share of any costs
that may be incurred as other divisions carry out aspects of a task
delegated to it. Such budgeting systems have been developed in both
the public and private sectors, but in either sector these systems are
complicated and often arbitrary in their assignment of costs.

The availability of summary evaluative statistics is a difficult
condition to satisfy in most public sector organizations. Profits and
growth, the most common of such statistics in the private sector, are
inappropriate. Money and organizational size are instrumental values
in public organizations, not ends in themselves. This situation forces
public administrators to seek measures of outputs or inputs and
develop them as comprehensive or summary statistics. Unfortunately, few of these statistics are reliable indicators of effectiveness.

There are, however, intergovernmental programs in which relatively good summary statistics may be available. In a housing allowance program, for instance, the number of participants successfully finding standard housing summarizes the success of much agency activity. Many agency functions in a housing allowance program—e.g., outreach, certification of eligibility, counseling, and housing inspection—may be involved in the successful placement of a participant. Monitoring agencies can allow local managers to select the mix of such functions they think appropriate to local conditions, yet still hold managers responsible for the number of eligible citizens placed in standard housing.[7]

Other statistics and constraints would be needed to supplement a statistic on the number of successful participants in a housing program. If managers are to be given broad discretion in the use of resources within the local division, they will need to operate within some sort of budget constraint. In a housing allowance program, the administrative budget could be based on the number of participants, with the allotment varying positively with the size of the allowance payment.

A second set of constraints would attempt to prevent "creaming" of the eligible population, allowing participants to rent or remain in substandard housing, or failure to screen out ineligible applicants. To prevent creaming, the monitoring government (e.g., state or federal regional offices) would conduct annual surveys to discover the size, income, racial, and age characteristics of the eligible population. Local agencies would need to justify any substantial deviations in the profile of their participants and the profile of the eligible population.

Errors or laxness in the certification of eligibility or in the inspection of housing would be monitored through a series of spot checks by the state and federal levels. If error rates were too high, local governments would be requested to reduce them. Local units would usually not be required to adopt one particular administrative process or another to correct a problem. Discretion as to the most appropriate way to alleviate a problem would be left to local officials and administrators.

To summarize this discussion on the availability of summary statistics, the aim has been to find a statistic or set of statistics which will permit an evaluation by the central office of the performance of local agencies. The availability of such statistics will allow the local agency or division to exercise a great deal of discretion in handling day-to-day operations, but still allow for oversight from the state or

federal levels. Such statistics will not be available in all programs
which are administered through an intergovernmental system. There
may be, however, more programs for which such statistics can be
found than has previously been thought.

The creation of an elite analystical staff at the federal and state
levels of an intergovernmental system is an important feature of a
multidivision form of organization. This staff evaluates local agency
performance, selects appropriate evaluative statistics, and adjusts
standards for evaluating performance to conform with observed
practices. Based on these analyses, actions would be taken to modify
or "improve" divisional performance. In more conventional termi-
nology, the federal and/or state government would be trying to get
local agencies to comply with broader standards of performance.

Obtaining compliance in an intergovernmental system is always
difficult and chancy, but the notion of general revenue sharing may
add a positive incentive to the essentially negative incentives
currently used. General jurisdictions in which the local "divisions" of
an intergovernmental system are performing well, could be given
additional general revenue-sharing funds as a bonus for good
management. These general revenue grants could also be offered to
local jurisdictions which reform their administrative, evaluative, and
budgeting structures so that they may function as divisions in an
intergovernmental administrative system. If the positive incentives of
such grants were not sufficient to gain compliance, the state and
federal governments could still use any of the older techniques for
persuading an errant jurisdiction. These techniques include "going
public" with adverse reports, threatening to cut off funds, and finally
cutting off all or some portion of the funds transferred to the
jurisdiction.

The preceeding three sections have examined a number of fields in
an effort to find techniques and concepts which may serve as a guide
to bring local governments more fully into an intergovernmental
administrative system. Developments were explored in administrative
theory which relate organizational structure with, first, the technology of the task to be performed and, second, the complexity of
the social environment of the organization. Vouchers were analyzed
to see the feasibility of using this device to create administrative
systems which will be sensitive to the preferences of consumers of
public goods but still channel expenditures into areas which satisfy
national interests (see also Porter, 1975). Finally, the possibility was
examined of adapting the multidivision form of organization to

intergovernmental systems. The ability of this organizational form to manage situations in which there are rather uniform central objectives but considerable diversity in local conditions suggests that efforts should be continued to adapt this form to the public sector.

REVENUE SHARING AND LOCAL REFORM

Since the Civil War, both public and private organizations have been growing larger and larger. A few hundred firms now produce half of the manufactured goods in the United States. A handful of huge government agencies account for billions of dollars in expenditures. Policies such as trust-busting and revenue sharing have sought to decentralize or break up some of these large organizations and regulate their growth. In the private sector, such policies have not succeeded. Oligopolies and conglomerates dominate many industries. It is also doubtful that revenue sharing will be much more successful in its efforts to turn back the growth of larger and larger organizations. The thousands of state and local governments aided by revenue sharing will, its advocates hope, be able to handle many of the problems faced by government more effectively. But large, national problems press ever more persistently, and these problems can only be addressed through institutions which can function at a relatively broad level.

The solution of these larger problems may not, however, require a single, central government to deal with them. In fact, research in administrative theory and practice is making it increasingly clear that very large organizations suffer substantial losses in effectiveness simply because of their size (Williamson, 1970). Central surveillance becomes more and more difficult because of the "bounded rationality" of the overseers. Workers within these organizations become more able to pursue their individual interests and to ignore the overall objectives of the organizations for which they work. Consumers have difficulty expressing their preferences and must settle for a product or service that satisfies an "average" consumer. There is a role for strong and vigorous local units, endowed with considerable discretionary powers, to counteract trends toward the production of undifferentiated or unwanted public goods or services.

In this paper, it is argued that the development of such local units as a part of an intergovernmental administrative system has not occurred. Local, general purpose governments are the least developed element in our national administrative structures.

Three strategies have been suggested for bringing local governments more fully into a system of intergovernmental administration. Each of these strategies suggests a broader role for local governments and citizen-consumers. No single approach seems capable of dealing with all the functions being administered through intergovernmental arrangements in the United States, but, when all three strategies are considered together, there is a strong case for giving serious attention to restructuring local governments.

Through a vehicle such as general revenue sharing, efforts to restructure local governments can build on basic institutions that already exist in American federalism. There is no need to abolish the political structures of state or local governments or even to try to bypass those levels in order for intergovernmental programs to be effectively executed. On the contrary, the politically sensitive structures of these two levels provide an essential element. It is unrealistic to expect a distant, central government to be as responsive to the demands of individual citizen-consumers as state and local civil servants can be.

General revenue sharing can be an important vehicle for encouraging reforms in general purpose governments. These grants are particularly suited to inducing changes in the structures and capabilities of general purpose jurisdictions. To build more effective intergovernmental systems, federal policy makers will need to have a conceptual framework to guide them. It is unlikely that sporadic, disjointed, and/or random restrictions on general grants will produce an integrated system of intergovernmental administration or strong responsive local governments. It is hoped that the three strategies explored in this paper might provide the basis for the elaboration of such a framework.

NOTES

1. Joseph F. Zimmermann, in a letter to the author in October 1974, noted that not all revenue-sharing funds pass to general purpose jurisdictions. "Counties in Alabama and Massachusetts, for example, are not general purpose governments, and many mid-west townships have very few functions."

2. For views pro and con on revenue sharing, prior to its passage, see Lincoln Institute and National Academy, 1971, and Reagan, 1972.

3. Morton Grodzins (1960) called these arrangements a "marble cake." There is no reason to argue with this description of intergovernmental relations. However, it is not clear that such a poorly articulated administrative system can meet the increasing demands being placed on it.

4. This interpretation of the early powers of municipal corporations runs counter to the

more legalistic treatments of the powers of local governments. Municipal corporations were, as a matter of law, subservient to state governments. Dillon's Rule was widely accepted. Even so, nineteenth century cities had considerable discretion in everyday governance because interdependencies were not so extensive. For a more complete analysis of the legal status of municipal corporations in the nineteenth century, see Porter, 1969.

5. Friedman is widely acknowledged as the intellectual guru of conservative economists. Christopher Jencks, a self-proclaimed socialist, directed the study which designed a voucher experiment in the Alum Rock School District in San Jose, California. (See Jencks, 1970.)

6. See Chandler, 1966; Williamson, 1970. Robert Anthony has finished a first manuscript (as of 1974) of a very important book on managerial accounting for nonprofit organizations. Such accounting techniques are essential to multidivision organizations. Rivlin (1971: 122-130) suggests the application of the multidivision form of organization in the decentralization of our federal system. She gives an excellent analysis of some of the advantages and problems in such systems and notes how both voucher and multidivision systems rely on the derivation of better measures of effectiveness.

7. Definitions of what is a "standard" home have filled books. In this paper we ignore the problems of definition and use the idea of standardness as if it were amenable to objective definition.

REFERENCES

BISH, R. L. (1971). The Public of Metropolitan Areas. Chicago: Markham Publishing.
CHANDLER, A. D. (1966). Strategy and Structure. New York: Doubleday.
EDWARDS, R. C.; REICH, M.; and WEISSKOPF, T. E. (1972). The Capitalist System. Englewood Cliffs, N.J.: Prentice-Hall.
ELDON, J. M. (1971). "Radical politics and the future of public administration." Pp. 19-42 in D. Waldo (ed.), Public Administration in a Time of Turbulence. Scranton, Pa.: Chandler Publishing.
FREDERICKSON, H. G. (ed., 1972). "Symposium on decentralization." Public Administration Review, 32(October).
FRIEDMAN, M. (1955). "The role of government in education." Pp. 123-144 in R. A. Solow (ed.), Economics and the Public Interest. New Brunswick, N.J.: Rutgers University Press. The same essay is included in M. Friedman, Capitalism and Freedom (Chicago: University of Chicago Press, 1962).
GALBRAITH, J. K. (1973). Economics and the Public Purpose. Boston: Houghton Mifflin.
––– (1972). The New Industrial State. Boston: Houghton Mifflin.
JENCKS, C. (1970). Education Vouchers. Cambridge, Mass.: Center for the Study of Public Policy.
KIRKHART, L., and GARDNER, N. (eds., 1974). "A symposium on organization development." Public Administration Review, 34(March/April).
Lincoln Institute, John C., and the National Academy of Public Administration (1971). "Problems and response in the federalism crisis." Washington, D.C.: National Academy of Public Administration.
NATHAN, R. P. (1973). "Essay on special revenue sharing." Paper presented at the Conference on Approaches to Accountability in Post-Categorical Programs, Stanford Research Institute, Menlo Park, California, August 20.
OATES, W. E. (1972). Fiscal Federalism. New York: Harcourt Brace Jovanovich.
OSTROM, V. (1973). The Intellectual Crisis in American Public Administration. University: University of Alabama Press.
PORTER, D. O. (1975). "Responsiveness to citizen-consumers in a federal system." Publius, The Journal of Federalism (Fall).

––– (1969). "The Ripper Clause in state constitutional law: An early urban experiment." Utah Law Review (April, June): 287-335, 450-491.

REAGAN, M. D. (1972). The New Federalism. New York: Oxford University Press.

RIVLIN, A. M. (1971). Systematic Thinking for Social Action. Washington, D.C.: Brookings Institution.

SCHMANDT, H. J. (1972). "Municipal decentralization: An overview." Public Administration Review, 32(October): 571-588.

SIMON, H. (1965). Administrative Behavior (2nd ed.). New York: Free Press. (First published in 1947.)

SUNDQUIST, J. L. (1969). Making Federalism Work. Washington, D.C.: Brookings Institution.

THAYER, F. (1973). An End to Hierarchy: An End to Competition. New York: New Viewpoints.

THOMPSON, J. D. (1967). Organizations in Action. New York: McGraw-Hill.

TULLOCK, G. (1970). Private Wants, Public Means. New York: Basic Books.

WILLIAMSON, O. E. (1970). Corporate Control and Business Behavior. Englewood Cliffs, N.J.: Prentice-Hall.

WRIGHT, D. S. (1974). "Intergovernmental relations: An analytical overview." The Annuals, 416(November): 1-16.

5

GENERAL REVENUE SHARING
AS A POLITICAL RESOURCE
FOR LOCAL OFFICIALS

SARAH LIEBSCHUTZ

State University College at Brockport

The purpose of general revenue sharing, enthusiastically endorsed by its supporters and never denied by its detractors, was to return power to the people. The State and Local Fiscal Assistance Act of 1972, the first legislative enactment of the New Federalism, reflects the clear intent of the President and the Congress "to shift some decision-making from Washington to State and Local governments" (U.S. Congress, House Intergovernmental Relations Subcommittee, 1974: 5) and, by so decentralizing, to improve the responsiveness of local officials to local problems. In contrast to the categorical aid programs of the 1960s which sought to mobilize community (i.e., extragovernmental) political participation, the State and Local Fiscal Assistance Act gives responsibility for allocating shared revenue to elected officials of general purpose units of government, allows them wide latitude in the uses of those funds, and does not require citizen participation. Because responsibility is coupled with latitude, an examination of the allocation decision procéss presents an unusual opportunity for political scientists to heed the counsel of the late V. O. Key (1964: 536) to learn about that "thin stratum of persons referred to variously as the political elite, the political activists, the leadership echelons, or the influentials."

One of the most widespread beliefs about the American political system is that it is biased toward the status quo, that "conservatism and self preservation rather than innovation and demand for change" (Polsby, 1963: 134) are its modal characteristics. Applying this assertion to the revenue sharing allocation context, we postulate that elected officials regard revenue-sharing funds as a resource to be used to enhance self-maintenance. While the possible foci for self-maintenance relationships are varied, including the bureaucracy and extragovernmental elites, our concern here is with ways in which revenue-sharing decisions assist local elected officials in their reelection efforts. We hypothesize that local officials behave so as to derive political gain from the availability and allocation of revenue-sharing funds.

Underlying the status quo bias is the familiar assumption "that those who propose change do so, clearly, with the expectation that they will benefit more from the new order than they did from the old" (Murphy, 1971: 4). A subsidiary hypothesis concerns innovation as an outcome of the allocation process. Here we make use of the notion of political entrepreneurship elaborated by Wallis in his explanation for the growth of social welfare activities in the public sector. Wallis advances the proposition that politicians, in order to engender electoral support, "seek new programs to put before the public, even though no appreciable part of the public is demanding them" (Tobin, 1968: 42). Unlike the businessman/entrepreneur who bears the costs of introducing and building consumer approval for new products and services, the

> . . . politician almost never can introduce a truly new program . . . because he has to persuade . . . before he can give a demonstration. For the political entrepreneur, the test is whether the proposal sounds attractive enough *in advance* to win the public's support for the man or party who proposed the innovation. . . . [T]he kind of innovation that meets the test of political entrepreneurship usually is not one that promises the voters a new service with which they are unfamiliar but one which brings them a service with which they are already familiar. [Tobin, 1968: 43-44]

The availability of revenue-sharing funds to finance new programs (services or capital investments) proposed by the politician/entrepreneur would seem to make such programs unusually attractive to the public. However, the political entrepreneur must still bear in mind the familiarity caveat, for voters must have some awareness of programs before they can perceive benefits from the allocation of revenue-sharing funds for them. Hence, we hypothesize that where shared revenue is allocated for innovative uses, these uses, whether new service undertakings or capital investments, will be regarded by elected officials as acceptable to the electorate on grounds of prior familiarity.

STUDY DESIGN

To test these hypotheses, we examine the allocations of shared revenue in four local governments of a single county in New York State for funds received for the first two and one-half years of the Act (January 1972-June 1974). Our data are longitudinal, obtained over an 18-month time period, January 1973-July 1974, through interviews with political elites in the city of Rochester and the towns of Chili, Greece, and Irondequoit. Within each jurisdiction, the chief elected officials, the mayor of Rochester and the town supervisors of the three towns, were interviewed on several occasions. These chief elected officials are the most visible politicians in the four governmental units and constitute our primary sample for purposes of testing the hypotheses about political motivation and entrepreneurship. Policy decisions, however, do not occur in vacuums. In order to appreciate the environments in which revenue decisions were made, the interview sample included other elites as well. These were appointed town and city officials, finance and budget directors, city manager and town clerks, and elected opposition party members of the town and city councils. In addition, the opponents of each chief elected officer in the November 1973 election were interviewed.[1]

The 18-month time frame of this study afforded opportunities to observe and evaluate initial and continuing reactions of decision makers to the availability of shared revenue and, since it encompassed a local election, the saliency of the electoral context for allocation decisions.

These four local governments in the sample, all located within the same fast growing urban county (Monroe) in western New York State, were selected for analysis because of anticipation that differences among them in urbanization levels would affect their decisions about allocating revenue sharing. The city of Rochester, first settled in 1812, is an old city whose fiscal resources are strained not only because costs of providing municipal services are rising but also because a steadily increasing portion of the city budget must be used to service debts incurred in the course of massive urban redevelopment undertaken since the early 1960s. During the five years prior to the receipt of revenue sharing, 1969-1973, the general operating budget for the city increased at a much faster rate (46%) than either assessed valuation (7%) or population. The latter actually declined by 8 percent between the 1960 and 1970 censuses.

The towns of Chili, Greece, and Irondequoit are all first ring moderate-income towns surrounding the city of Rochester. All three experienced considerable population growth and land development during the decade of the 1960s, which translated into sizable increases in general operating budgets during the five years prior to revenue sharing. The smallest (1970 population: 19,609) and least developed of the three towns is Chili. A report prepared in 1973 explained the growth of 75 percent in population since 1960 on the basis of "an ample supply of relatively inexpensive land available for residential building" (Deegan and Jackson, 1973: 2). Greece, the largest of the three towns (1970 population: 75,136) also experienced rapid growth during the recent period. Greece, like Chili, remains relatively undeveloped; 55 percent of its land is currently vacant or agricultural, which means that expansion can be expected to continue. The very large growth of 84 percent in the town's operating budget during the five years prior to revenue sharing occurred because of wage and benefit increases to town employees, particularly policemen, and increases in expenditures for town planning and engineering functions. Irondequoit (1970 population: 64,897) is almost fully developed, with only 2 percent of its area still available for development. In contrast to Chili and Greece, where assessed valuation of taxable property increased about 22 percent in each town during the five years prior to revenue sharing, in Irondequoit the increase was only 7 percent. Its prospects for future increases in assessed valuation are dismal.

DECENTRALIZATION, ACCOUNTABILITY, AND GENERAL REVENUE SHARING

President Nixon, in his 1971 State of the Union message, told Congress that one of his "Six Great Goals" was to "strengthen and renew our state and local governments." Noting the dramatic growth of federal power since the 1920s, Mr. Nixon declared, "The time has now come in America to reverse the flow of power and resources from the states and communities to Washington and start power and resources flowing back from Washington to states and communities and, more important, to the people all over America." Nixon asserted on another occasion that federal resources would be better managed if they were controlled by state and local governments, that paternalism by central authority in Washington results in bad and costly decisions, and that "by returning more power to the people and their state and local governments . . . people can decide what is best for themselves" (1972b).

This theme, that New Federalism in general and revenue sharing in particular would improve the responsiveness of local officials to deal with local problems, was echoed by public officials from urban, suburban, and rural areas, in testimony before the House Ways and Means Committee.

> Revenue sharing . . . will demand and command more local initiative and creativity. Revenue sharing should stimulate a new type of citizen participation. . . . Cities will be forced to call upon greater citizen input to help order these priorities . . . to draw more local resources—both public and private. [U.S. Congress, House Committee on Ways and Means, 1972: 661]

Officials from urban areas in particular stressed their perception of revenue sharing as new money, "infusing funds and independence into city governments . . . to increase our total governmental capacity to cope with the large social crises of the 1970s" (U.S. Congress, House Committee on Ways and Means, 1972: 711).

Opponents of the decentralization-democracy theme warned that political accountability at the local level would not be enhanced by general revenue sharing. Former HEW Secretary Wilbur Cohen (National Journal, 1972: 1920-1921) stated bluntly:

> We have to have federal programs with strings attached because it is the only way that the disadvantaged, the poor whites and the poor blacks will get their fair share. . . . Unlike the federal government, city councils are controlled by the real estate and industrial development interests and they will divert the money to their ends.

He also stated that state and local administrators are not competent to

> . . . solve the problems of mass transportation, mental retardation, the disadvantaged child and the impoverished family . . . [and that] if Nixon

wanted to really move the New Federalism forward he should loan 25,000 or 50,000 competent federal experts to work in State and Local government.

Another witness before the Ways and Means Committee stressed the mediocrity-of-local-officials theme in this way:

> It is a fact that 55 percent of all Americans living in urban areas now reside in the suburbs. [There is] an almost total lack of administrative personnel even aware of the barest extent of Federal programs now available. Planning, the inveterate apex of all suburban problems, is, in most cases, handled by ill-trained building inspectors and engineering technicians. City managers are tied to the past of status quo laissez-faire development to maintain job security. The beginning input of new-breed activist city managers is stifled by councils replete with lack of education, unable to accept the need for change, although they are aware that such need exists.
>
> Local government operates in a vacuum relating only to itself, effectively isolating the citizenry which is resigned to the guaranteed continuum of built-in mediocrity in local government. [U.S. Congress, Committee on Ways and Means, 1972: 769]

A related theme, citing the general lack of involvement and concern by the public with the local budgetary decision-making process, projects doubt that "revenue sharing would increase their attention . . . or their impact on the process" (Caputo and Cole, 1973: 38).

General revenue sharing, a key aspect of the President's New Federalism program, was passed by Congress and signed into law in October 1972.[2] Two important features which distinguish the State and Local Fiscal Assistance Act of 1972 from categorical aid legislation are its widespread geographical extension of federal funds and its potential for strengthening the autonomy of governors, mayors, and town and county supervisors in determining their own priorities. The fact that 50 states, 323 Indian tribes, and over 38,000 general-purpose units of local government automatically qualify for shared revenue contrasts markedly with the lengthy process of gaining approval from appropriate federal agencies for grants-in-aid applications. A second major difference is that the State and Local Fiscal Assistance Act permits the use of funds for a broadly defined list of eight expenditure categories to give eligible jurisdictions "the flexibility that they need to use the funds for the most vital purposes in their particular circumstances" (U.S. Congress, Joint Committee on Internal Revenue Taxation, 1973: 1).[3]

Although the act mandates periodic public reporting by recipient governments on their uses of shared revenue and although it contains antidiscrimination, antimatching, and wage-rate level provisions, it can be characterized on the whole as a "no-strings" approach of federal assistance, allowing for much greater flexibility across the board than either categorical or bloc grant programs. President Nixon (1972a) emphasized when signing the act that decentralization of decision making would be facilitated by its enactment:

> Under this program, instead of spending so much time trying to please distant bureaucrats in Washington . . . officials can concentrate on pleasing the people. . . . When we say no strings we mean no strings. This program will mean both a new source of revenue for state and local governments —and a new sense of responsibility.

As we have suggested above, there was no consensus while revenue sharing was being considered by the Congress that decentralized decision making would lead to revitalization of government at the local level. Those who supported the proposition maintained that local leaders would now have the necessary resources as well as the desire to respond to local needs articulated by citizens now more involved in local decision making; those who questioned the proposition argued that local leaders would merely continue to be responsive to their traditional areas of political strength and would not consciously encourage the presently noninvolved to become involved. Both positions seem to share the assumption that local officials would behave so as to derive political gain from revenue sharing, either by using it to win approval (votes) from new segments of the electorate or by using it in ways designed to maintain traditional patterns of electoral support.

ANTICIPATION OF REVENUE SHARING PRIOR TO ENACTMENT OF THE LAW

There was considerable variation in the anticipation of revenue sharing in the four local governments—ranging from aggressive activity by Rochester's mayor to awareness, but passivity, by the three town supervisors. Two explanatory factors are useful in explaining the variation: the perceived fiscal status of the jurisdiction prior to revenue sharing and its previous experience with federal funding.

The city of Rochester was widely perceived to be under severe financial pressure prior to the passage of the State and Local Fiscal Assistance Act. The mayor, in testimony before the House Ways and Means Committee in June 1971 described Rochester as a city whose fiscal resources are strained and whose people are burdened by "heavy reliance on the real estate tax . . . which bears little relationship to a person's ability to pay and to the services it finances."

Since 1962, when a massive urban renewal program was begun, Rochester's elected and appointed officials had been accustomed to monitoring federal legislation and to dealing directly with the federal government. Although Rochester is the nation's forty-ninth largest city according to the 1970 census, its urban renewal program is alleged to be the thirteenth largest in the nation. Twenty-six million dollars in federal categorical grants was administered by city governmental agencies in 1973 (City of Rochester, 1973). The mayor, reacting in March 1973 to the proposed 1974 federal budget, estimated that Rochester would lose more than $32.7 million in direct federal grants if the administration's budget were adopted. He asserted:

> Since Rochester's revitalization progress is largely due to its active and successful participation in the federal funding process, it is clear that the impact of federal cutbacks would be greater for us than most urban centers. To compensate for loss of federal revenues, we will have to reduce programs significantly or increase taxes, resulting in added hardships for already overburdened taxpayers. [May, 1973a]

The Rochester mayor was an active participant in the lobbying efforts of the United States Conference of Mayors and the Big City Mayors of New York State for the passage of revenue-sharing legislation. He testified before the House Ways and Means Committee stressing that general revenue sharing must be "new revenue available to cities large enough to have a significant impact on our ability to effectively deliver public services . . . and must be made available for general municipal purposes as determined by the local government, with no strings attached" (U.S. Congress, Committee on Ways and Means, 1973: 711). In addition, he actively urged Congressman Barber Conable, member of the Ways and Means Committee whose district includes half of the city of Rochester to remove a "local-maintenance of effort" provision, which would require localities to spend revenue-sharing funds for increased services and not use them to reduce taxes (Thompson, 1973: 93). Mayor May was also a frequent visitor to the office of Rochester's other Congressman, Frank Horton, to urge him to support the closed rule for debate on revenue sharing, and to the office of Senator James Buckley of New York to urge support for the Senate version of revenue sharing.

The progress of the legislation was thus monitored closely by the mayor and other city officials, with the optimistic expectation that it would pass the Congress. When the Ways and Means Committee reported out the bill on April 26, 1972, the city manager, with the mayor's approval, made a firm decision to incorporate federal shared revenue into anticipated revenues for the city's 1972-1973 budget. That budget was adopted by the Rochester city council on June 13, 1972, four months before revenue sharing became law.

In contrast to the clear awareness of revenue sharing, activity to ensure its passage, and anticipation of funds by the mayor of Rochester, the attitude toward revenue sharing, prior to the law's enactment, among chief executive officers in the three towns sampled can best be described as passive. The three supervisors indicated in interviews early in 1973 that they had been aware of the fact that general revenue sharing was under consideration by Congress and that their towns would benefit. But none engaged in any lobbying activities with their representatives to indicate personal or town support for the legislation or attempted to project the sums to be realized by their towns. None of the 1973 budgets for these towns, all adopted in October 1972, included revenue-sharing funds in the revenue projections.

In the case of Greece and Chili, both of which are represented by Congressman Conable, the explanation may lie partly in the fact that Conable himself was an early and strong advocate of revenue sharing. Through his news releases, Congressman Conable attempted to keep his constituents informed about the protracted legislative struggle over revenue sharing. Conable (1972) stated, "We are down to the wire on revenue sharing. . . . I have been one of the central figures, though not necessarily the leader, of the struggle to initiate this type of aid over the past three years." Clear evidence of the failure to anticipate revenue sharing is shown in the case of Greece, where the town clerk as late as October 1972 projected a deficit for 1972 and recommended that the town board increase the property tax rate by 18 percent for 1973. The deficit later turned out to be a considerable surplus a month later after receipt of the town's first revenue-sharing check.

All three towns, by their own self-descriptions, were, at the end of

1972, in sound financial condition. Relatively stable property tax rates over a period of five budget years in view of substantially increased general operating budgets were reconciled with growth in assessment bases and increases in per capita state aid. None of the three towns was receiving federal grants during 1972, and neither elected nor appointed officials had had extensive experience up to that point in time in dealing with the federal government. During 1972, the Greece supervisor for the first time had applied for Federal Law Enforcement Assistance funds and had been in contact with federal officials concerning flood relief funds. However, the federal government was not regarded as a normal source of revenue for the town. The supervisor of Chili applied for a HUD multipurpose community center grant in 1972, which was unsuccessful because of an impoundment decision by the Nixon Administration. He contrasted revenue sharing with the unrealized HUD grant in saying that he was "grateful to have revenue sharing and glad the town didn't have to go through a long complicated process to get it." That sentiment seemed to be shared by the political elites sampled in all three towns.

ALLOCATION DECISIONS
FOR THE FIRST THREE ENTITLEMENTS

Decisions in the four governments concerning the spending of the initial revenue-sharing checks for the period January 1972-June 1973 were largely influenced by philosophies of the chief executive toward the concept and interpretations of flexibility afforded them under the law. Attitudes ranged from regarding revenue sharing as undifferentiated general revenue to regarding it as "windfall" to be treated as separate and special.

Decision makers in the city of Rochester from the beginning saw it as general and relatively unrestricted revenue. In the 1972-1973 budget, adopted even before the revenue-sharing law was enacted, they did not stipulate the expenditure category for which the projected funds were to be applied. It was not until November 1972, after instructions from the New York State Department of Audit and Control that the city council amended its previous budgetary approval to stipulate that the revenue-sharing funds were to be equally allocated between salaries of firemen and policemen. These categories were selected on the advice of the budget director, who stated that public safety maintenance and operating expenses were an allowable use and that this allocation "facilitated the accounting process." Despite the mayor's prior urgings to the Ways and Means Committee that revenue sharing be "new" and additional revenue for hard-pressed cities, it was clear by early 1973 that the financial squeeze on cities who had been receiving substantial federal categorical grants was even greater. The mayor, in March, expressed his "continuing support for the President's New Federalism concept," but he emphasized "concern about the crunch of the transition period" (May, 1973a).

Hence, revenue sharing from the outset was perceived as revenue to "keep a sinking ship afloat." The shared revenue actually received for the first three entitlement periods represented only 4 percent of the 1972-1973 budget, but as we shall see later it was publically presented as a substitute for funds that would otherwise have accrued from a tax increase higher than the one actually adopted for 1972-1973.[4]

Attitudes toward general revenue sharing among supervisors of the three towns seem to have been largely influenced by the philosophy of Arthur Levitt, Comptroller of New York State, which was transmitted in Revenue Sharing Workshops for Local Officials held immediately after the law was enacted. Levitt (1973: 1-2) asserted that revenue sharing is "a trust . . . not cheap dollars to be squandered . . . [but] to be use[d] . . . with prudence and planning —not just for today, but for tomorrow." The "planning for tomorrow" aspect of Levitt's philosophy was taken to heart by all three supervisors. For all three towns, the first three entitlement period checks represented a substantial influx of new money—that is, unanticipated increments of 11 percent (Greece), 14 percent (Irondequoit), and 16 percent (Chili) to their 1973 budgets.

The philosophy of the Irondequoit supervisor that shared revenue "should be used for one-time, non recurring expenses and projects . . . to stabilize tax rates not reduce them" underlay his directive in December 1972 (after the first revenue-sharing check was received) to all town departments heads, asking them to submit long-range capital requests. This was a deliberate effort on his part to force them to assess their current equipment inventories and to project future capital needs. Responses to the solicitation included items ranging from a hockey rink to a small tool. The hockey rink, categorized by the supervisor as a "luxury item," was rejected, but the other requests were approved by him and then presented to the town board for ultimate approval. The supervisor's own preference for revenue sharing to be used to purchase new highway equipment to replace the town's deteriorating stock was clearly evident in the recommended list. Even so, the amount of revenue sharing anticipated for the 1972 calendar entitlement periods was greater than the amounts approved and forwarded to the town board. The supervisor commented that we "had to look for ways to spend this substantial [$265,000] sum of money." He then advanced the idea of a capital improvement fund for a future addition to the town hall.

The emphasis on capital nonrecurring expense allocations of the town's revenue-sharing funds was shared by all town board members. The only Republican town board member agreed that items with "a long range of life . . . that Irondequoit could point to 5-10 years from now and say that federal revenue sharing was responsible" should be funded. He argued, however, that recreational facilities would have a "longer functional life" than trucks and that the town's revenue-sharing funds should be more directed toward this purpose.

The decision process, allocating anticipated revenue sharing for the first three entitlement periods, deviated from the normal budgetary process in terms of timing and consensus achieved among town board members. Because revenue sharing had not been anticipated and incorporated into the 1973 budget (adopted in October 1972) spending decisions necessarily were made well into the budget year. Additionally, the supervisor and town board members expressed the attitude that federal revenue sharing was "special" and required their careful, collective attention. In contrast to public disputes along partisan lines over town budgets, discussions among Irondequoit town board members concerning the allocation of revenue sharing were unanimous regarding the emphasis on capital investment, and decisions were consensual. The final allocation decision for use of the anticipated revenue sharing for Entitlement Periods 1-3 reflected both the supervisor's preferences for highway and town hall capital investments and the minority board member's preference for investment in recreation facilities.

Whether these allocation decisions reflected the preferred alternatives of any segments of the population of the town was not a consciously expressed concern of the supervisor or the opposition party board member. The supervisor made no deliberate attempt to engender participation outside the town government in the decision-making process, and he reported no efforts by town persons to exert influence. However, his concerns for tax stabilization as the net effect of revenue sharing and his preferences for allocating the funds for what the public would find as familiar and acceptable (highway equipment, town hall addition, playground equipment) rather than as luxury (hockey rink) can be interpreted as having been calculated for electoral approval.

There are many similarities in attitude toward revenue sharing and the decision process between Chili and Irondequoit. The Chili supervisor and town board members who were interviewed also regarded revenue sharing, from the outset, as separate funds to be used for special purposes. One town board member asserted that "revenue sharing is a windfall and will always be treated as such." Failure to anticipate revenue sharing, coupled with skepticism about the constancy of any federal funds, caused the supervisor to propose special, closed, informal meetings of the entire town board to decide the allocation of funds. In contrast to Irondequoit, where requests were solicited from department heads by the supervisors, each Chili councilman acted as an advocate for the appointed town commission (recreation, library, etc.) to which he was liaison, and the only actor from the town government itself to directly request funds was the commissioner of public works.

The allocation process was described as highly informal, closed to the public, involving minority town board members, and was also apparently highly consensual. Two projects, all reflecting a capital, nonrecurring use philosophy were allocated 1972-1973 funds: remodeling of the town hall and establishment of a new community recreation center fund. These are projects, according to the supervisor, which the "town could do without but would like to have . . . projects that will add to the worth and services of the town, but won't involve a great deal of money to sustain once they are completed." Moreover, both projects were perceived by the supervisor as being highly acceptable to town residents. The remodeling of the town hall would enable all of the town services to be administered in one location, seemingly beneficial to both administrators and residents. The community center, for which HUD funds had been unsuccessfully sought in 1972, was specifically promoted by appointed town recreation commission members, who argued that it would benefit the entire spectrum of town people, from preschoolers to senior citizens.

Again, the consensus surrounding revenue-sharing allocations was in clear contrast to decisions on the regular budget, which are characterized by public and partisan conflict. The closed, informal nature of the revenue-sharing allocation process tended to facilitate consensus. But the attitude of Chili decision makers toward treating federal money with "kid gloves lest it be taken away" would seem to have been the major factor promoting harmony. For both Chili and Irondequoit, decisions to use revenue sharing for capital investment were consonant with the "special money with fiscal payoff for the future" interpretation.

The supervisor of Greece, the largest town in our sample, viewed revenue sharing as part of an overall revenue picture for the town; and information in the Treasury Department reporting forms essentially reflected bookkeeping rather than substantive decisions. The supervisor in December 1972 directed town department heads to look on revenue sharing as "additional and available funds, but not as a Christmas gift" and requested them to present proposals for "new programming in areas where it can be justified." The emphasis on programming rather than capital needs was eventually translated into the reported use of a large part of the Entitlement Periods 1-3 revenue sharing for current operations. These programming proposals were requested by the supervisor to be projected for the future, not only for the 1973 budget year. Hence, revenue sharing in Greece, as in Irondequoit, was an incentive for developing a long-range project inventory.

The actual approval process for revenue-sharing allocations in Greece was similar to that in the other towns. To comply with reporting and publishing requirements special town board meetings were convened. Both minority and majority board members looked on revenue sharing as a "windfall" to be viewed in the context of the town's overall comfortable fiscal status, to be used to initiate new programs which could be "maintained even if revenue sharing stops at the end of five years." Unlike the other towns, where planned and actual use reports bore a close relationship to the projects specifically tied to the advent of revenue sharing, the official Greece reports for this period do not reflect the program innovations that actually got under way.[5] Interviews with the supervisor and town board minority members show that the net effects of revenue sharing were to expand police and recreational services and to fund a sidewalk building program which had been recommended two years previously by a citizen's committee. All these uses were justified as acceptable to the public; the origin of the sidewalk building program was always cited as a citizen's committee report.

Decision makers in all three towns were familiar with Congressman

Conable's view that "one of the chief purposes of the program is to give tax relief to local taxpayers." "What a travesty," the congressman wrote in a release carried in local newspapers, "if this program became a justification for forcing spending rather than a means of reducing the local tax burden" (Conable, 1972). Yet none of the elites interviewed advocated direct use of shared revenue for reduction of property taxes; and several, alluding to the tax effort variable, spoke of adverse effects on future revenue-sharing allocations from tax cuts. A minority member of the Greece town board asserted that as long as revenue sharing allocations did not lead to large tax decreases, "rich suburbs would get richer." The Chili supervisor wrote in his 1973 annual report that "the effect of a tax reduction by a local municipality . . . is to reduce its revenue sharing allocation in the ensuing year in relation to that of a municipality which did not reduce its taxes."

We have seen for the four local governments under study that initial attitudes toward revenue sharing, whether regarded to help close current revenue-expenditure gaps or to expand present services or undertake special long-range investments, were mirrored fairly closely in allocation decisions for the first three entitlement periods. Moreover, we have shown that decisions were always rationalized as acceptable to the residents of the local governments, either on grounds of the benefits of tax stabilization, expansion or improvement of already agreed on government services or new undertakings with which some sector of the town seemed to be already familiar.

ALLOCATIONS FOR THE 1973-1974 ENTITLEMENT PERIOD

Because the towns had not anticipated shared revenue in their 1973 budgets, they considered it during the 1973 fiscal year, too late to affect the property tax rate for that year. The necessity of filing and publishing a Planned Use Report for 1973-1974 by August 1973 meant that decisions about allocating these anticipated funds had to be made in the context of their impact on the 1974 town budgets. Nonetheless, the allocation distribution patterns which we have described for the first three entitlement periods persisted for the 1973-1974 period. That is, the mayor and city council of Rochester continued to approve the budget director's equal designation of shared revenue for police and fire salaries. The city manager asserted that he "would love to use revenue sharing for nonrecurring capital expenditures, but we don't have the option." The towns of Irondequoit and Chili continued, without apparent discord among town board members, to designate major portions for capital expenditures. Irondequoit, stressing highway equipment, recreation, and town hall improvements, and Chili, featuring the future community center and a new highway garage fund, allocated 90 percent (of $329,000) and 80 percent (of $98,000) respectively for capital projects in their Planned Use Reports for the fourth entitlement period. The town of Greece designated 72 percent of its 1973-1974 allotment for current costs of police and landfill operations and used the remainder for the sidewalk construction program.

Despite these similarities in allocation patterns for Entitlement Periods 1-3 and Entitlement Period 4 in the sampled governments, there were key differences in the decision-making environments for the two time frames. The first was that each government, as it convened to consider the 1973-1974 allocations of revenue sharing, had now experienced the regular receipt of its quarterly checks from the Office of Revenue Sharing and could confidently anticipate that the checks would be continuing until the end of 1976.[6] Thus, revenue sharing could now be regarded as regular, anticipated revenue.

In the second place, decisions about dispersing the 1973-1974 entitlements could become an issue in the elections that would be held in November 1973 since the mayor and supervisors in our sample were all candidates for reelection.

For three of the four governments, there was now candid recognition of revenue sharing as a source of normal revenue with no particular restrictions. The supervisors of Greece and Irondequoit stated at the time that the 1973-1974 Planned Use Reports were filed that the anticipated shared revenue would "pay for many town projects that otherwise would be funded with tax money" (Irondequoit supervisor) and that "taxes can be cut because the town is receiving federal revenue sharing" (Greece supervisor). Approval by the two town boards for the 1973-1974 Planned Use Reports could be described as perfunctory and pro forma.

The 1973-1974 city of Rochester Budget Document showed estimated general revenue sharing as a line item under Intergovernmental Aid and Reimbursements. Preparation and filing of the Rochester Planned Use Report for 1973-1974 was treated by majority and minority city council members as an internal administrative matter, not even requiring separate council approval.

Only elected officials in Chili continued to view revenue sharing in a separate category and continued to hold special executive meetings to discuss allocation of the yearly "windfall." Consonant with this view, the Chili supervisor, in his 1973 Annual Report mailed to town residents in October 1973, solicited suggestions for spending revenue sharing "for areas which need additional funding in the future." It should be noted, however, that this request for public input was made some two months after the fact of determining the 1973-1974 allocation pattern. Nine months later, the supervisor stated that he had no response respecting that solicitation.

Despite the recognition of revenue sharing as ongoing anticipated revenue, seen for the most part in the context of the total budget picture, the allocation decisions continued to be consensual and nonpartisan. The total 1974 budgets for the three towns sampled were presented for public hearing and town board decisions in October 1973, several months after the 1973-1974 Planned Use Reports had been published. The 1973-1974 city of Rochester budget had been adopted in June 1973. In spite of increases in operating expenses for all four governments, particularly large for Greece, property tax rates were increased only slightly for Chili and Rochester and decreased slightly for Greece and substantially for Irondequoit. (See Table 1.) Revenue-sharing allocations were not a matter for public discussion at any of these hearings.

In the absence of conscious efforts to engender public interest or input in the revenue-sharing allocations, the governmental elites had seemed to rely on their own sense of community needs.[7] The attitude of the Greece supervisor, that citizens should be interested "in the entire budget process" and that revenue sharing funds are not

Table 1. CHANGES IN BUDGETS AND PROPERTY TAX RATES: 1973-1974

	General Operating Budget			Property Tax Rate per $1,000 Assessment		
	1973	1974	% Change	1973	1974	% Change
Chili	$ 1.1 mil.	$ 1.2 mil.	+ 9	$16.37	$16.39	a
Greece	4.6 mil.	5.7 mil.	+24	18.25	18.10	b
Irondequoit	3.5 mil.	3.7 mil.	+ 6	20.60	17.54	−15
Rochester[c]	86.9 mil.	94.4 mil.	+ 8	38.51	39.79	+ 3

a. Increase less than 1%.
b. Decrease less than 1%.
c. 1972-1973 and 1973-1974 budgets (the fiscal year being July 1-June 30).

"extra funds for special groups to disburse," was shared by the other elites interviewed. This attitude, it can be argued, could have the effect of defusing any incipient public interest in revenue-sharing funds while focusing greater interest on the budget document as a whole *and,* at the same time, enable incumbent decision makers to justify property tax reductions and/or program expansions on grounds of good, overall management. As we shall now discuss, it was his role as manager of the total government finances that each incumbent chief executive stressed in campaigning for reelection, and not revenue-sharing allocations per se.

REVENUE SHARING AS AN ELECTION RESOURCE

We have already seen that attitudes toward revenue sharing were widely shared among elites within each local government and that decisions about allocating it were consensual and nonpartisan. While there were differences in initiative among the chief elected officials toward obtaining and allocating shared revenue, their actions had the clear approval of minority and majority legislators. Revenue sharing was not itself a conflict-producing issue involving leaders and followers, winners and losers. Since there were no sides to take, how could it have been a campaign issue? The broad answer to the question is that revenue sharing per se was not projected by the incumbent mayor and supervisors as a campaign issue. Rather, it became a subtle and secondary justification for a primary issue—i.e., farsighted yet prudent leadership of the government. Within that broad "issue" were a cluster of subsidiary claims.

The Greece supervisor during his reelection campaign said that, under his leadership, the town had expanded police and recreation services, had changed the nature of the budget process such that budgets were now adopted prior to election day, had initiated critical staff changes in the finance and planning areas. He talked about the need for his continuing leadership in future planning of the development of the town. When asked whether he had discussed revenue sharing during his campaign, he responded, "Nobody asked me about it!"

The Greece supervisor's (unsuccessful) opponent stated in an interview after the election that he had tried to make revenue sharing an issue, but that the local newspapers "ignored what I said" and "citizens didn't think about it." He alleged that the "Town Hall used revenue sharing to reduce taxes to make the town government look good," but he concluded by saying that "debate on local issues between the parties is insignificant."

The reduction of the Irondequoit property tax rate for 1974 by about 15 percent was explained by the Irondequoit supervisor as resulting from his stress on fiscal responsibility, that is, a "tight rein on spending while at the same time . . . [providing] improved and expanded services. Because of this very conservative fiscal policy we have been able to accumulate a very healthy surplus the past two years" (Irondequoit Press, 1973b).

The Irondequoit supervisor had two opponents, both unsuccessful. One alleged that the tax reduction was possible because "the federal revenue sharing program had produced more funds than originally anticipated in the town budget . . . and a mild winter . . . saved thousands of dollars on snow plowing." The other opponent simply declared that the money which the supervisor is "giving you back in the tax decrease is your own tax dollar coming back from Washington."

The supervisor, after his reelection, reflected that revenue sharing was itself not a major issue. After all, he had on several occasions reminded his opponents and the public that all decisions on the Planned Use Reports had been reviewed very thoroughly by all town board members and "the final determinations were approved unanimously" (Irondequoit Press, 1973a).

The use of revenue sharing in the town of Chili was apparently not publicly referred to at all in the reelection campaign of the supervisor. In contrast to Greece and Irondequoit, where the issues, such as they were, were variations on a "good management" theme, there was a specific and highly salient policy in Chili on which all candidates for every office involving town voters focused. It concerned the proposed conversion of part of a county park within the town to a county-operated landfill. As one observer of the election comments, "All the candidates attended anti-landfill meetings, each saying he hated landfills more than the other. With this to occupy them, revenue sharing allocations were never raised as an issue" (Gardella, 1974: 10).

Both the Chili supervisor and his opponent agreed that revenue sharing was not an issue in the campaign. A minority town board member observed however, that because people are generally unaware of the sources of town revenues, they tend to give credit to the supervisor when they see such manifestations of new programs as the sign marking the proposed community center site.

The mayor of Rochester, in contrast to the supervisors of the three towns, could not point to a stabilized property tax in the context of increased budgetary commitments. What he did do, however, was to suggest that Rochester's financial situation would have been even worse if not for his successes as chief lobbyist for the city with the federal government. During his campaign, he stressed his efforts to keep federal funds flowing to Rochester, citing the "leadership role public officials play in aggressively seeking these funds . . . and his close working relationship with Republicans who run the state and federal governments, [his] membership on state and national committees and boards which disperse funds, and [his] lobbying efforts with other mayors" (May, 1973b). The mayor also spoke specifically of his support for the concept of New Federalism and the enactment of federal general revenue sharing and attributed the passage of the legislation to "vigorous lobbying efforts by mayors across the nation and particularly New York State" (May, 1973c).

CONCLUSION

Both hypotheses posited at the outset of this paper are supported by the data we have presented. Revenue-sharing funds did represent a political resource used in various ways by the chief elected officials, from specific campaign references to it by Rochester's mayor, to keeping it all quiet, allowing voters to draw their own conclusions about the efficiency of the town supervisors.

The second hypothesis, viewing the chief elected official as political entrepreneur, also finds support. Innovative allocations were made in the towns where shared revenue enhanced already sound financial bases. In each case where services or capital costs not committed prior to revenue sharing were undertaken with revenue-sharing funds, those innovative projects were perceived by the elites to be acceptable on grounds of community familiarity and acceptability. The Chili community center and the Greece sidewalk program were viewed as long standing community high priority items, and the Irondequoit town hall addition was not regarded as the novelty for town residents that the rejected hockey rink would have been.

Advocates of general revenue sharing contend that the availability of unrestricted federal funds will facilitate decentralization of decision making and will stimulate greater accountability and revitalization of local government. In this paper we have looked at revenue sharing as a political resource for governmental elites. We have found that while only one of the chief elected officials had actively sought these funds, all four welcomed them and took quite seriously the business of their allocation.[8] Further, we found that allocation decision processes in all four governments were consensual and nonpartisan, and confined to the governmental actors. Finally, we found that how the chief elected officials perceived present and future fiscal prospects for their jurisdictions and whether they regarded shared revenue as ordinary or as special shaped their allocation preferences.

In these four local governments, the expectation that revenue sharing "should stimulate a new type of citizen participation" (U.S. Congress, House Committee on Ways and Means, 1972: 661) is not supported. Rather, the process we have described here fits a model that asserts that government policy makers pursue their policy preferences in relative freedom. We conclude, in agreement with the general proposition of Hawkins (1971: 118) that inputs from elites within the system—i.e., "demand with inputs"—may be as important for scholars to focus on as extragovernmental "demand inputs" in understanding the allocations of general revenue-sharing funds at the local level.

NOTES

1. Rochester has a council-manager form of government in which the mayor is elected by the city council. The chief elected official for Rochester in this study is the man who served as mayor from January 1970 to December 1973. As a member of the Republican majority of the city council, he ran for reelection as an at-large candidate in November 1973. The city council candidate who was the chief spokesman for the Democrats on fiscal matters in the campaign is regarded as his opponent in this study.

Town supervisors in New York State who serve as chief executive and fiscal officers and presiding officers of town boards are elected for two year terms at general elections in odd-numbered years.

2. See Thompson (1973) for the legislative history of revenue sharing, and Nathan et al. (1975) for discussion of the provisions in the State and Local Fiscal Assistance Act of 1972. See also Reagan (1973) for an analysis of federalism in the American context.

3. Local governments may use shared revenue for maintenance/operating and capital expenses for public safety, environmental protection, public transportation, health, recreation, libraries, and social services for the poor or aged. Capital expenditures only are allowed for education. State governments are given complete flexibility within all of the categories. High priority local operating uses not permitted are some social welfare categories and education. See U.S. Congress, Joint Committee on Internal Revenue Taxation (1973: 20).

4. The 1972-1973 Rochester Budget Document states that the revenue-sharing funds

projected to be received during that fiscal year had the effect of diminishing the absolute property tax rate increase from a potential $8.95 to the actual $4.83.

5. For a fuller discussion of misinterpretations which can be derived from reliance on the Treasury Department reports, see Nathan (1975: 234-244).

6. Each of the towns in the sample was notified in July 1973 that it would be receiving additional increases for the fourth entitlement period because of the favorable results of recalculations by the office. The city of Rochester, on the other hand, was informed that it would be receiving some $700,000 less than anticipated.

7. This observation conforms to the finding of Prewitt and Eulau that among 82 city councils in the San Francisco area "as many as 36 did not in any discernible manner seem to act in response to any politically organized views in the public. These 36 councils seemed to rely on their own sense of what the community needs were" (1969: 429).

8. This is the dominant pattern among the 38,000 governmental units receiving revenue sharing. Only 130 governments were reported to have told the Office of Revenue Sharing "to stop sending them Federal revenue sharing money. their reasons [were] both practical and philosophical. . . . 'It's not worth the worry of having the Government . . . looking down our necks,' said the letter from Mayor W. A. Montroy of Shortsville, Mo." (New York Times, 1973).

REFERENCES

CAPUTO, D., and COLE, R. L. (1973). "Revenue sharing and urban services: A survey." Tax Review, 34(October): 37-40.

City of Rochester (1973). Federal Programs Inventory. Rochester: Office of Public Information.

CONABLE, B. (1972). Washington Report, June 22.

DEEGAN, R., and JACKSON, J. (1973). Cost-Benefit Analysis of Proposed Community Center in Town of Chili, New York. Rochester: University of Rochester.

GARDELLA, D. (1974). "General revenue sharing and the town of Chili." SUNY Brockport Independent Study Paper (unpublished).

HAWKINS, B. W. (1971). Politics and Urban Policies. Indianapolis: Bobbs-Merrill.

Irondequoit Press (1973a). "Deming sets the record straight." September 20: 3.

––– (1973b). "Tax rate down for '74." October 4: 1.

KEY, V. O. (1964). Politics, Parties and Pressure Groups. New York: Crowell.

LEVITT, A. (1973). Federal Revenue Sharing Information. Albany: Department of Audit and Control.

MAY, S. (1973a). Statement on the Effects of the 1974 Federal Budget on Rochester, New York (March). Rochester: Office of Public Information.

––– (1973b). "Statement on issues for channel 21" (October 1). Rochester: Office of Public Information.

––– (1973c). "The mayor's role in city's survival." About Time Magazine (October).

MURPHY, R. (1971). Political Entrepreneurs and Urban Poverty. Lexington, Mass.: Heath.

NATHAN, R., et al. (1975). Monitoring Revenue Sharing. Washington: Brookings Institution.

National Journal (1972). "New Federalism III: The opposition." 4(December): 1920-1925.

New York Times (1973). "Revenue sharing a red-tape bore to some towns" (November 23).

NIXON, R. (1972a). "Statement on signing of the State and Local Assistance Act of 1972." Weekly Compilation of Presidential Documents, 5(October 23): 1534-1535.

––– (1972b). "The philosophy of government: Nationwide radio address." Weekly Compilation of Presidential Documents, 5(October 30): 1546-1548.

POLSBY, N. (1963). Community Power and Political Theory. New Haven: Yale University Press.

PREWITT, K., and EULAU, H. (1969). "Political matrix and political representation: Prolegomenon to a new departure from an old problem." American Political Science Review, 63(June): 427-441.

REAGAN, M. (1973). The New Federalism. New York: Oxford University Press.

THOMPSON, R. (1973). Revenue Sharing: A New Era in Federalism? Washington, D.C.: Revenue Sharing Advisory Service.

TOBIN, J., and WALLIS, W. A. (1968). Welfare Programs: An Economic Appraisal. Washington, D.C.: American Enterprise Institute for Public Policy.

U.S. Congress, House Committee on Ways and Means (1972). Hearings on the Subject of General Revenue Sharing, 92nd Congress, 1st Session. Washington, D.C.: Government Printing Office.

U.S. Congress, House Intergovernmental Relations Subcommittee (1974). Replies by Members of Congress to a Questionnaire on General Revenue Sharing, 93rd Congress, 2nd Session. Washington, D.C.: Government Printing Office.

U.S. Congress, Joint Committee on Internal Revenue Taxation (1973). General Explanation of State and Local Fiscal Assistance Act and the Federal-State Tax Collection Act of 1972, 92nd Congress, 1st Session. Washington, D.C.: Government Printing Office.

PART III

ENVIRONMENTAL POLICIES

6

INTERGOVERNMENTAL COORDINATION IN THE IMPLEMENTATION OF NATIONAL AIR AND WATER POLLUTION POLICIES

ROBERT D. THOMAS

Florida Atlantic University

The majority of grant-in-aid programs enacted by the Congress in recent years are characterized by national objectives to be carried out through state and local governmental processes (Sundquist, 1969; Reagan, 1972). In these programs, intergovernmental coordination is a particularly intense problem for federal administrators, inasmuch as they are required to achieve national objectives—for which Congress holds them accountable—by relying on the initiative, the ability, and in some cases the willingness of state officials.[1] Some of the difficulties of coordination are obvious. National problem solutions do not neatly fit all states. Federal officials must find problem solutions with insufficient data on causes and effects, on reactions and consequences. They must deal with fragmented jurisdictions and patterns of authority and responsibility (Wengert, 1967). Furthermore, some state officials may not have the technical expertise, legal authority, or propensity to implement national policies. And some may simply be politically hostile.

The Clean Air Act of 1970 and the Federal Water Pollution Control Act Amendments of 1972, in their complexity, their legislative detail, and their economic, social and political implications, epitomize the dilemma confronting federal administrators responsible for accomplishing national program objectives through diverse state and local processes. The basic implementation problem confronting Environmental Protection Agency (EPA) officials in both of these acts is reconciling the "principle of national supremacy" with the "principle of non-centralized government."[2] On the one hand, national air and water pollution objectives are established. Congress has placed ultimate responsibility for achieving these objectives in the bureaucratic hands of EPA officials by specifying that if state officials do not work toward national pollution objectives as directed by national legislation, then EPA officials must carry out pollution control for them. On the other hand, EPA officials must work with and through the political and administrative machinery of the states in implementing national objectives. However, in both the Clean Air Act of 1970 and the Federal Water Pollution Control Act Amendments of 1972, Congress prescribed more than incremental problem solutions.[3] In doing so, Congress provided EPA officials with an implementation framework within which the agency has to reconcile problem solutions that are outside the normal order of things (incrementalism) with state and local processes that are geared to incrementalism.

The EPA has established management strategies for implementing national air and water programs. In both programs, the EPA is emphasizing the states as key actors through whom national pollution control programs should be implemented. Through the requirements of the Clean Air Act of 1970, the EPA has established a framework within which states are setting emission standards for existing air pollution sources in order to achieve national standards. Each state is required to establish a state process for meeting air quality standards by developing State Implementation Plans (SIPs), which are subject to the EPA's approval and the EPA's development if a state submits an unacceptable plan.

Like the Clean Air Act of 1970, the Federal Water Pollution Control Act Amendments of 1972 placed the states in the pivotal role of implementing national water pollution standards. The 1972 amendments "require states to develop a comprehensive and continuing planning process for water quality management; submit annual reports to the EPA that inventory all point sources of pollution, assess existing and anticipated water quality, and propose programs for non-point source control" (Council on Environmental Quality, 1973: 170). Furthermore, based on the premise that key state and local elected officials are instrumental in coordinating federal, state, and local pollution control activities, the 1972 amendments placed new responsibilities on the governors, mayors, and other state and local elected officials.

The EPA has set forth a direct implementation strategy for accomplishing the intentions of the 1972 amendments (U.S. environmental Protection Agency, 1973). The two central elements of this strategy are (1) to promote the participation of the states in implementing national water pollution control objectives by establishing a framework for them to assume the major responsibility for basin and area-wide planning, permitting, enforcement, and grant review and (2) to establish an ongoing federal-state management process which integrates planning and program formulation. Overall, therefore, the water strategy is very similar to the air strategy. It emphasized the states as the key actors by requiring them to establish processes through which they can coordinate local and substate regional pollution control. And it directs financial and technical assistance to the states to help them manage pollution control.

Program grants are the principal mechanism being used to encourage states to carry out federal requirements. Grants give substance to national standards by providing EPA officials with a monetary sanction to be used to encourage the states to work toward national objectives. At best, however, the grant device is a precarious tool for coordinating state pollution control activities. Other than the threat of losing federal aid and to some extent court action, the states are subject to no real discipline, or incentive, to work toward national pollution control standards. Withdrawing federal aid does not solve the dilemma for EPA officials; rather it intensifies it. Withdrawing federal aid places EPA officials in the position of performing pollution control activities for the states when the EPA is no better equipped with adequate resources (funds and personnel) than the states and is certainly ill-equipped to deal politically with either governmental or private polluters in the states. If EPA officials had to carry out pollution control and abatement for a state, it would slow down activities both in the state and nationally, because EPA officials would have to put aside their own work to do the state's work.

The principal objective of this study is to shed some light on the characteristics of intergovernmental policy coordination as reflected in the EPA's implementation of national air and water pollution control agency grants.[4] It shows that while the EPA has developed processes for centralized coordination, states are afforded the opportunity to bargain on the application of national objectives and negotiate for their definition of how these objectives should be applied. As such, they are able to tailor the implementation of national objectives to fit their perceptions of specific geographical and political circumstances. Some of the factors influencing this tailoring process are uncertainty in federal grant administration; the difference in leadership styles; the complexity of problem definition, program solution, and problem responsibility; and the representativeness of the American federal system.[5]

CHARACTERISTICS OF INTERGOVERNMENTAL COORDINATION

UNCERTAINTY

Many of the current state and local air and water pollution control activities were given their impetus by federal legislation. With only few exceptions, almost all of the local creation of separate air pollution control agencies came after the enactment of a national air program which offered program grant assistance. The federal water pollution control program has also changed the scope of state activities. Prior to intensive federal involvement, most states dealt only with the health effects of water pollution, and responsibilities for pollution control in most instances were in state health departments. After the federal government redefined the scope of water pollution problems to include not only health but also aquatic and aesthetic conditions, states have likewise redefined the problem, and many have removed pollution control authorities from health departments and placed them in environmental or pollution control departments.

Federal assistance has become a necessary part of state and local air and water programs. Since federal assistance is contingent upon the states and their localities meeting certain federal conditions, state and local officials need to know, in planning for pollution control, what they will receive in federal grant assistance from year to year in time to plan for individual programs. However, the federal granting process is not consistent. Congressional appropriations may or may not match congressional authorizations. The timing of congressional appropriations also contributes to inconsistency. Budget approval may come prior to the beginning of the fiscal year (July 1), but in many years it comes after the beginning of the fiscal year.[6]

This inconsistency is carried over to program implementation. Federal administrators are formally obligated not to commit grant funds until they have been appropriated by Congress. Informally, in some cases, federal administrators utilize this inconsistency to coerce state administrators to seek more funds from their legislators if it appears less federal money will be available, or to undertake additional or expanded program activities if it appears more federal money will be available.

Both the inconsistency of congressional appropriations and the timing of grant allocations create uncertainty for state administrators who must integrate federal grant allocations into their budgets to plan for the most optimal pollution control program. Deil S. Wright has shown that "a frequent problem associated with grants is the uncertainty of estimating available federal funds. Uncertainty may seem to be an abstract and minor matter to the uninvolved and unfamiliar observer. To a state the issue can pose the difference between continuity and chaos in the conduct of programs" (Wright, 1972: 23).

Table 1 illustrates how uncertainty was generated in the states of California, Arizona, and Nevada in fiscal year 1974. This table shows that federal grant allocations, which contain state program planning and budgeting conditions, follow state budgeting by as much as six or seven months in California and Nevada (August to February) and up to three months in Arizona (October to February). In all three states, federal advice of upcoming funding lagged behind the submittal of the state budget to the legislatures by one month.

There are two consequences of this uncertainty on the states. First, the states must go through two (one state and one federal) program planning and budgeting cycles. Second, the states' budgets for air and water programs must be prepared without a complete understanding of federal funding.

How does this affect the EPA's coordination of national objectives with state diversity? One of the major effects is the nullification of central direction from the EPA on substantive program issues. The EPA is unable to direct state activities toward national program objectives through the utilization of grants as a management tool. The promise of federal grant monies offers little incentive to state administrators to engage in substantive program utilization of federal funds, since it is uncertain how much is being promised. Rather, a more typical characterization of grant administration is gaming, with the major question concerning state administrators being not How

Table 1. COMPARISON OF STATE BUDGET CYCLES IN ARIZONA,
CALIFORNIA, AND NEVADA WITH FEDERAL AIR AND
WATER GRANTING CYCLES

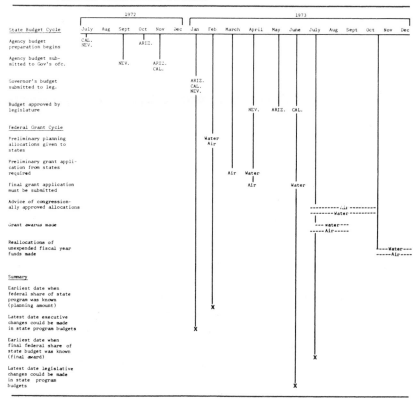

can we optimally use federal funds to achieve pollution control objectives? but rather What strategies must we follow to get federal funds?

The uncertainty in the federal granting process is not altogether disapproved of by state program administrators. Some state administrators utilize the uncertainty as a bargaining tool with their legislatures to negotiate for their agency's survival and growth. State pollution control officials generally must go to their legislatures for budget approval between January and April (for those states on a July-June fiscal year). In presenting their budget requests, state pollution control officials are asked what federal funds will be available. It is a generally understood rule of the game among state officials and EPA regional personnel that they should not depend on federal funds in excess of the previous year's allocations (i.e., they should not indicate any higher figure to their legislatures). In recent years, as federal requirements have been intensified as well as federal dollars increased, it has been the strategy of many state administrators to argue for more state money to meet federal requirements even when there is a strong indication that more federal funds will be available than in the past year.

The uncertainty of federal allocations not only works as a bargaining tool for state administrators to negotiate with their legislators, it also works for them as a bargaining tool in their negotiations with federal administrators. State administrators contend that they cannot plan comprehensively; that they cannot accomplish federal requirements without assurance of federal money in time to plan. As a result, state administrators use the uncertainty of federal money to define pollution problems in terms of state priorities rather than national priorities.

While some state officials utilize, cultivate, and encourage the continuation of uncertainty in the federal grant process, others contend that it slows down and stifles state pollution control activities. One of the major problems cited by these officials is that their legislatures are reluctant to match federal dollars without knowing for certain what amount the state is going to receive. The legislatures have developed a cautious approach to appropriating either matching funds or state funds.

Uncertainty in grant administration forces the EPA to establish coordination not through central direction, but through negotiations. Uncertainty offers state administrators a means of negotiating for state control of national program implementation as it applies to their perceived needs. It also diminishes the EPA's clout in asserting federal authority. In essence, federal program implementation provides part of the setting for state budgeting and state political behavior and in turn has implication for state policy outputs.

PROBLEM COMPLEXITY

One of the most striking characteristics in the implementation of national air and water pollution policies is the inability of the EPA to define clearly the nature of environmental problems. The inadequacy of data on air and water pollution problems leads to a situation in which intergovernmental coordination is achieved not through central direction from the EPA but through bargaining and compromise.

Notwithstanding its detail, national air and water pollution legislation only defines the problem parameters in the most general terms. Congress has legislated in generalities (as indeed it must) and left it to the discretion of the EPA to define the problem dimensions in more detail. The EPA has defined the problems in terms of national averages, which rarely apply to the diversity of the 50 states and the numerous localities.

The legislatively defined problem parameters and the administrative clarification of these parameters in program implementation affect coordination. Data or information about the nature of the problem is not generally used to define substantive problems and generate solutions to these problems. A typical characterization of this occurrence is supplied by a federal bureaucrat: "Our information [data] is about one-half step behind major policy decisions. Data are not used in major decisions, rather they have been used as status reports after the fact."

Since data are unavailable in most major policy decisions, what we find in the implementation of air and water policies is "data lag" or "the unavailability of data" being used as a bargaining tool by state and local pollution control officials to negotiate for their definition of their states' priorities to meet their problems if these priorities differ from the EPA's. This characteristic of policy implementation requires the EPA to accomplish coordination through processes other than central direction. Problem complexity in this situation changes designated congressional policy prescriptions and administrative strategies to implement them. Problem complexity, as it is responded to by public officials, ends up structuring the nature of political processes (Jones, 1972: chap. 2).

Two scenarios will illustrate the use of data as a bargaining tool in negotiation:

1. *"We give you the data, but they are not complete."*

In developing a traffic control strategy, as part of the SIP, for the Phoenix, Arizona metropolitan area, Arizona state administrators, after working closely with EPA regional personnel for several months, concluded that they did not have the capability to develop the strategy. As a result, the state administrators provided the EPA with their data and asked the EPA to write a traffic control strategy for the Phoenix area. One of the principal solutions proposed by the EPA after analyzing the data was bus laning. The data, according to EPA officials, showed that automobile pollution during peak rush hours was the major pollution problem. When initially informed of the EPA's plan, Arizona administrators approved. At a later public hearing to approve the plan, state officials categorically rejected the EPA's proposal. Reason? The solution proposed by the EPA was based on inadequate and incomplete data. The EPA was then forced to negotiate for a politically acceptable alternative.

2. *"You don't understand our unique problem. We've been in the business longer and know the problem; therefore, our solutions are the best for us."*

The Los Angeles County Air Pollution Control Agency has been in the air pollution control business since 1948. The agency has a highly competent staff. In the application of national air quality standards to Los Angeles County, the EPA is confronted with the problem of operating on highly technical basis. Los Angeles officials are extremely skeptical of the EPA's expertise to deal with photo-chemical smog. Los Angeles officials have the attitude that the EPA does not understand their problem, that it bases solutions on unsubstantiated data, and that to find an acceptable solution all the EPA needs do is consult the Los Angeles staff. In this situation the EPA is placed in the position of overturning engrained procedures of dealing with the problem in Los Angeles. With the experience gained over the years, the Los Angeles agency is able to counter the EPA's analysis of problem solutions at every turn. This type of confrontation over technical interpretation of air pollution problems has led to nonnegotiated bargaining between the EPA and the Los Angeles agency.[7]

In both of these examples, policy coordination is taken out of the realm of investigating the technical aspects or from central direction from the EPA. Rather, coordination centers on negotiation, bargaining, and compromise. The EPA cannot say for certain, based on available data, that its solutions will produce the most optimal results; therefore, it is placed in a defensive position from the outset. In sum, even on very technical policy issues such as air and water pollution, there is not exact data on the nature of the problem. State and local policy makers use the lack of data as a bargaining tool to modify the implementation of national standards as they apply to the states.

A related aspect of problem complexity on coordination, especially since implementation is linked to matching grant programs, is the determination of the division of responsibility between the federal government and the states. V. O. Key (1937: 381) succinctly stated the difficulty as follows:

A perennial problem in the American federal system has been to make the most appropriate assignments of jurisdiction to the states and to the national government. The question whether a given function should be undertaken by the federal or by the state governments recur constantly.

What is found in policy implementation is that the division of federal-state responsibility is never absolute. Difficulties in problem definition, state and local agencies' dependency on federal grants, federal dependency on the states, all contribute to a fluctuating EPA involvement from state-to-state. Federal involvement in state-local pollution control is continuously changing in the process of implementation. In one state at one point in time, there may be a heavy federal involvement because the state seeks federal participation. In another state there may be a heavy federal involvement because the state is recalcitrant. In still another state, federal involvement may be minimal because the problems are minimal or because the state can handle its own problems. Since involvement is not absolute, coordination is not absolute. Problem complexity forces discretion into implementation in terms of program priorities pursued by federal regional officials with individual states.

LEADERSHIP

The EPA's regional officials are middlemen in the implementation of national air and water programs. As such, regional administrators confront probably the most difficult coordinating tasks that exist between the federal government and the states. The problems of coordination for the regional administrators, as spelled out by an EPA study team (December 1972), include

> ... achieving some balance between national and regional objectives; between headquarters' desire for uniformity and consistency and the regional offices' desire for operational latitude; and, between categorically separate national program aims and the aims of EPA program integration in the regions.

How do EPA regional administrators confront these problems and achieve coordination? In the four regional offices investigated for this study, each regional administrator followed a different pattern of finding the appropriate course of action to deal with the problem of coordinating national program objectives with state and local diversity.[8] These four leadership approaches to coordination can be placed on a continuum running from strong federal control and direction to almost no control and direction. The middle positions were found to be (1) understanding the states' problems and attempting to blend national objectives to state objectives and (2) "authority of expertness"—that is, educating the states to national program objectives by disseminating information on research conducted nationally and on information learned from other states.[9]

Each of these approaches was molded by the uniqueness of the regions and by the philosophies of the regional administrators concerning how to approach regional problems in the context of a national program. For example, the regional administrator who adopted direct control did so because he viewed the objectives of national air and water programs as an attempt to standardize the programs across the 50 states:

> What we are trying to do is standardize a program from the point of view of the 50 states. How do you do this for states as diverse as those in this region?
>
> My philosophy is not to put my people into the states on a permanent basis. If I did this my objectives would go astray. Look at what I would confront. In California, my people would get eaten alive. California is the most sophisticated state in water pollution, but weak at the state level in air pollution. It would be difficult to know where to send my people. If I sent my people to Nevada or Arizona, they would overwhelm the state people. If I sent my people to Hawaii, they would get lost out there. In effect, I can best accomplish my objectives by keeping my people at home—the characteristics of the states in the region necessitate that I do.

Compare this style of leadership to that of the regional administrator whose philosophy is to blend national priorities with state priorities:

> We must get out and understand the states' problems. We're not going to understand their problems or the proper solution to their problems from Washington, or from the regional office. Sure, by sending federal regional people out to the states (on a permanent basis) they may be coopted but so what; they'll understand the local situation and be able to blend solutions to the needs of particular circumstances.

His reason for this approach is explained by the problems faced in his region:

> Our major pollution problems center around water. The air program generally takes care of itself because the problems are not severe, so we don't have to pressure the air agencies anyway. In water the national

legislation focuses on point source control through permitting. I agree that
this is a useful national approach and it applies in this region to a limited
extent. However, our biggest problem here is non-point source control.
This requires us to emphasize land use planning and resource utilization
and focus on pollution from such sources as logging, construction, and
various types of runoff; therefore, we must modify the national strategy to
blend with the particular problems and needs of the states in this region.

These constrasting styles of leadership result in different attitudes
about the use of the grant-in-aid as a device for coordinating
federal-state relations. Central control, according to the regional
administrator on the control end of the continuum, requires that
grants be used to their full potential to direct state actions. "If we
use grants as a management tool, we can force changes. We must
consider grants as the driving force to accomplish national objectives." On the other hand, the use of grants by the regional
administrator interested in more state input is as follows: "We've
overworked the blackmail effect. I don't see the advantage of forcing
states to do the job in exactly the way the feds want. I don't think it
would hurt to put all the funds into special revenue sharing."

SEEKING REPRESENTATION

In recent years, federal pollution control legislation has stimulated
state and local governments to institute considerable changes in
organization, regulatory activities, and services. These changes, most
required by federal law to undertake expanded pollution control
functions and as requisites to federal funding, are creating dissatisfaction among state and local pollution officials. Many pollution
officials do not agree with either national legislative objectives or the
EPA's administration, contending that in many cases congressional
generalities and the EPA's averages do not fit their problematic
situations.

How do state and local pollution officials seek representation of
their views when they disagree with the administration of national air
and water program implementation? What access points do they use?
How do they use these access points? This study suggests several
conclusions.

First, in seeking representation of their interests, state and local
pollution officials are afforded multiple access points both through
bureaucratic channels and elected channels (i.e., congressional
delegations, individual congressmen). Of course, one of the most

common forms of seeking representation of state and local views is though routine, everyday administrative dealings. The temper of these and their success for state and local officials vary considerably depending on the professional abilities of the state involved. For example, California can easily obtain representation of its views through professional, routine administrative practices. Its water administration at the state level is highly competent, well staffed, and always abreast of federal requirements. California's local air agencies, especially in Los Angeles, have been in the air pollution business longer than most. They are confident of their position, and have support from the state Air Resources Board. Michigan, Wisconsin, and to some extent Texas and Oregon also exhibit these characteristics.

By contrast, state administration in both air and water pollution control in Arizona and Louisiana is understaffed and overburdened with both state and federal work. They are not confident of their ability to obtain representation through routinized bureaucratic channels; therefore, they seek alternative access points through informal bureaucratic contacts and through their congressional delegations.

Second, seeking representation in policy implementation, while similar to seeking representation before an elected body, appears to be more subtle and more complex. Seeking representation before an elected body is expected, encouraged, and fairly well defined on issues along pro-con lines, and involves fundamental questions. Representation in policy implementation of national air and water programs generally adheres to a norm of working out differences between federal implementation and state positions in the spirit of compromise. However, finding a compromise varies by states and generally follows an escalating sequence on the part of state and local pollution officials. The general sequence observed is displayed in Table 2.

The most common method utilized by state and local pollution officials in seeking representation of their views is negotiation with EPA bureaucrats in the regional offices. State and local problem differences in this context center around routine technical and administrative questions. They are resolved by investigating mutual problems and are highly cooperative.

During the course of routine administration of pollution policies a tactic commonly utilized by state and local officials is a minor bluff. A typical characterization is: "If you (EPA) are not flexible in your

Table 2. SEQUENCE OF STATE AND LOCAL POLLUTION OFFICIALS SEEKING REPRESENTATION IN NATIONAL POLICY IMPLEMENTATION

Seeking Representation	Questions Involved	Principal Actors Involved	Type of Relationship Between EPA and State and Local Officials	Type of Problem Resolution Between EPA and State and Local Officials
Through Administrative Channels:				
Negotiations among Bureaucrats	Routine technical and administrative	EPA regional officials; state/local pollution executives and administrators	Highly cooperative	Cooperative investigation of mutual problems
Minor Bluff	Routine technical and administrative; sometimes more fundamental questions of jurisdiction and authority are raised	EPA regional officials; state/local pollution executives and administrators. Bluff may be that scope of involvement will be expanded to other administrators, (e.g., EPA Hdq., OMB)	Cooperative	Negotiated bargaining
Major Bluff	Fundamental questions of jurisdiction and authority	(Same as minor bluff). Bluff may be that scope of involvement will be expanded to not only other administrators but to Congress and courts	Cooperative to conflicting	Negotiated and non-negotiated bargaining
Through Other Access Points:				
Congress	Fundamental questions of jurisdiction and authority	EPA executives and bureaucrats, regional and Washington, as well as other agencies (e.g., OMB); elected officials	Conflicting	Non-negotiated bargaining
Courts	Fundamental questions of jurisdiction and authority	Bureaucrats; elected officials; judges	Conflicting	Non-negotiated bargaining

application of the law, we'll dump the responsibility on you." As one state administrator expressed it:

> If Congress decided pollution control is solely a federal matter, then there is no room for flexibility. But I don't think Congress has done this. Therefore, the EPA will have to be flexible in our transportation control strategies, because some of the things the EPA is telling us to do are antagonistic to this state and its metropolitan areas. If we don't reach an accord we'll simply dump it on the EPA and let them develop transportation control strategies and then enforce the plan. If decisions concerning this state are going to be made in Washington, then let them carry them out from there.

Minor bluffs occur during routine bureaucratic relationships between EPA regional administrators and state and local pollution officials. The bluff may involve state and local officials threatening to expand the scope of involvement to other bureaucratic channels within the EPA (e.g., going to EPA administrators in Washington) or to other federal agencies with jurisdiction (e.g., the OMB). The relationships are still cooperative. Generally, routine administrative and technical questions are the issue; however, minor bluffs are a prelude to more fundamental disagreements over such issues as jurisdiction and authority.

In the sequence of negotiating for their point of view, when routine negotiations and minor bluffs do not succeed, state and local officials offer major bluffs. Major bluffs are offered in negotiated bargaining (i.e., face-to-face negotiations) and in nonnegotiated bargaining through other administrative and political channels and through the media. An example of a major bluff through an administrative intermediary is illustrated below, when the EPA discontinued funding for four local air agencies in Texas. A state Air Resources Board official stated the bluff as follows:

> We receive a letter from the EPA regional office advising us (state ARB) that EPA in Washington has ordered all Class III air programs be cut. Now, I've checked with my friends in EPA in Washington—I'm a retired Public Health Service officer and know many people back in Washington—and they tell me Washington said Class III programs should be cut down, but not cut completely. What we have here is the regional office attempting to use its discretion to cut some needed programs. My advice to the local agencies was to send a letter to the regional administrator telling him we're going to seek advice from our city attorney and from our congressman on the propriety of his action.

An example of a major bluff offered in the context of negotiated bargaining is illustrated by a Louisiana pollution official:

> If EPA continues to hold up our program on insignificant things in our grant application, we'll go to our congressional delegation. I wanted to go the congressional delegation route last year, but EPA finally came through. But this year is a different matter. EPA is really being nit-picking. They are attempting to slap our wrist like children by letting us know they control the purse strings. Well, I don't think they can get away with it. It's not what Congress intended and we're going to let Congress know about how they are treating us.

When routine bureaucratic negotiations and minor and major bluffs fail to bring about resolution of differences, other access points are open to state and local officials through Congress and the courts. This study reveals that state and local officials go to their congressional delegations or individual congressmen to seek representation of their interests in federal program implementation; however, actually contacting congressmen and asking for their representation occurs generally after resolution of differences have been attempted through routine bureaucratic channels and after minor and major bluffs have been offered. When state and local pollution officials seek representation through their congressmen, the scope of participation in program implementation is expanded to all bureaucratic channels and to elected channels. Under these circumstances, negotiated bargaining between the EPA and state and local officials breaks down and nonnegotiated bargaining ensues through congressional intermediaries.

Resolving differences through the courts is the last alternative and is generally avoided, even when attitudes about the EPA's implementation are that the EPA is operating on the edges of the law. Court decisions are too final. They are made in black and white terms. Both federal and state officials attempt to avoid this finality in resolving their differences. Thus, while the bluff of going to court is used, the practice is avoided.

COORDINATION AND IMPLEMENTATION: SOME IMPLICATIONS

In national air and water pollution programs, the grant-in-aid device provides a mechanism through which Congress has established the parameters of state and local pollution control without overturning the integrity of "noncentralized" government. The EPA's implementation strategies are designed to accomplish national objectives through central direction. They do not appear to accomplish this objective. Paradoxically it seems that the grant-in-aid device allows the EPA to encourage states to assume expanded pollution control responsibilities without completely overturning their authority to chart how these responsibilities will be exercised.

In coordinating national policies with state and local diversity, the EPA adheres to a general overall blueprint for intergovernmental relations. When this blueprint is placed over the states and their localities, it undergoes constant adjustments. The EPA must adopt flexibility in its implementation to achieve any semblance of problem solution. Coordination processes are not applied absolutely from state to state. They are adjusted according to the problems within the states and the states' ability to cope with their problems. They are adjusted according to their perceived applicability by administrators charged with using them. And they are adjusted according to the political disposition of the states. What occurs in the coordination of national policies with state and local diversity through the grant-in-aid device is a continuous restructuring of not only federal-state relations but also state-local relations.

There is evidence that, in the first instance, state and local interests are the initiators of this restructuring. Heinz Eulau (1973: 155), for example, implies this by arguing that it is in Congress (particularly the House) "where federalism and representation meet." Reagan (1972: 81) explains that individuals and groups (presumably this would include state and local officials) who cannot develop policy coalitions in their individual states can mount a campaign in the 50 states to develop a policy coalition before Congress, and out of this what is deemed to be national is what Congress says is national. These arguments suggest that in policy formulation state and local interests are determining their own destiny by demanding the restructuring of certain state and local functions under the umbrella of a national program.

This allows states to undertake program expansion and program experimentation with the least amount of political risks. They can demand that a national program be established as a way of increasing the states' role in a functional area, when they do not have the clout to undertake expanded program functions under state authority. They can also demand that the states be given the major responsi-bility—with, of course, federal assistance—in carrying out national objectives. However, when a federal agency attempts to coordinate national objectives through the states by relying on the grant device, state and local officials can deny these applications as being detrimental to them and their programs. In program implementation state and local officials have the opportunity to bargain for the alteration of national objectives as they apply to them if meeting these objectives becomes politically restrictive or if these objectives bring a greater alteration than anticipated or deemed desirable.

The EPA's coordination of national objectives with state diversity involves more than just the application of solutions to public problems. It involves problem identification, albeit with difficulty. It involves a constant reaffirmation of the legitimacy of legislative enactments and administrative regulations through bargaining and compromise. It involves a recurring definition of federal and state authority and jurisdiction. It involves a continuous appraisal of the technical, administrative, and political feasibility of activities. It involves a variety of political processes that cut across federal, state, and local legislative, executive, judicial, and administrative channels, both vertically and horizontally.

NOTES

1. According to Charles E. Lindblom (1965: 11, 25-28), coordination processes prevade the political system. They include cultural processes of language, historical experiences, moral rules, and standards of evaluation; socialization processes found in personal and small group relations and in the schools and the mass media; the processes "that maintain coordinating subcultures, like those that . . . explain coordination of decision making." Lindblom characterizes four types of coordination that occur among decision makers. The first is central coordination in which decisions are adapted "to one another on instruction from a central decision maker." At the opposite extreme is mutual adjustment, which is a process of coordination where "no central mind or decision maker exercises any coordinating responsibility. The most familiar mutual adjustment process is negotiation." There are two types of coordination between the extremes of central coordination and mutual adjustment. One is coordination by cooperative investigation of mutual problems rather than through bargaining, negotiation, or any other technique of mutual adjustment. The other is coordination through agreed rules of behavior which are "sufficient to specify how each decision . . . is to be adjusted to [an] other."

2. Daniel J. Elazar (1965: 11-12) argues that early in the nation's history "Congress . . . acquired the authority to legislate very broadly under the constitution" and that "from the first [there] was the inherent superiority of the federal government as a raiser of revenue because of the tax sources available to it and the reluctance of the people to allow equally substantial state and local tax levies." Elazar says that "these two trends . . . firmly established the principal of national supremacy." Equally important, he argues, was that the "states . . . were simultaneously cast in the role of managers and administrators of these functions," which embodies the important facet of policy-making for federal programs. This means that "the states, as of right, share in the initial development of most cooperative programs."

3. According to Charles O. Jones (1974: 438-464), the changes in the Clean Air Act of 1970 do not fit the model of incrementalism. Instead of "nibbling away at the problem" Congress enacted air pollution policy in 1970 that "contrast sharply with earlier policy." For a discussion of the changes that the Federal Water Pollution Control Act Amendements of 1972 brought, see Robert D. Thomas and Ralph Luken (1974: 43-63).

4. Control agency grants are categorical grants established on a matching basis to assist state water pollution control agencies and state and local air pollution control agencies. In both programs, these grants are linked to all program functions. In the air program, for example, control agency grants are the major dollar incentive that the EPA uses to encourage state and local agencies to work toward national objectives. In the water program, control agency grant requirements are tied to the award of construction grants for waste water treatment plants. Since construction grants are now the largest funded public works program, the states have an added incentive to meet the conditions of control agency grants.

5. The data were derived mainly from 122 interviews with federal, state, and local public officials. Twenty officials in the EPA's Washington headquarters were interviewed. These interviewees were not selected with any thought of randomness or executive position; rather the objective was to interview persons knowledgeable about the programs. Thirty-five officials in four of the EPA's 10 regional offices (Chicago, Dallas, Seattle, and San Francisco) were interviewed. (The EPA also has regional offices in Boston, New York City, Philadelphia, Atlanta, Kansas City, and Denver.) These interviews, while still open-ended, were more systematically conducted. They were conducted with the major regional executives (e.g., regional administrators, deputy regional administrators) and the principal program heads (e.g., planning, permitting, research, monitoring, enforcement, and grant administration) and focused mostly on coordinating national objectives within the regions. Within the four regions, 67 state and local officials in seven selected states (Michigan, Wisconsin, Texas, Louisiana, Oregon, California, and Arizona) were interviewed. State officials interviewed included not only program executives and administrators but also officials in other agencies with direct or indirect responsibilities in pollution control (e.g., attorneys general, governors' planners and budget officials, key legislators, and legislative staffs). Local officials interviewed were principally in air agencies; however, local and substate regional water agency officials were also interviewed.

6. The inconsistency may be amplified in the pollution control programs because of the various organizational and program changes in recent years. For example, in less than a decade, the federal water pollution control program moved from the Department of Health, Education, and Welfare (HEW) to the Department of the Interior to EPA; and the air program from HEW to EPA. Also, massive changes, as indicated above, were made in both programs by the Clean Air Act of 1970 and the Federal Water Pollution Control Act Amendments of 1972. However, the fluctuations of congressional budgeting affect all programs.

7. Lewis A. Froman, Jr. (1967: 22) uses the term nonnegotiated bargaining to apply to situations of coordination which do not involve face-to-face negotiation (i.e., an actual interchange between two or more people).

8. Leadership displayed by regional administrators is conceptualized according to Robert Eyestone's definition of policy leadership as "a special form of political leadership that may be exerted in a problematic situation" (Eyestone, 1971: 3). The policy leader is concerned with finding the appropriate course of action to deal with the problem in order to reach certain desired goals.

9. This is a notion developed by Herbert A. Simon (1957: 136-139). This concept is used in an analysis of the administration of federal grants-in-aid by E. Lester Levine (1969: 177-182).

REFERENCES

Council on Environmental Quality (1973). Environmental Quality: The Fourth Annual Report. Washington, D.C.: Government Printing Office.

ELAZAR, D. J. (1965). "The shaping of intergovernmental relations in the twentieth century." The Annals, 359(May): 11-12.

EULAU, H. (1973). "Polarity in representational federalism: A negative theme of political theory." Publius, 3(Fall): 153-171.

EYESTONE, R. (1971). The Threads of Public Policy: A Study in Policy Leadership. New York: Bobbs-Merrill.

FROMAN, L. A., Jr. (1967). The Congressional Process: Strategies, Rules, and Procedures. Boston: Little, Brown.

JONES, C. O. (1972). An Introduction to the Study of Public Policy. Belmont, Calif.: Wadsworth.

--- (1974). "Speculative augmentation in federal air pollution policy-making." Journal of Politics, 36(May): 438-464.

KEY, V. O., Jr. (1937). The Administration of Federal Grants to States. Chicago: Public Administration Service.

LEVINE, E. L. (1969). "Federal grants-in-aid: Administration and politics." In Daniel J. Elazar et al. (eds.), Cooperation and Conflict: Readings in American Federalism. Itasca, Ill.: F. F. Peacock.

LINDBLOM, C. E. (1965). The Intelligence of Democracy. New York: Free Press.

REAGAN, M. D. (1972). The New Federalism. New York: Oxford University Press.

SIMON, H. A. (1957). Administrative Behavior. New York: Free Press.

SUNDQUIST, J. L. (1969). Making Federalism Work. Washington, D.C.: Brookings Institution.

THOMAS, R. D., and LUKEN, R. (1974). "Balancing incentives and conditions in the evolution of a federal program: Some perspectives on construction grants for waste water treatment plants." Publius, 4(3): 43-63.

U.S. Environmental Protection Agency (1972). An Assessment of Decentralization in EPA (December). Washington, D.C.

--- (1973). Water Strategy Paper: Statement of Policy for Implementing Certain Requirements of the 1972 Federal Water Pollution Control Act Amendment (April). Washington, D.C.

WENGERT, N. (1967). "Perrennial problems of federal coordination." In L. K. Caldwell (ed.), Papers on the Politics and Public Administration of Man—Environment Relationships. Bloomington: Institute of Public Administration, Indiana University.

WRIGHT, D. S. (1972). "The states and intergovernmental relations." Publius, 1(Winter).

7

INTERGOVERNMENTAL POLICY DEVELOPMENT:
THE IMPORTANCE OF PROBLEM DEFINITION

SHELDON EDNER

Eastern Michigan University

The field of intergovernmental relations might be characterized as the hidden dimension of government. . . . [P]erforming as almost a fourth branch of government in meeting the needs of our people, it nonetheless has no direct electorate, operates from no set perspective, is under no special control, and moves in no particular direction. [U.S. Senate, Committee on Government Operations, 1965: 2]

Perhaps the greatest lack in the many analyses, both direct and indirect, of intergovernmental relations (IGR) is the absence of any consideration of IGR as a policy-making process. Despite our contentions to the contrary, we seem to maintain a layer-cake view of IGR—we view policy as formulated on each level but not between levels of government. The policy aspirations and goals of each level of government, although fixed to some extent at the outset of the process of intergovernmental interaction, become altered and re-arranged during the process. In a very important way, intergovern-

AUTHOR'S NOTE: *The initial research upon which this study is based was supported with grant assistance from the Water Resources Research Center, University of California at Davis (OWRR Grant A-045-Cal). In addition, the Social and Behavioral Science Research Center of the University of California at Riverside provided much needed supporting services. This paper is based upon the findings initially reported in my "Formula Grants and Intergovernmental Relations: The Politics of Effluents," a doctoral dissertation filed with the University of California, Riverside, December 1973, and my paper "The Implementation of Federal Water Pollution Control Policy," which was presented at the annual meeting of the Western Political Science Association, April 1973, in San Diego, California. I am indebted to the constructive criticism of Professors Michael D. Reagan and Patrick Egan, who reviewed earlier drafts of this paper.*

mental relations constitute not just a procedural relationship but another policy-making process. This is, perhaps, the true import of the quote from Senator Edmund Muskie above.

An overly simplistic approach to the nature of "public problems" may be partly responsible for the deficiencies noted above. The notion of a "public problem" is a difficult concept to grapple with, but this difficulty has often been attributed to the term "public" rather than "problem." I will leave the intricacies of the term public aside and focus primarily on the nature of problems. Problems are often assumed to be clearly identifiable. One simply points his finger and says with authority that a particular segment of the populace is suffering from poverty or a lack of education or inadequate housing. However, what constitutes poverty or inadequate education or housing? As an example, we can arbitrarily identify many factors as components of poverty: insufficient income, cultural deprivation, or a lack of proper medical facilities. Yet these may reflect only part of the problem or all of it, depending upon the political and socioeconomic definitions of poverty which may be advanced. The nature of poverty as a problem is open to many conflicting definitions, none of which may totally encompass all of the parameters which could feasibly be identified with it. The focus of this paper is to show how the conflicting interpretations of problems and necessary policy solutions serve to affect the interaction of state and federal governments during the course of their intergovernmental relations. "Policy problem," as a concept, will be linked with the concepts of "policy substance" and "legitimacy" to identify types of intergovernmental relationships.

THEORETICAL APPROACHES TO INTERGOVERNMENTAL RELATIONS

From a theoretical perspective, IGR is a virtual wasteland. Only a few rather tottering steps at even a middle-range theory have been taken (Grodzins, 1966; Elazar, 1962; Segal and Fritschler, 1970; Wright, 1972). Much of the literature has been confined either to political rhetoric and speculative analysis or a fragmented, piece-by-piece look at some of the elements of intergovernmental relations —i.e., specific programs (Steiner, 1966; Sundquist, 1969; Derthick, 1973), administrative and professional contact between levels (Weidner, 1955 and 1959; Adrian, 1965; Anderson, 1959), and most thoroughly on the fiscal aspects of the system.[1] Little, if any, work has been done to try and trace the policy implications of the results of these studies. The primary emphasis has seemingly always been the question of which level of government ought to make decisions and take responsibility for the implementation of programs.

The central difficulty with existing studies seems to lie in their approach to IGR—there is a lack of focus on IGR as a political, policy-making process. This is not policy making in the classic sense of congressional enactment of laws or even from the sophisticated systems approach of policy development and legitimization. For the most part, these works have focused on the process of intergovernmental relations and particularly the manner in which the fiscal relationship has altered the conduct of the partners. A rigorous approach to the impact of IGR on the goals and objectives of the respective governmental partners is needed.

We find this approach only tangentially in the study of substantive programs (Steiner, 1966; Derthick, 1973). The focus should shift to an analysis of the interaction (or "struggle" if you wish) between the levels of government in implementing their priorities and the manner in which this interaction refashions or creates policy. The policy aspirations and goals of each level of government as it seeks to meet the requirements of its particular constituency, although fixed to some extent at the outset of the process of interaction, become altered and rearranged *during the process.* In this sense, IGR is not just a relationship, but can be another form of the policy-making process in our governmental system. As such, it must be subjected to a rigorous analysis, not just in terms of its proceses but also in the light of the manner in which public goals and objectives are represented in the subsequent policy decisions or nondecisions.

What is needed is a more analytically sophisticated approach to IGR. The issues of decentralization versus centralization remain, but not necessarily in the context of the either-or form of which level of government should make the decisions. A new approach should emphasize the location of decision making, on what basis, who's values are being served, and with what consequent result? One way of attempting to gain an understanding of these problems would be through an approach emphasizing the substantive problems with which the intergovernmental system deals and their relationship to the process of implementing intergovernmental programs. It is not enough to identify the sources of funds, the presence of spending

requirements and limitations, and the existence of certain perspectives among administrators. We must begin to deal with the policy
objectives of the participants and the way in which they define the
substantive nature of problems that the intergovernmental system
faces. In addition, we must also confront the manner in which these
perspectives are altered and affected by constraints on program
implementation. Derthick (1970, 1973), Pressman and Wildavsky
(1973), and Wright (1972) have made a start in this direction, as has
Ingram (1973). We must continue to push this attempt further in
order to obtain answers to the questions posed above.

As a means of meeting the challenge posed in the above discussion,
I would like to propose a framework for analysis which will attempt
to link the aspects of implementation, substance, and actor perspective in the implementation and policy making of intergovernmental
programs. As the central theme of this proposal, I will consider the
manner in which intergovernmental actors deal with the nature of
policy problems and how these problems are linked to their actions
associated with intergovernmental relationships. The framework will
offer a definition of "policy substance" as a means of shedding light
on problem definition and will tie this to the critical element of
intergovernmental "legitimacy" as the key in establishing or creating
various types of intergovernmental relationships.

POLICY SUBSTANCE

The importance of political symbols for public policy has been
demonstrated by Edelman (1969). They relate to policy through the
context of defining just what actions or activities are intended by
governmental design and implementation of programs and of the
nature of the problems they are intended to alleviate. In the context
of intergovernmental relations, our primary concern is the nature of
the partners' attempts to convince each other of the appropriate
structures and objectives of programs. Thus, we might point to a
specific program and the state-federal relationship therein as affected
most significantly by the differences of opinion pertaining to their
respective views of the purposes and goals of the program.

At least in part, this is the significance of "policy substance" for
IGR. "Policy substance" is not easily defined. Most definitions
offered in the literature focus on an after-the-fact, what-is-the-
impact-of-policy approach,[2] or on policy content as stated in the

legislation or regulations governing a program,[3] or on the structure of demands.[4] The definition posited here focuses on substance as the meaning given to policy prior to and after formalization. It encompasses both the definition of the problem for resolution and the alternative formulations of policy advanced by political actors (in the broadest sense). In its overall context, policy making is a definitional activity which selects the particular definition of a policy problem and the appropriate solution from a broad array of alternatives through the political process of decision making. Within this framework, policy substance encompasses both the definitions of problems and the solutions necessary to deal with them, since solutions tend to grow out of the particular definition given to a problem. Policy substance is a composite of the ideas, issues, facts, and action elements which form the substance of any problem or policy. This comprehensive, before-and-after focus considers (1) the meanings given to a particular policy area before one particular set or definition of policy substance has been "formalized" and (2) the meaning attributed to the content of a particular policy.

The "idea" element of policy substance concerns the intellectual concepts or constructs which activate political action—e.g., freedom, alienation, spaceship earth. These ideas serve an "umbrella" function since they link together the other three elements of policy substance—issues, facts, and action. In addition to serving as an expression of general conceptual identity, ideas also involve a value component. The examples of ideas given above are associated with particular preferred states of existence—values or goals. These values and goals help structure the perceptual views of individuals and institutions (broadly defined) defining facts, issues, and action. In the simplest (but not simplistic) sense the "idea" element of policy substance represents a "world view" or cognitive map.

The "issue" element of policy substance represents the operationalization of the intellecutal element. It is one thing to posit intellectual concepts, but for political and, hence, policy action, it requires some real world referent to make it meaningful. Such a referent could be a particular formulation of a perceived problem —e.g., the "poverty" of a large segment of the populace, or the "degradation" of natural resources, or the "repression" of a portion of the citizenry. In each case the nature and extent of the problem, and the issues related to them, are conditioned by the intellectual interpretation of the nature of the conditions surrounding and causing it. The relationship between ideas and issues is intimate, since the intellectual realm will in fact frame the issues which are identified.

"Facts" (not necessarily in the conventional terms of the scientist) are the specific items which help pinpoint the extent of the issue and the possible solutions to these issues. In a more direct sense, facts substantiate the existence of a problem. Again, there is a reciprocal relationship between ideas, issues, and facts. Facts, in a pure sense, do not speak for themselves. Their meaning is derived from the context (intellectual and real world framework) which indicates their significance. For example, an annual income of $4,000 per year for a family of four is a "fact" concerning the standard of living for that family. Whether this level of income indicates a state of poverty for that family is dependent not only on the direct purchasing power of the family but also on the social and political interpretation of an adequate standard of living and on whether or not it is the purchasing power alone which is the key to establishing the existence of poverty.

Finally, "action" represents the operationalization of the solutions suggested by the analysis resulting from the identification of ideas, issues, and facts. It includes both programs for governmental implementation and organizational patterns for government. Thus, "action" represents all of the collective arrangements of society which relate to the resolution of policy problems.

Policy substance is a composite of all four elements. Defining substance in this fashion leads to a perception of policy making as a selective, definitional activity—i.e., the selection of one particular set of ideas and related issues, fact, and action over another or perhaps a mixture of alternative policy substances. In this framework, formalized policy becomes a definition of the course of government action, based on the selection of a substantive framework or parts of different substantive frameworks. It is also useful to employ this conception of policy substance as a key to understanding the manner in which policy is implemented and obeyed in the political system. Vague policy such as that identified by Lowi (1969) is likely to be reinterpreted by actors in the political system to fit their version of policy substance. Conversely, a well-specified policy and program may lead to political conflict as a reaction to its proposals which may be negatively perceived by some members of the polity. Bailey's *Congress Makes A Law* is a good example of the interplay of different views of policy substance in the policy-making process.[5]

LEGITIMACY

This preliminary formulation of the substance of policy is advanced in order to suggest a framework for depicting the characteristics of intergovernmental relations. Before continuing with this framework, however, it is necessary to consider one more concept—legitimacy. This concept has a history as old as that of political theory. In the context of this discussion, I interpret it quite specifically in terms of the mutual respect held by actors on different levels of government. Within the context of IGR (for the most part), this bears on the respect and confidence shared by state and federal actors for each other. This respect is a product of the perception of an actor that another actor is making a valid and respectable effort to implement or organize a viable program. To an extent this approach to legitimacy draws upon Arendt's definition of authority.[6]

Authority as a concept contains legitimacy within it as a major component. Authority is, by definition, legitimate. It is an attribute recognized within an individual by another individual. It has been suggested by Adrian (1965), Price (1963), and others[7] that there is a distinction between "professional" authority (legitimacy) and "political" authority (legitimacy). This distinction implies a clear separation of the political and professional elements of government and different criteria of authority. Through this implication there is also an implicit distinction that the actions and substantive efforts of professionals and politicians are somehow different from one another. The classic distinction between administration and legislation dictates that the activities of these groups are different. However, in the light of Lowi's analysis and the evidence of other studies, it becomes difficult to maintain that the formulation and implementation of policy can be clearly allotted to one or the other of these groups. Therefore, it is clearly inappropriate to maintain that there is a qualitative distinction to be made concerning the substance of their efforts.[8] Further, there may be insufficient evidence to make even this distinction of professional and political legitimacy based upon their respective sources of authority—i.e., training versus electoral mandate. Many congressional leaders are recognized as "experts" in particular fields not because of constituent support but because of long-term commitments to understanding particular policy areas. Some professional administrators are recognized as political "experts" because of their ability to develop constitutencies to support their professional ideas for policy programs.[9]

In light of the above discussion, legitimacy in the context of IGR is derived not from the professional or political background of an individual but from his position of respect and acknowledgement from other intergovernmental actors who may come from either of these groups. Moreover, it is tied not to the program that an actor may espouse, but to his credibility as an effective representative of his constituency (i.e., level of government). Therefore, the relationships between levels of government will be dependent upon the ability of governmental representatives, both professional and political, to obtain recognition of their legitimacy through conscientious representation of their constituencies' interests.

Therefore, it is possible to suggest that intergovernmental relationships are more political than the focus on administrative procedures and technical questions suggests. Political scientists have tended to treat intergovernmental relations as an extension of the administrative process, rather than as a truly political relationship. State administrators are not just professionals sharing the same values as their federal counterparts. They are also political representatives of their governments.

The resulting federal-state relationship, therefore, is aimed at establishing a mutually acceptable set of objectives and values and accommodating these to the solution of the problems of different political constituencies. In order to be effective in this light, the respective administrators must first achieve, regardless of their respective views of policy substance, a degree of legitimacy in order for them to be effective in persuading their counterparts as to the validity of their particular views on policy issues and programs. Thus, we can make a clear distinction between the definition of policy problems and the ability of federal and state representatives to obtain recognition from their counterparts of their inherent capability to function effectively as representatives of their particular constituencies.

A PRELIMINARY MODEL

At this time we can employ these concepts (substance and legitimacy) in an heuristic framework (see Figure 1). Although the boxes may represent ideal types, they suggest a manner of identifying the reasons for the particular character of an intergovernmental relationship. The two dimensions of legitimacy and

	LEGITIMATE	NONLEGITIMATE
SUBSTANTIVE AGREEMENT	MUTUAL ACCOMMODATION OF PROGRAMS 1	TACIT NONCOOPERATION 2
SUBSTANTIVE NONAGREEMENT	INTERACTION AIMED AT ESTABLISHING A MUTUALLY ACCEPTABLE FRAME OF REFERENCE 3	CONFLICT 4

Figure 1.

agreement on policy substance are exhibited here as either-or categories, although in all probability they are continua. Further elaboration of the fundamental bases of these two categories will be necessary in order to operationalize them. At this time, I wish to demonstrate their usefulness in the analysis of a particular inter-governmental area (water pollution control) and suggest prospects for further refining them for intergovernmental and policy analysis.

The four types of relationships that this framework suggests characterize intergovernmental relations, based on the degree to which the state and federal programs are substantively compatible and the manner in which the respective state and federal actors perceive each other. In the case of box number one, the relationship is characterized as one of mutual accommodation between programs based on the mutual compatibility of program substance and the respect and confidence that each of the two levels of government has in each other. Because these conditions exist, the mutual imple-mentation of the respective state and federal programs becomes mostly a matter of administrative tinkering in order to mesh the programs. The mode of discourse between the two partners takes place in terms of bargaining over the specifics of bringing the two programs into compatible alignment. In the specific case of a grant-in-aid program, for example, the state will receive federal funds; and federal grant requirements and, hence policy objectives, will be met.

Box number two represents a situation in which the policy approach of the federal and state participants is mutually compatible but the working relationship between the partners is constrained by a lack of respect and confidence in the administrative and political procedures and activities of the individual actors (or perhaps governmental structure as a whole). In such a situation, the interaction between federal and state actors will probably be minimal, characterized by a tacit understanding of a mutual hands-off approach to their respective programs. Because the substantive efforts of their respective programs are similar, they can exist without a cooperative framework and feel assured that the eventual results will be predominantly mutually acceptable. The federal grant funds would be made available to the states, to return to my previous example of a grant-in-aid program, since the federal policy objectives will probably be met in the course of the state implementing its program. The important distinctions here lie in the "accident" of the similarity of the federal and state programs and the fact that the federal government realizes this in its review of grant applications. Thus, the federal grant or agency would allow this course of events to continue as long as it is satisfied that there is sufficient similarity of programs such that its major objectives were being met.

The third box characterizes a relationship of mutual trust and respect such that despite significant differences in programmatic approach, the two levels of government still feel that they can work together to arrive at a mutually satisfactory frame of reference over the course of time. The mode of discourse in this type of relationship will be "persuasion" in an attempt to convince each other to accept a particular definition of policy substance with regard to the program they are attempting to implement. The result in terms of the implementation of federal policy may be ambiguous since a mutuality of programmatic objectives does not exist.

Yet, there may be some accomplishment of federal objectives either as the state accepts federal views on acceptable policy objectives or as the federal agency adopts the state position on policy. In this type of relationship, federal grant funds would be awarded to the state since the federal agency has confidence that some form of mutually acceptable set objectives will eventually be established, and to withdraw aid might jeopardize this possibility.

The final form of relationship is best characterized in terms of conflict between federal and state actors predicated on a complete absence of any similarity in approach to programs and an absence of respect and confidence in the governmental efforts each puts forward. In such a situation the mode of discourse between the two levels of government will be couched in terms of forceful effort to change each other's programmatic efforts. In this context, federal policy objectives will go unrealized unless the state is compelled to adopt them. The initial response of the federal government in a grant-in-aid program would be to deny federal funds to a state. If the federal agency is unsuccessful in forcing the state to acquiesce to federal requirments and objectives, the federal program will go unimplemented in that state.

WATER POLLUTION: ARIZONA, CALIFORNIA, AND THE U.S. EPA

The following, based upon previous work by the author, provides an illustration of the application of this framework. It draws upon an analysis of the California and Arizona water pollution control agencies' experience with a federal grant program which provides funds to these agencies for the administration of their programs. Two caveats should be acknowledged before this example is broached, however. First, the assumption is that the two levels of government must both see each other as legitimate in order to fall within the category of legitimacy. If this situation does not prevail, the relationship will fall in either box two or box four. Second, the federal government must be actively attempting to insure that its policy program is being implemented in the states. If the federal government adopts a passive approach to state programs, then we must assume that whatever the states are doing meets the federal requirements. Pertaining to this last situation is the source of the federal drive to implement the federal program. The federal motivation in implementing a program may lie either with the federal administrative unit or with an outside agent (e.g., Congress, the President). If there is insufficient support for the federal agency from the national executive or Congress, then the states may be able to avoid the pressure of the federal program by appealing to one or the other of these institutions for support against the federal agency. This may alter the entire structure of and basis for the intergovernmental relationship.

California's relationship with the U.S. Environmental Protection Agency seems to fall more in box two than in box one. Although the liaison between the top administrative levels of the two agencies appears to point to a relationship of mutual accommodation, the relationship between the lower and middle levels of the two agencies seems to indicate that the legitimacy that they accord one another may be a facade to cover up some serious difficulties in their relationship.

Additionally, although the state and the EPA are for the most part highly compatible in their substantive approach to water pollution control—i.e., they are in "phase" in terms of their policy approaches —there are some points of disagreement on policy goals. This disagreement is not severe enough, however, to place the state more toward box four in terms of its relationship with the EPA. Thus, I am led to conceive of the California-EPA relationship in terms of tacit noncooperation on most *specific* elements of policy and program.

The Arizona situation most appropriately falls in box four, although with some qualification. In 1972 the EPA attempted to withhold from Arizona grant assistance for its administrative program. Additionally, some of the comments of state administrators who were interviewed indicated a distinct disrespect for federal administrators. The converse was also true for the federal administrators' view of the state officials. In 1973, however, a new director of the state Division of Water Quality Management was appointed. His appraisal of the substantive orientation of the federal program is a great deal more favorable than his predecessor's and perhaps his superiors'. Therefore, he is more inclined to adopt additional elements of the federal program for the state. More important, however, is his appraisal of the federal administrative efforts which are more positively oriented. This orientation on his part and the more concerted effort of the EPA, since the exercise of the withholding action, to cooperate with the state tend to suggest that it may be that the Arizona-EPA relationship is moving toward box three. Additional support for this contention comes from the fact that federal funds were awarded to Arizona despite the fact that even after revisions were made in the state program there were still areas that the EPA felt that the state could improve.

One of the assumptions made above was that the federal agency was actively pursuing a program to realize specific policy objectives. Such a mission-oriented approach to a grant-in-aid program or any form of intergovernmental program fits the commonsense notion of the federal stake in a policy area. However, this mission-oriented approach to policy poses serious problems in an intergovernmental program, not so much in itself, but in one of its by-products. As noted in the discussion of legitimacy, the crucial aspect of this concept was the respect and confidence felt between intergovernmental actors. The problem in a mission-oriented program is the tendency to disregard this aspect of the intergovernmental relationship because of an inward focus on accomplishing the objectives of one's own program. This is particularly important when the pressure is on an administrative agency either from the legislative or executive elements of the level of government it serves or from the public it represents.

This denial of legitimacy has been operating in the federal relationship with the states in water pollution control. It is not that the EPA has completely downgraded the efforts of the states. Rather, it is more of a tension between the need to respect the states and the need to accomplish the federal program objectives. As the pressure is applied to accomplish the national policy goals, the "rights and responsibilities of the states" seem to become second in priority in the face of the necessity to meet the federal objectives. In this program the federal administrators are on the horns of a dilemma when they must achieve the development and implementation of a national program, but allow the states to make independent policy decisions which might negate the success of this program. The causes of this dilemma lie in part with the problem of establishing precisely what the needs and objectives of a national program are and what makes them unique in regard to the states. If Lowi (1969) is right and policy has been set by Congress in such a fashion that it is ambiguous, thus leaving the administrators the task of providing clear specification, then the response of administrators in defining the federal mission may be to overly specify the federal objectives to the exclusion of the states' role. It becomes easy to do this when the common federal conception of the states is that they are backward and parochial, thus overlooking the fact that perhaps the states have made a conscious choice to adopt the policy programs they have adopted because they want them in that fashion.

An additional problem is one of defining the "publics" served by the states and the federal governments and attempting to understand that they may be different or at least concerned with different problems. The drive for national uniformity often tends to downplay the uniqueness of the states in an attempt to accomplish the federal objectives. It may be a misconception to view the national public as a homogeneous whole.[10] The states do serve segments of the national constituency which, when viewed as state publics, may exhibit unique perspectives on policy goals. The problem for the federal administrator is that the polity he serves—i.e., his mission—in all probability has not made these distinctions for him. Thus, he responds, perhaps, by overstating the federal role to the neglect of the states.

This overspecification of the federal mission poses severe difficulties for the state administrator who knows full well that he serves a government which is responsive to a different public than is the federal government. He must accomplish the goals of the state, but do so in the face of the federal program which may be asking or compelling him to meet the federal requirement first. The pressure on the state administrator to accomplish the state objectives is most direct since his future may be determined more by what he does in the state than by whether he meets the federal requirements. Therefore, in the case of a grant-in-aid program, if the federal requirements are framed with the intent of accomplishing the federal objectives without considering the state's objectives, the state administrator may respond in a negative fashion to the federal administrator. The result, therefore, is to perceive the federal program from this negative perspective.

One of the major findings of the author's previous study was that the success of the federal objectives through the influence exercised in a grant-in-aid program depended on the willingness and cooperation of the states more than on the coercive capability of the federal agency. In other words, the success of the federal program depended either on the compatibility of the state and federal programs initially or on the responsiveness of the state administrators to the persuasion of the federal administrators. In the first case, the success of the federal program in terms of the state program occurs because of the accident of the similarity of their substantive orientation. In the second situation, a feeling of mutual legitimacy is necessary in order that state and federal personnel can carry out a meaningful interchange.

The above discussion points to the importance of boxes one and three in the framework posited earlier. Boxes two and four are not useful from the federal and state perspectives since they permit the implementation and accomplishment of cooperative objectives only by chance or not at all. If anything, in their pure forms, these boxes suggest a negative attitude toward cooperation. This negativism is antithetical to the accomplishment of joint intergovernmental objectives since it does not permit a cooperative approach to a policy problem. In the terms suggested by Elazar and Grodzins this is a nonsharing arrangement. (Boxes one and three are most useful for a cooperative program since they establish a mutuality of credibility and the potential for the accomplishment of shared objectives.)

It is box three that we should consider most closely. The substantive similarity of programs can be enhanced through federal persuasion of the states or conversely through state persuasion of federal officials. There may never be a complete mutuality of substance which in itself is an important consideration to realize. Where there is a mutuality of substance then both partners can be satisfied. The important consideration is that the partners can also realize the importance attributed to the non-shared portions of substance. They are important to the respective programs of each level. The mutual feeling of legitimacy each partner holds for the other allows this situation to exist because they feel capable of working with one another and potentially reaching a greater similarity of substance in the future. Thus, box three might represent a more valid view of the "real world" and a more desirable one, if the partners can perceive the credibility of each other's efforts. It is also the "crux" of the political and policy-making nature of inter-governmental relations.

SUMMARY

From this perspective we can perceive the importance not only of legitimacy in intergovernmental relations but also of policy sub-stance. Policy substance, in effect, is another approach to the problem of clearly identifying the nature of the policy issues. It is often convenient to assume a single definition for policy issues and problems, but anyone who has tried to grapple with the definition of pollution control, for example, can only conclude with Davies (1969: 2) that the definition of pollution is political. In recognizing this fact, we are led further along the path to an understanding of why intergovernmental relations work the way they do, and to some extent as to why public policy works the way it does. However, since this framework is still in its infancy, it requires further development before it can be fully applied to the analysis of intergovernmental relations or public policy issues.

The four elements of policy substance described above are at best general categories which need further refinement before they can be fully operationalized. It is easy to posit "ideas" as a major component, but any political theorist who has ever tried to wrestle with the concept of ideology knows full well how difficult it is to pin this concept down. Further, we need some method of clearly defining issues. The act of identifying issues in itself may be a definitional activity which will prove difficult to clearly specify. These same difficulties may also prove true of the other two categories. Moreover, I have posited substantive nonagreement and agreement as meaningful categories. If they are in fact continua, as suggested, then how can we identify points along that continua? Is agreement-disagreement on one category enough? Is the fact that it is probably more difficult to reach agreement on the definition of issues than on the meaning of programs for action significant in distinguishing between agreement and nonagreement? These are questions which need to be addressed to operationalize what is now only a heuristic framework.

The importance of this framework is that it clearly indicates that in the conduct of intergovernmental programs a similarity of approach and identification of policy problems and solutions should not be blithely accepted. The formation of policy is a political activity. It does not cease being political simply because we have something identified as formalized policy. As Bailey (1950) has indicated the formation of the Employment Act was a process which revolved around the definition of what "fair employment" really meant. The alternative views of policy simply do not go away. Ours is a multiple crack system, to use Grodzin's term, wherein there is a continuous feedback of ideas on policy as the experience with its implementation is gained. It would not be a feedback system if we clearly could identify at the first cut what the policy problems, issues, facts, and solutions really were. Politicians and professional administrators must continuously be aware of the multiplicity of policy definitions if they are to function effectively either in the intergovernmental realm or in the other realms of our political system. Where differences exist between state and federal programs in an intergovernmental situation, the accommodation of these differences will depend on the partners' abilities to overcome different definitions of policy problems. These efforts will require in many cases creative approaches to intergovernmental cooperation.

NOTES

1. The fiscal aspect of intergovernmental relations has been widely recognized as the "cutting edge" of federal-state-local relationships. It is impossible to document all the

studies which have addressed this topic without in effect writing a separate paper. From my perspective the core of this literature is represented by Heller (1967), Break (1962), Pechman (1970), and Oates (1972).

2. In general see Ranney (1968) and Froman (1968). Also see Lowi (1964: 677-715) and Dolbeare (1970: 85-111).

3. To some extent the nature of policy content was addressed by Reagan (1967). However, this initial attempt at grappling with the concept only raised the issue and did not take us very far. Jones (1970) has given us a better insight, but this approach is still treacherous.

4. The approach initiated by Lowi (1964) was elaborated upon by Salisbury and Heinz (1970) but still has its pitfalls as those who have used this approach know.

5. As Bailey notes, the interplay of political actors during the long struggle to formulate the Fair Employment Act was critically focused on the issues of what "fair employment" meant and what the federal government's role should be.

6. Arendt in her essay "What is Authority" (1968) argued that authority is not a product of the exercise of political power. In her terms, power is a phenomenon of group activity, whereas, for others, authority is an attribute accorded to an individual or institutional entity. In the intergovernmental arena, where the authority of the participant may not be clearly granted or established by legislation, it must be a product of the participants perceptions of one another.

7. The trappings of professional authority as suggested by Adrian (1965) and Price (1963) grow out of the shared experiences of professionals–i.e., their similar schooling and professional frame of mind–whereas political authority is supposed to grow from the electoral and leadership mandate of the politician. I question whether this distinction can honestly be made. Although the sources of authority may be different, the process by which it is achieved is the same–the recognition of some personal attribute which enables one to achieve the respect of others. The key here is not so much the knowledge of a particular policy area, which admittedly may be more extensive in the case of the professional administrator, but the manner in which the individual carries out his responsibilities. Thus, we can make a distinction between the authority (legitimacy) of the intergovernmental actor and his position or view on a particular policy substance.

8. The individual politician may know less about a policy issue but he may try as hard or harder than the professional to implement his view. Thus, the distinction between professional and political authority is not one of quality or quantity of knowledge but of quantity and quality of effort. Effort which engenders respect and the accord of legitimacy is no different for politician or professional.

9. Anyone who has ever indulged in budgetary research soon acknowledges that the successful professional administrator is a politician at heart.

10. Elazar (1974) has clearly raised the differences in political culture among the many states and regions of this country. This is just one indication that the United States is not a homogeneous whole.

REFERENCES

ADRIAN, C. (1965). "State and local government participation in the design and implementation of intergovernmental programs." The Annals, 359(May).

ANDERSON, W. (1959). Intergovernmental Relations in Review. Minneapolis: University of Minnesota Press.

ARENDT, H. (1968). Between Past and Future. New York: Viking.

BAILEY, S. (1950). Congress Makes A Law. New York: Vintage.

BREAK, G. G. (1962). Intergovernmental Fiscal Relations. Washington, D.C.: Brookings Institution.

DAVIES, J. C. (1969). The Politics of Pollution. New York: Pegasus.
DERTHICK, M. (1970). The Influence of Federal Grants. Cambridge, Mass.: Harvard University Press.
——— (1973). New Towns, In Town. Washington, D.C.: Urban Land Institute.
DOLBEARE, K. (1970). "Public policy analysis and the coming struggle for the soul of the post-behavioral revolution." Pp. 85-111 in P. Green and S. Levinson (eds.), Power and Community: Dissenting Essays in Political Science. New York: Vintage.
EDNER, S. M. (1973a). "Formula grants and intergovernmental relations: The politics of effluents." Unpublished Ph.D. dissertation, University of California, Riverside.
——— (1973b). "The implementation of federal water pollution control policy." Paper presented at the Annual Meetings of the Western Political Science Association, San Diego, California (April).
ELAZAR, D. (1962). The American Partnership. Chicago: University of Chicago Press.
——— (1970). Cities of the Prairie. New York: Basic Books.
——— (1974). American Federalism: A View from the States. New York: Crowell.
——— et al. (1969). Cooperation and Conflict. Itasca, Ill.: Peacock.
EDELMAN, M. (1969). The Symbolic Uses of Politics. Urbana: University of Illinois Press.
FROMAN, L. A., Jr. (1968). "The categorization of policy contents." In A. Ranney (ed.), Political Science and Public Policy. Chicago: Markham.
GRODZINS, M. (1960). "The federal system." In M. Grodzins (ed.), Goals for Americans. New York: Columbia University Press.
——— (1966). The American System. Chicago: Rand McNally.
HELLER, W. (1967). New Dimensions of Political Economy. Cambridge, Mass.: Harvard University Press.
INGRAM, H. (1973). "Policy implementation through bargaining: The impact of federal grants-in-aid." Unpublished manuscript, University of Arizona, Tucson.
JONES, C. O. (1970). An Introduction to the Study of Public Policy. Belmont, Calif.: Duxbury.
LOWI, T. (1964). "American business, public policy, case studies and political theory." World Politics, 16(July).
——— (1969). The End of Liberalism. New York: Norton.
MACMAHON, A. W. (ed., 1955). Federalism: Mature and Emergent. New York: Russell and Russell.
OATES, W. (1972). Fiscal Federalism. New York: Harcourt Brace Jovanovitch.
PECHMAN, J. (1970). Federal Tax Policy. Washington, D.C.: Brookings Institution.
PORTER, D. O., and WARNER, D. C. (1973). "How effective are grantor controls?: The case of federal aid to education." In K. Boulding (ed.), Transfers in an Urbanized Economy. Belmont, Calif.: Wadsworth.
PRICE, D. K. (1963). The Scientific Estate. New York: Oxford University Press.
RANNEY, A. (1968). "The study of policy content: A framework for choice." In A. Ranney (ed.), Political Science and Public Policy. Chicago: Markham.
REAGAN, M. D. (1967). "Policy issues: The interaction of substance and process." Polity (Fall).
SALISBURY, R., and HEINZ, J. (1970). "A theory of policy analysis and some preliminary applications." In I. Sharkansky (ed.), Policy Analysis and Political Science. Chicago: Markham.
SEGAL, M., and FRITSCHLER, A. (1970). "Policy-making in the intergovernmental system: Emerging patterns and a typology of relationships." Paper delivered at the sixty-sixth annual meeting of the American Political Science Association, Los Angeles, California (September).
STEINER, G. (1966). Social Insecurity. Chicago: Rand McNally.
SUNDQUIST, J. L. (1969). Making Federalism Work. Washington, D.C.: Brookings Institution.

U.S. Senate (1963). The Federal System as Seen by State and Local Officials. Washington, D.C.: Government Printing Office.

––– Committee on Government Operations, Subcommittee on Intergovernmental Relations (1965). The Federal System as Seen by Federal Aid Officials. Washington, D.C.: Government Printing Office.

VILE, M.J.C. (1961). The Structure of American Federalism (3rd ed.). New York: Oxford University Press.

WEIDNER, E. (1955). "Decision-making in a federal system." In A. W. MacMahon (ed.), Federalism Mature and Emergent. New York: Russell and Russell.

––– (1959). Intergovernmental Relations as Seen by Public Officials. Minneapolis: University of Minnesota Press.

WHEARE, K. C. (1953). Federalism. New York: Oxford University Press.

WILDAVSKY, A., and PRESSMAN, J. (1973). Implementation. Berkeley: University of California Press.

WRIGHT, D. S. (1968). Federal Grants-in-Aid: Perspectives and Alternatives. Washington, D.C.: American Enterprise Institute.

8

WATER POLLUTION AND
COMPLIANCE DECISION MAKING

B R U C E P. B A L L

Angelo State University

The purpose of this study is to identify the factors that influence the administration of federal programs by nonfederal officials. The enforcement of water pollution legislation has consistently involved questions and issues of intergovernmental relations. Legislation has continually emphasized three themes: (1) the structuring and development of a grant-in-aid program; (2) the steady extension of federal jurisdiction in establishing water quality standards; and (3) the extension of enforcement or compliance strategies available to enforcement officials. All of these are either directly or indirectly linked to the development of an intergovernmental administrative subsystem responsible for the enforcement of water pollution legislation.

The federal grant-in-aid program for water pollution began with the 1956 amendments to the Water Pollution Control Act of 1948. (See Table 1 for a review of the water pollution legislation.) The program was limited by funds, a project grant ceiling, and a small

AUTHOR'S NOTE: *I would like to acknowledge the helpful comments of Charles O. Jones of the University of Pittsburgh, Robert D. Thomas of Florida Atlantic University, and James F. Torres of the University of Wisconsin, River Falls. This is a revised version of a paper presented at the 1974 Annual Meeting of the American Political Science Association, Chicago, Illinois, August 29-September 2.*

Table 1. ANNOTATED COMPILATIONS OF SIGNIFICANT WATER POLLUTION LEGISLATION

Date	Act
1899	*Refuse Act of 1899* (Section 13 of the Rivers and Harbors Act, 30 Stat. 1152). The act prevented dumping of effluents into navigable streams and lakes. Although it was passed with navigation–not water quality–in mind, it has lately been used to stop offshore drilling and dumping of untreated effluents into navigable waters. The act provided for a permit procedure to be handled by the Corps of Engineers. (Only recently have the provisions been used to improve water quality.)
1948	*Water Pollution Control Act* (P.L. 80-845). The act provided for the establishment of the Federal Water Pollution Administration in the Public Health Service. Loans were made available to municipalities for the construction of treatment plants. Of the $22.5 million authorized per year, little was ever appropriated. Abatement authority rested almost solely with state and local agencies; federal authorities could be introduced only with the states' consent. A two-step compliance process was outlined. The legislation was to be in force for only three years.
1953	The 1948 Act was extended for three years.
1956	*Amendments to the Water Pollution Control Act* (P.L. 84-660). Of primary significance was the establishment of the compliance process: conferences, public hearings, and litigation. Financial arrangements were changed allowing federal grants. However, the grants were not to exceed $50,000,000 per year and $250,000 per project. Half of the funds appropriated were to be used by communities under 125,000. Federal authority, still weak, could be invoked only in those cases in which (1) interstate waters were involved or (2) a state requested federal intervention.
1961	*Amendments to the Water Pollution Control Act* (P.L. 88-668). The main feature was the extension of federal authority to navigable waters, not just interstate waters. It also raised authorized grants to $80 million for FY 1962, $90 million for 1963, and $100 million for 1964 through 1967. However, the single grant project limit was raised to only $600,000 and the federal sharing continued at 30 percent.
1965	*Water Quality Act* (P.L. 89-234). The main feature was the establishment of federally approved state water quality standards by June 30, 1967. It also authorized a grant total of $150 million in 1966 and 1967. The individual grant ceiling was raised to $1.2 million; the research and development program was expanded. The "180-day notice" provisions allowed for a streamlined abatement effort taking only 180 days between notice of pollution and commencement of legal action.
1966	*Executive Reorganization Plan No. 2* (under authority granted to the President by the Reorganization Act of 1949). The plan suggested the transfer of the Federal Water Pollution Control Administration from the Department of Health, Education, and Welfare to the Department of Interior. Under the legislative veto procedure the burden was placed on Congress to reject the proposal within 90 days or let the plan stand. It stood unchallenged.
1966	*Clean Water Restoration Act* (P.L. 89-753). Of importance was the changing of the granting formula from 30 percent to 50 percent federal share if the state government committed itself to funding 25 percent of the project. An added 10 percent of the federal share—net reduction of 5 percent of the project cost—would be taken up by the federal government if an area-wide metropolitan plan was available. The act removed the ceiling for individual grants. Authorizations for grants were also increased to $450 million in FY 1968, $700 million in 1969, $1 billion in 1970, and $1.25 billion in 1971.

Table 1 (continued)

Date	Act
1970	*National Environmental Policy Act* (P.L. 91-224). Significant was the provision that all federally funded projects must include a statement as to the impact of that project on the environment.
1970	*Reorganization Plan No. 3.* The plan suggested the creation of the Environmental Protection Agency, an independent agency to consolidate nearly all environmental quality efforts and programs. The agency was approved in the fall of 1970.
1972	*Water Pollution Act of 1972.* The act substantially expanded federal financial commitments to deal with water pollution. The act called for a $30 billion outlay over a six-year period. The federal commitment also included a 75-25 matching formula for construction grants.

city preference clause. However, the precedent was established, and the grant program was steadily developed to a point where today $3 billion per year has been authorized as the federal share—up to 75 percent of the cost—for the construction of waste treatment plants.

Federal jurisdiction has also steadily expanded. Initially the federal government's authority over water pollution was limited to "interstate" waters. Later federal authority was extended to "navigable" waters. More recently legislation mandated federal approval of state water quality standards. This gave the federal government indirect control over all water quality standards.

Likewise, enforcement strategies have been expanded. Initially, federal authorities were restricted to a three step compliance process where recalcitrants were brought to a water pollution conference, a public hearing, and finally litigation. More recently federal legislation has added a "streamlined" 180-day notice provision to this compliance process. In addition, the courts have expanded a 75-year-old permit program to include environmental concerns.

Charles O. Jones (1974) suggests that this increased federal presence is not unique to the water pollution issue-area. In examining air pollution policy activity, Jones argued that intergovernmental relations in the regulatory area consistently move toward a more prominent federal presence. Figure 1 schematizes five intergovernmental linkages suggested by Jones. A federal role is initially evident

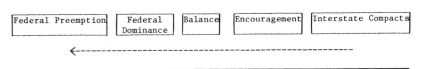

Figure 1.

with the (federal) encouragement position. Encouragement or inducement programs include grants-in-aid, tax breaks, subsidies, and effluent fees. With the further development of a federal presence, these encouragement policies give way to a more active, forceful enforcement effort by federal officials. These include tighter federal controls over the grant program (i.e., the requirement of secondary treatment for all federally funded waste treatment plants) as well as *federally approved* water quality standards.

Table 2 illustrates the linkage between the Jones schema and the classical enforcement strategies noted above. To be sure, it is a rough and superficial association, but it is suggestive of a patterned development that has led to a strong federal presence. This is, however, not to imply that the current federal dominance has totally excluded state and local participation in the enforcement effort. Thomas and Luken (1974) observed that the most recent federal legislation has provided a significant role for state and local enforcement officials and programs.

An intergovernmental administrative subsystem is thus evident in the water pollution issue-area. The federal presence is strong and growing; however, federal legislation has provided for a significant enforcement role for both state and local officials. How this diffuse (vertical separation of power) decision-making system works is the central concern of this study.

In attempting to answer this question, we have chosen the case study method. By examining the abatement process related to a specific case, we will identify those factors that have a positive as well as those factors that have a negative effect on the abatement program. In developing these findings we borrowed heavily from compliance theory, particularly as it has been developed by students of the court.

Table 2.

Organizational Development Stages	Classical Enforcement Strategies	Water Pollution Legislation
Interstate compacts	Voluntary compliance	Pre-1956
Encouragement	Grants, loans and other economic subsidies	1956-1964
Balance	Continuation of above with some federal concern for quality of state and local programs	1964-1967
Dominance	Effluent fees, permits, standards, and controlled grants	1967-1971
Preemption	Nationally coordinated use of all appropriate strategies	?

THE WATER POLLUTION COMPLIANCE
DECISION-MAKING SYSTEM

We "arbitrarily" chose the case of Omaha.[1] A thorough examination of the case proceedings, as well as personal and written interviews with case participants supplemented the *Omaha World Herald*'s rather thorough coverage of the compliance proceedings. (See Table 3 for a sketch of the case.) These several sources produced the data necessary for the following analysis.

Table 3. ANNOTATION OF THE OMAHA CASE

Period	Compliance Activity
1950-1956	The federal regional office in conjunction with lower Missouri River Basin States provided a Lower Missouri River Plan that called for treatment of all sewage by users of the river. However, no action was taken to further treat the effluents.
1957-1964	Under authority of the 1956 amendments to the Water Pollution Control Act a water pollution conference was called by federal officials. At the conference Omaha outlined a five-project multimillion dollar plan and schedule that would intercept all of the city's 28 outfalls to the river and treat (primary) the effluents. The program was to be completed by 1960.
	Delays in financing the projects (initial voter rejection of revenue bonds and a restrictive city debt limit) caused slippage in the abatement program. However, the program as presented was completed in early 1964. The treatment plant packers (23) continued to introduce untreatable effluents into the municipal sewage system, by consent of the city.
1964-1967	A second conference session was called at which Omaha suggested an additional project, a pretreatment plant, that would pretreat the packers effluents before it was received by the city treatment plant. The new project would be funded through a lease-purchase agreement between a nonprofit corporation, the city, and the packers.
	Questions concerning the nontaxable status of the bonds to be issued caused a three-year delay in the issuance of the bonds.
1967-1969	A third conference session was called by impacted states at which they asked for a public hearing. Federal officials indicated that such a hearing would be warranted if further delays occurred. In mid-1969 the pretreatment plant as well as the entire abatement project was put on line.
1969-1971	The system continued to function as projected. The by-products of the pretreatment plant were to be sold for a profit. However, the operation proved less successful than intended and the contracting company operating the plant forfeited their annual payments in 1971.
1971-Present	The city continues to operate the pretreatment plant at an annual $600,000 loss. In addition, the city is under orders to draw up plans converting their present primary treatment system to secondary treatment.

An analysis of the Omaha water pollution case produced two major conclusions. First, the compliance decision-making system has three distinct components. Each component is identified below, and the link between the components and compliance behavior is developed. Second, an intergovernmental decision-making system is evident.

COMPLIANCE DECISION-MAKING COMPONENTS

Below are identified and annotated the three components of the compliance decision-making system: the legitimating decision, the enforcement system, and the issue-public response. (See Figure 2.) Many of the linkages with compliance behavior have been previously suggested by studies of the court system; however, the components and linkages discussed below were active ingredients of the subject-case studied here. (Especially noteworthy are Dolbeare and Hammond, 1971; Wasby, 1970.)

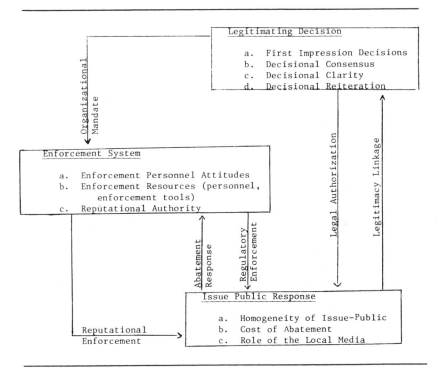

Figure 2: COMPLIANCE DECISION-MAKING SYSTEM

Legitimating Decision

Policy or legislative decisions function to authorize governmental activity in a legal sense (Dolbeare and Hammond, 1971: 134-135). But previous impact research has indicated an equally important dimension to such policy level decisions. While decisions might legally authorize governmental action, this authorization does not automatically insure that those affected, the issue-public, will grant such legitimacy to the governmental activity. Judicial impact research and the observed pollution case both demonstrate certain decisional characteristics bearing significantly on the question of decisional legitimacy. Those characteristics found active in the Omaha water pollution effort were initial or "first impression decisions," decisional consensus, decisional clarity, and decisional reiteration.

Perhaps most important of these decisional characteristics is the first impression decision (Wasby, 1970: 43). These decisions are made on the frontiers of the public-private sector. They are the first efforts made by government to regulate behavior or redistribute resources in an issue-area. Government regulation of behavior and activity, whether it be corporate or personal, is viewed by many as acceptable only as a last resort. Correspondingly, state and local regulatory policies seem to provide less anxieties than do federal initiatives. As a result, initial regulatory thrusts by the federal government are especially susceptible to problems of compliance. The issue-public's rights have been newly abridged, and the traditions of governmental regulation are absent. Therefore, first impression decisions are especially open to questions of legitimacy by the issue-public.

Because the official Omaha proceedings began in 1957, shortly after the passage of the 1956 amendments which expanded federal jurisdiction, the question of federal governmental legitimacy was apparent. Repeatedly, state, local, and even federal officials argued that the issue was one of a state and local concern, not an issue for federal intervention. This argument was voiced by President Eisenhower in vetoing the 1960 Water Pollution Control Amendments:

> Because water pollution is a uniquely local plight, primary responsibility for solving the problem lies not with the federal government but rather must be assumed and exercised as it has been, by state and local governments. This being so, the defects of H.R. 3610 are apparent. By holding forth the promise of a large scale program of long term federal

support, it would tempt municipalities to delay essential water pollution abatement efforts while they waited for federal funds. [Jennings, 1969: 90]

M. Kent Jennings and James Sundquist narrate the early efforts at formulating water pollution legislation. Both essays point to the question of whether the water pollution issue was properly a federal issue: "In the early 1950's hardly a word was spoken in the Congress to suggest that the beauty of the countryside and the city, the pollution of air and water, the pressure of population upon outdoor open space were national concerns" (Sundquist, 1968: 332).

Interviews with Omaha participants acted to reinforce this suspicion. A local administrator noted: "We really didn't know how serious the 'feds' were. From 1948 to '56 they really didn't do much, and even after the conference [in 1957] we hardly saw them. We thought we should be pretty much left on our own." Other remarks and actions by Omaha and Nebraska officials substantiated this apparent confusion bordering on indignation at federal intervention.

Thus, early legislative efforts were held in some question by federal officials, as well as state and local officials. The question of the legitimacy of federal intervention clearly acted to slow local abatement efforts.

Three other decisional characteristics were seen to have an influence on these questions of legitimacy. Each of these character- istics—decisional consensus, decisional clarity, and decisional reiter- ation—act to reinforce the legitimacy of the decision with the issue-public or exacerbate the questions of legitimacy with the issue-public.

Decisional consensus, by the authorizing body, has been directly linked to the issue-public and that public's granting of legitimacy to the decisions. Judicial impact research has shown that decisional consensus, as represented by lopsided or unanimous votes by the authorizing institution, increase the propensity for the issue-public to comply with the decisions (Wasby, 1970: 44; Muir, 1967: 132-133; Levine, 1972: 107). Voting represents division or consensus, a united stand for or against an issue, or a hope for those negatively affected that a subsequent decision may reverse the impact of the former. A unanimous or consensus decision carries the full weight of the decision-making body—or an increased proportion. Not only is the recalcitrant faced with little hope of reversal, but there is a symbolic or psychological dimension to such unanimity.

Like many other concepts in the social sciences, credibility lacks precise definition, yet it offers immense potential for understanding the decision-making process. Perceptions surrounding a decision are often as important as the realities of the decision. Thus, the perception of decisional consensus by the issue-public enhances the credibility of the decision and diminishes the likelihood of non-compliance.

Likewise, the lack of decisional consensus—especially when complemented by a first-impression decision—seems distinctly counter-productive to compliance behavior. Case data revealed that the initial legislative forays were far from uniformly supported by either Congress or the executive. Support did increase until today the question is not whether, but how much.

This change in legislator attitudes and decisional consensus corresponds with increased federal enforcement activity. Although we are inclined to speculate that there is a linkage between the developing consensus and enforcement, the relationship must be noted as speculative, not empirical—even in the case study. Thus, decisional consensus does seem to have a positive link in water pollution compliance decision making, albeit a nebulous and/or speculative linkage.

Decisional clarity has also been shown to be effective in influencing compliance behavior. Several links have been suggested relating decisional clarity to compliance behavior. Thomas Barth (1968: 314) has suggested, "Ambiguity of a decision increases the likelihood that it will be misunderstood by the other actors in the political process and that the policies of the other participants will not be adjusted to conform to the decision." A second linkage is suggested by Lawrence Pettit (1969: 271), who has argued that clarity in the court's decision nullified regional and local norms that might influence a more ambiguous decision.

Evident in the Omaha case were decisional ambiguities concerning *what* to do to comply, and *how* to do it. Although their abatement program was accepted by the water pollution conference, there was no specific stipulation as to what should be the primary objective of the program. Questions regarding the speed and quality of the abatement program and whether to consider advanced treatment methods (secondary and tertiary treatment) were left undiscussed. Procedural questions were left almost entirely to Omaha. They received little direction as to *how* to proceed. It is perhaps fair to surmise that what should have been done and how it should have been done were implicit; however, the lack of complete clarity allowed Omaha some self-discretion. Consciously and unconsciously (there is reason to suspect) officials were able to rationalize a slower abatement program than if the decisional objectives and the procedures for compliance were explicit.

Finally, first impression decisions can be strengthened by reiteration of the initial decision (or objectives of that decision). The effect of periodic reiteration of a decision has the same effect as decisional consensus in giving added assurance that the decision will not be reversed. This makes noncompliance more difficult to reconcile with previous behavior.

Decisional reiteration may occur in several ways. In the judicial system it may be a follow-up decision by the Supreme Court, or a decision by lower courts based on the Supreme Court's decision. In the legislative system such reiteration can be indicated by long-term legislative commitments: repeated program appropriations, continuing verbal-symbolic support by policy leaders, and/or new legislative initiatives.

Such reiterations were evident in our case examination. Throughout the compliance effort, federal legislative initiatives included larger appropriations, rhetoric by national policy leaders, and stronger enforcement efforts. Each action by federal policy makers seemed to act to reinforce a permanent commitment to the policy goals. The possibility of noncompliance then lost acceptability.

Thus, compliance seems enhanced when a decision is perceived by an issue-public as a legitimate exercise of governmental activity. Early regulatory thrusts tend to post questions of legitimacy with their issue-public. Compliance depends upon the development of decisional consensus, the clarity of the decision, and its reiteration. When all three factors are present, the legitimacy given a decision by its issue-public seems to increase.

ENFORCEMENT SYSTEM

Previous compliance research has dealt with the enforcement system in a variety of ways. Specifically, the enforcement personnel attitudes and the available enforcement resources were found to be influences on water pollution compliance activity.

A major facet of the enforcement system influencing compliance is the attitudes of the enforcement personnel toward the issue and the issue-public. A decision agreed to by the administering personnel will have a better chance of achieving compliance. (See especially Dolbeare and Hammond, 1971; Milner, 1972: 297-313.) A bureaucracy in agreement with a decision is more likely to administer the decision vigorously, for they are committed to the goals of the decision both professionally and emotionally (Rourke, 1969). Personal and written surveys of conference participants revealed that there was a commitment in Omaha to comply. However, this commitment was very difinitely tempored. The restraint felt by federal enforcement officials was evoked by a concern for the economy of the community as well as a recognition of limited enforcement tools. (See Table 4.) Nebraska's restraint, on the other hand, was produced by a lack of fiscal and regulatory resources to induce compliance. Omaha city officials were restrained by a primary concern for the city's economy. Table 4 illustrates results of a mail survey of Omaha, Nebraska, and federal officials directly responsible for abatement programming.

In short, there was evidence of a concern to abate the problem. The financial outlays of the city are testimony to this. However, at all three governmental levels attitudinal restraints operated to neutralize a complete commitment by administrators. The result was a failure to address the problem in a sustained, systematic way.

The availability of enforcement resources—personnel and enforcement tools—has been linked also to a higher propensity for compliance behavior (Dolbeare and Hammond, 1971: 134-136; Wasby, 1970: 43-44; Levine, 1972: 109). The adequate staffing of an enforcement system is linked to compliance behavior in two ways. First, adequate monitoring of abatement activity is of concern. The desirability of self-regulation is questionable in the first place. However, self-regulation without outside monitoring has been consistently linked to a poor compliance record. The "visibility" issue

Table 4. IN RESPONSE TO THE QUESTION: "WHICH BEST REPRESENTS YOUR POSITION CONCERNING OMAHA'S WATER POLLUTION ABATEMENT PROGRAM?"[a]

	Omaha	Nebraska	Federal
(1) Abatement as soon as possible	0	1	1
(2) Abatement as soon as other economic and business considerations can be resolved	6	2	4
(3) Abatement is not important	1	0	0

a. There are five possible federal respondents, nine possible Omaha respondents, and five possible Nebraska respondents.

has been posited as a second link between enforcement system staffing and compliance behavior. Monitoring, supervision, and so on must be visible to the recalcitrant to reinforce and support the abatement orders.

The impact on compliance of the lack of adequate staffing is clearly demonstrated in our water pollution case. State (Nebraska) officials had neither the desire (Table 4) nor the staff to support an active, ongoing monitoring program. As a result, local officials were allowed almost total discretion in procedural questions (day-to-day decisions) as well as project level decisions. This situation was further exacerbated by the lack of a federal presence until 1969. Although regional (federal) officials made sporadic visits, there was no systematic federal monitoring or supervising program by federal officials. Indeed, federal administrative policy was voiced by the conference administrator when he said:

> We [the federal administrators] do not presume to tell you how or what to do. The purpose of the conference sessions is to identify the problem and the proper methods of treatment. The federal government is interested in helping you, not in dictating to you. [Stein, 1957]

This attitude did change. But the Omaha proceedings suggest that it was not before 1968-1969 that a federal presence was apparent at either the state or the local level.

In conjunction with an enforcement staff are the tools available to the staff. There are two general types of enforcement tools or alternatives: coercive (fines and penal ties) and inducive (financial and technical support). An adequate enforcement system must have both alternatives available to confidently deal with the problems of enforcement (Dolbeare and Hammond, 1971: 135-137; Murphy, 1959: 390; Freeley, 1972: 60-63). It is the lack of these enforcement strategies that is illustrated in the case. Federal legislation only recently has provided any criminal or financial penalties for pollutors. Although some have raised questions about whether charges of obstructing justice and other malfeasances were not implicit in noncompliance activity, there has not been a judicial test of such an argument. Although financial penalties now exist for both public and private noncompliance, the few state and federal litigated cases indicate a strong reluctance on the part of judges to use such penalties in any punitive way.

On the other hand, federal grants-in-aid have been available to support local abatement efforts since 1956. Although these federal inducements for compliance now reach as high as 75 percent of the cost of the abatement program, this is a maximum limit, one that cannot always be met, and it pertains only to specific facets of the abatement effort. During much of the Omaha proceedings, the city was eligible for 30-33 percent of federal matching money. However, the five-project average was just under 15 percent. Omaha paid for 85 percent of the abatement costs. State aid is a more recent development, and Omaha received no financial aid from the state of Nebraska until the 1970s.

What this demonstrates is that an understaffed federal and state enforcement system lacked adequate enforcement tools (coercive and inducive) to enhance compliance with water pollution legislation. Our methodology does not permit us to examine the relative influence of each of these variables on the laggardly abatement program. However, the aggregate of these clearly hampered compliance activity.

In summary, each of the above enforcement system characteristics have distinct features influencing compliance activity. All seem to increase the compliance decision-making system's capability to react to a compliance problem quickly and with discretion. An enforcement system with trained personnel, committed to the goals and objectives of the enabling legislation, with available enforcement resources, has been directly and positively linked to the compliance effort by our case.

Reputational Enforcement. Above are noted several facets of the enforcement system that have been linked to compliance activity. Each acts to strengthen the enforcement system's capability to act. However, enforcement can be attained short of overt activity. While overt regulation is one method of effecting compliance, the potential for effective enforcement (perceived, covert, or reputational regulation) can be as strong, if not stronger, in inducing compliance. If the certainty of enforcement is "credible" the necessity for coercive measures is reduced.

The Omaha case indicates that the threat of enforcement was not perceived as credible by the issue-public. Indeed, the dual role played by the city (enforcer and pollutor) plus the lack of a federal or state enforcement presence severely restricted a credible enforcement potential. For Omaha, then, the benefits of noncompliance outweighed the costs of noncompliance. (See Table 5.) There was little reason for quickened compliance activity in Omaha inasmuch as the "costs" for noncompliance—short of possible public indignation—

Table 5. COST-BENEFIT COMPLIANCE EQUATION

Perceived Costs of Noncompliance	Perceived Benefits of Noncompliance
(Fines and penalties)[a]	Continued economic well-being
(Federal and state indirect financial sanctions, i.e., nonpollution grant-in-aid cutoffs.)	Continued low and stable taxes
Public indignation	(State and federal financial aid)

a. The designation (   ) indicates potential but not credible or available enforcement costs or benefits.

were perceived as insubstantial. If the enforcement system had presented a credible potential to inflict more costs, the equation might have been different.

This suggests the "reputational authority" argument discussed by scholars of non-decision-making. (See especially Crenson, 1971.) Before an administrative organization can rely on reputational authority it must demonstrate its ability to impose overt regulatory measures. The implications of this suggestion are "Catch 22ish." Those administrative systems which lack resources and staff and which could most use reputational authority do not generally possess such authority. On the other hand, large established organizations which no longer have acute compliance problems do have, almost by definition, enforcement status or reputational authority.

In summary, neither regulatory enforcement (actual overt enforcement activity) nor symbolic enforcement (covert or reputational enforcement) was a substantial incentive for a quickened compliance response in the Omaha case. Regulatory enforcement was restricted by the lack of resources; and symbolic enforcement was restricted because of the embryonic state of organizational development, lack of overt enforcement activity, and the paucity of enforcement resources.

ISSUE-PUBLIC RESPONSE

The third and final component of the compliance decision-making system is the issue-public. Those directly impacted by the decision play a major role in determining the speed and extent of compliance with water pollution laws. Three significant characteristics of the issue-public can be linked to compliance activity: the homogeneity of the attentive issue-public, the cost of the abatement effort, and the influence of the local media.

Court decisions involving obscenity and school prayers have detailed a linkage between the homogeneity of a community and its propensity to comply. The findings support statements such as: "Non-compliance with the Supreme Court's church-state rulings seems to have been greater in religiously homogeneous communities than in those heterogeneous communities with significant religious minorities" (Blaustein and Ferguson, 1957: 96).

Implicit in these studies is an elite issue-public or an "attentive" issue-public. In other words, the collective citizenry of Omaha was not the noncompliant. The question of compliance was confined to the city government and the packing industry. Thus, while the community as a whole was heterogeneous, the noncompliant element was much more homogeneous.

The implications for compliance is clear. A homogeneous issue-public restricts acceptable alternatives. If the attentive public is inclined toward compliance, decision makers will more likely be inclined toward compliance. However, if the attentive issue-public is negatively inclined, then rapid compliance is constrained. In Omaha the attentive issue-public (the packing industry, elected, and administrative officials, and the media) dictated that economic considerations be valued along with environmental concerns.

A second factor influencing the issue-public's response are abatement costs. As abatement costs go up (either financially or by the abridgement of strongly held beliefs), the likelihood of voluntary compliance declines. Most previous research has explored the effect of attitudes on compliance. Relatively little interest has been shown for issues requiring technological changes. While some issues are almost totally reliant on attitude change, others need large inputs of technology for resolution. Still others demand nearly equal amounts of each.

We can hypothesize that as an issue becomes more technological, the monetary cost of compliance increases; and, in turn, as an issue becomes more attitudinal in nature, the potential high costs of compliance will involve attitude and behavioral changes. While compliance with obscenity decisions might necessitate large costs in terms of behavior alterations, the high costs involved in water pollution compliance are financial.

Omaha is illustrative of these high fiscal abatement costs. Over $30 million was spent, and an estimated $50 million more must be appropriated to provide secondary treatment. The cost was not totally borne by the recalcitrant. As the federal government's

Table 6. CONTENT ANALYSIS OF *OMAHA WORLD HERALD*'s **TREATMENT OF THE WATER POLLUTION ISSUE**

Year	Total Number of Articles[a]	News Stories			Feature Articles[b]			Editorials		
		Positive	Neutral	Negative	Positive	Neutral	Negative	Positive	Neutral	Negative
1953	6	0	2	1	0	0	0	0	0	1
1954	5	1	2	0	0	1	0	0	1	0
1955	10	2	3	0	1	1	0	1	0	0
1956	12	2	1	2	1	2	0	2	3	0
1957	20	3	10	1	2	1	0	2	0	0
1958	13	2	8	1	1	1	0	0	0	0
1959	11	1	7	0	2	1	0	0	0	0
1960	13	0	6	0	1	2	0	2	1	0
1961	15	1	11	0	1	0	0	1	1	0
1962	10	1	6	0	0	1	0	1	1	0
1963	18	4	10	0	3	0	0	3	0	0
1964	38	3	12	1	3	1	0	2	3	2
1965	33	3	15	0	4	2	1	3	4	0
1966	23	3	10	0	4	1	0	2	2	0
1967	25	4	15	0	1	0	0	2	2	0
1968	14	1	10	1	0	1	0	0	1	0
1969	12	1	9	0	1	0	0	1	0	0
1970	10	1	8	0	0	1	0	0	0	0
Totals	278	35	145	7	22	16	1	21	19	3

a. Totals do not necessarily correlate because those items too difficult to classify were counted only in the totals.

b. Feature articles are distinguished from news stories by the presence of a by-line.

contributions became more prominent, compliance activity seemed to increase. The activity in Omaha tends to support the present policy assumptions by the federal government that substantial increases in grant-in-aid funds are a positive inducement to compliance activity. With increased state aid, the abatement program seems to be strengthened by reducing the cost of abatement to the noncompliant municipalities.

A final influence on the issue-public's response was the local media. William Muir's study (1967) of "Midland's" acceptance of the *Schempp* decision suggests the crucial role of the local news media. Few citizens were acutely aware of governmental decisions and it was through the local press that the ramifications of a decision were narrated. As a result, initial opinions were influenced from this source of information. The media may define the issue as a problem, argue its nonapplicability to the local setting, or characterize the issue as a nonproblem. Thus, if the issue is treated as a nonproblem by the local media, noncompliance could be more easily justified.

The data, as shown in Table 6, illustrate the critical roles played by the local media. The *Omaha World Herald* campaigned consistently for the abatement program. Early in the proceedings the *World Herald* acknowledged the problem and supported the abatement plan (which acknowledged both the need to deal with the problem, but within a context that would consider the economic implications to the city). The campaign was waged on the editorial page, as well as in numerous articles printed at appropriate times during the city's negotiations. These articles tended to "visualize" the issue as a problem.

The issue-public's response can, therefore, be seen as affected by at least three different factors. The homogeneity of the attentive issue-public, the high (financial) costs of compliance, and the role played by the local media were all found to be critical in explaining the recalcitrant's response to abatement orders. The influence of these three factors dictate the extent and means of response to the enforcement orders. A homogeneous issue-public that would incur high attitudinal and/or financial costs by complying is less likely to respond positively to the order. This situation is further complicated by the local media's definition of the issue as a problem or a nonproblem. The study does not shed light on the kinds of responses that might be expected, nor can we say with any confidence what the relative weight of each of these three factors is on compliance activity. Rather, the findings point only to the significance of these three features in influencing the issue-public's response.

SUMMATION AND CONCLUSIONS

Analysis reveals three active components in the water pollution compliance decision-making system. The legitimating decision is of central importance not only for its role in providing needed enforcement resources but for its function in providing legitimacy for the enforcement action. Four decisional characteristics were found to be of prime importance: the juxtaposition of the decision (a first impression decision), decisional clarity, decisional consensus, and decisional reiteration.

The nature of the enforcement system was also seen as critical in understanding the compliance decision-making system. The attitudes of the enforcement personnel and the availability of enforcement resources were all found to influence the enforcement system's capabilities in dealing with the compliance problem. When these enforcement features act to provide credibility to the enforcement structure, reputational enforcement was posited as a result. Correspondingly, the lack of these enforcement structure features were seen as constraints in the development of covert authority.

The issue-public was identified as the third component of the compliance decision-making system. To be sure, the effects of the legitimating decision and the enforcement structure bear directly on the issue-public's behavior; however, independent of these external influences are three internal features affecting the issue-public's behavior. These characteristics included the homogeneity of the attentive issue-public, the cost of abatement, and the influence of the local media.

The implications of these findings are both policy related and methodological. Clearly the study is suggestive of future policy options. *How* decisions are rendered are seen to be as important as the *substance* of the decision. In turn, decisional substance—especially as it reduces the cost of compliance and enhances the credibility of the enforcement structure—is an important variable in compliance decision making.

There are also methodological implications. The study is suggestive of a need for multicase analysis—perhaps drawing on a modification of our suggestions above—in which variables and characteristics of decisional components could be more systematically studied. The questions of variable linkage to compliance behavior, as well as the organizational component affecting such behavior, should be examined (next) in a comparative context, but with a theoretical backdrop such as is provided here.

NOTE

1. I mean to suggest that there was not a systematic examination of all possible cases. Rather Omaha was chosen because of the relative access of case materials to the author.

REFERENCES

BARTH, E. E. (1968). "Perception and acceptance of Supreme Court decisions at the state and local levels." Journal of Public Law, 17: 310-316.
BLAUSTEIN, A. P., and FERGUSON, C. C. (1957). Desegregation and the Law. New Brunswick, N.J.: Rutgers University Press.
CRENSON, M. (1971). The Unpolitics of Air Pollution. Baltimore: Johns Hopkins Press.
DOLBEARE, K. M., and HAMMOND, P. E. (1971). The School Prayer Decision. Chicago: University of Chicago Press.
FREELEY, M. (1972). "Coercion and compliance: A new look at an old problem." Pp. 59-68 in S. Krislov (ed.), Compliances and the Law. Beverly Hills, Calif.: Sage.
JACKSON, C. O. (1970). Food and Drug Legislation in the New Deal. Princeton, N.J.: Princeton University Press.
JENNINGS, M. K. (1969). "Legislative politics and water pollution control." Pp. 72-109 in F. N. Cleaveland (ed.), Congress and Urban Problems. Washington, D.C.: Brookings Institution.
JONES, C. O. (1974). "Federal-state-local sharing in air pollution control." Publius, 4(Winter: 69-85.
LEVINE, J. P. (1972). "Methodological concerns in studying Supreme Court efficacy." Pp. 99-111 in S. Krislov (ed.), Compliance and the Law. Beverly Hills, Calif.: Sage.
MILNER, N. (1972). "Comparative analysis of patterns of compliance with Supreme Court decisions: Miranda and the police in four communities." Pp. 297-313 in S. Krislov (ed.), Compliance and the Law. Beverly Hills, Calif.: Sage.
MUIR, W. K. (1976). Prayer in the Public Schools. Chicago: University of Chicago Press.
MURPHY, W. F. (1959). "Constitutional ambiguity and legislative decision-making: The establishment clause and aid to higher education." Pp. 268-283 in L. K. Pettit and E. Keynes (eds.), The Legislative Process in the United States Senate. Skokie, Ill.: Rand McNally.
Public Administration Review (1972). "Symposium on regulatory administration." Vol. 33(Fall-special issue).
ROURKE, F. E. (1969). Bureaucracy, Politics and Public Policy. Boston: Little Brown.
STEIN, M. (1957). "Conference in the matter of pollution of the interstate waters of the Missouri River—Omaha area, first session, June 14, 1957." Washington, D.C.: Government Printing Office.
SUNDQUIST, J. (1968). Politics and Policy: The Eisenhower, Kennedy, and Johnson Years. Washington, D.C.: Brookings Institution.
THOMAS, R. D., and LUKEN, R. A. (1974). "Balancing incentives and conditions in the evolution of a federal program: A perspective on construction grants for waste water treatment plants." Publius, 4(Summer): 43-63.
WASBY, S. L. (1970). The Impact of the United States Supreme Court: Some Perspectives. Homewood, Ill.: Dorsey Press.

PART IV

SOCIAL-REMEDIAL POLICIES

9

IMPLEMENTATION OF MODEL CITIES AND REVENUE SHARING IN TEN BAY AREA CITIES: DESIGN AND FIRST FINDINGS

RUFUS P. BROWNING

San Francisco State University

DALE ROGERS MARSHALL

University of California, Davis

The social problems of American cities such as poverty, decay of services, and racial discrimination have been a focus of national concern over the last decade. The federal government hurriedly developed a vast array of grants for cities; cities scrambled madly to grab the money; and the evaluators have rushed into print with their assessments of the "success" or "failure" of the grants. The intergovernmental game of capture-the-grants has run into a barrage of criticism from all sides, and there has been a surge of disillusionment with the federal government's ability to cope with urban problems (Banfield, 1974).

In the belief that this negative conclusion is based on incomplete and perhaps misleading information, we have started a longitudinal

AUTHORS' NOTE: *The authors are grateful for the support provided for this project by Lloyd Musolf, Director of the Institute of Governmental Affairs, University of California, Davis; and by Eugene Lee, Director, and Todd LaPorte, Associate Director, Institute of Governmental Studies, University of California, Berkeley; and for the research assistance of Bob Waste, University of California, Davis and Jim Desveaux, University of California, Berkeley. This essay is an adaptation of a paper prepared for delivery at the annual meeting of the American Political Science Association, September 1974.*

study of the implementation of Model Cities and general revenue sharing in ten Bay Area cities. Our objective is to describe the implementation and to specify the effects of these two federal grant programs, primarily their effects on city governments and local political systems: leadership, structure, personnel, decision processes, and outputs. Then we seek to explain changes over time, and differences between the cities, in program implementation and effect.

We are interested, in other words, in what these federal grants to cities have accomplished and why implementation and results differ from city to city. We recognize that we are not the first to ask these questions about public policies. But while the many efforts to answer such questions have advanced our understanding, the quality of our knowledge is still deficient. Concentrating on ten cities in the San Francisco Bay Area of course forces us to accept limits to our capacity to generalize. At the same time, it affords us the opportunity to apply innovations of concept and design to the difficult knowledge problems in the field of policy implementation and impact.

What follows is a preliminary discussion of work in progress. The first section briefly describes our research design, and the second presents findings from exploratory field work.

RESEARCH GOALS AND DESIGN

The design of our research has evolved from an awareness of the limitations of existing studies. Here we briefly indicate shortcomings in the literature of policy implementation and evaluation and for each gap, we lay out a corresponding element of our research design.

SCOPE OF IMPLEMENTATION

Political scientists, until recently, have given more attention to policy formulation than to policy implementation. Implementation was seen as a relatively simple mechanistic process. The very term "implementation"—implements are tools after all, never obstacles—seems to imply rational, purposive, administrative, technical processes carried out by subordinate and neutral instruments of higher authority.

This view of implementation has been challenged in the 1960s by the increasing awareness that policies often do not have the expected results. Political scientists have begun to realize that decisions following legislation, like those which precede it, involve a complex interaction of multiple processes and not just technical or administrative ones (Pressman and Wildavsky, 1973; Bardach, 1974; Rein and Rabinovitz, 1974). Aiken and Alford (1970) point out that urban political and organizational systems are important to explanations of differences in policy implementation.

Our research builds on this view of implementation as a political process—the policy-making process of the city—which is a complex and shifting sequence of interactions in an open, fragmented network of partly autonomous organizations and leaders who sometimes work independently, sometimes cooperate, sometimes conflict with each other. Implementation is shaped by the interaction of these forces over extended periods of time—such as the conflicts they start with, the agreements they are able to come to, the coalitions they are able to form, the initiatives they take, their accustomed ways of reaching decisions, their expectations of and demands upon each other, their skills both political and administrative.

> *Design goal:* To take a broad view of the implementation process in an intensive study of the political and organizational interactions which explain differences in policy implementation and out of which program effects, if any, will arise.

Policy studies tend to be either large sample correlational analyses (Aiken and Alford, 1970) or intensive, largely narrative studies of one or a couple of cities (Greenstone and Peterson, 1973). Findings of the correlational studies need to be interpreted and supplemented by longitudinal studies of the political and organizational processes that shape city responses to federal programs (Rossi and Williams, 1972; Kirlin and Erie, 1972). But endless case studies are not adequate either. A conceptualization is needed that puts the seeming uniqueness of events over time in different cities into a common analytical framework. Descriptions of process must incorporate common concepts and observations, so that valid comparisons can be made across cities and policies and so that analyses are replicable.

COMPARISON ACROSS POLICIES

Studies of the implementation of federal programs usually focus on only one policy (Austin, 1972; Kramer, 1969; Marshall, 1971a,

1971b; Sundquist, 1969; Washnis, 1973). But research limited to one policy cannot readily address questions about what effects alternative policy designs may have or whether there are systemic constraints within cities which will operate regardless of the content of federal policy.

> *Design feature:* Implementation process of two broad federal grant programs are compared: Model Cities and general revenue sharing. (As time passes and resources permit, the comparison will be extended to special revenue sharing programs.)

Model Cities and general revenue sharing were selected for comparison because both grants distribute money directly to city governments to increase their problem solving capacity. But the two programs embody contrasting assumptions about how urban problems can be solved. Model Cities consists of money and many rules which set forth conditions to be met by the cities in order to get the money. General revenue sharing, on the other hand, consists of money and the minimum of rules. The amount of revenue sharing funds received by cities are determined by formula and are not contingent upon annual federal approval. Revenue sharing assumes that local governments are the best judges of how to deal with their problems; Model Cities assumes that federal controls are necessary to force local governments to make the redistributions which the federal government judges necessary. Thus Model Cities involved money and controls with a redistributive thrust. Revenue sharing lacks the controls and redistributive aspect.

We are asking whether the difference in federal grant policies generates a difference in city response. Lowi (1964) and Salisbury and Heinz (1970) have suggested that different types of policies are associated with different decision processes and coalitions of interested parties. To what extent does this generalization apply to the implementation of Model Cities and general revenue sharing? We want to know whether the difference between the grants gives rise to different implementing coalitions at the city level. Does it result in different kinds of changes in the institutions of city government and in the decisions these institutions yield?

SCOPE OF EFFECTS

Studies of the effects of implementation are often concerned with a restricted range of program effects. They do not see programs as parts of larger social trends and political contexts and thus may miss unintended but important effects of the programs.

Both Model Cities and general revenue sharing may have effects on individual beneficiaries (e.g., reduced unemployment, new benefits) and on city government and politics. We do not propose an intensive analysis of the effects of Model Cities and general revenue sharing on individual beneficiaries, in part because it is so hard to follow individual beneficiaries over time and to disentangle program from other causes. Instead we propose a close study of changes in city government and politics because effects which are to be lasting should be institutionalized there.

Design goal: To describe changes in institutions, agenda, decision processes, officeholders, participation, organization, coalitions, programs, allocations, and beneficiaries. To ascertain whether observed changes can be traced to forces set in motion by the federal grant programs.

TIME SPAN

Many policy studies use cross-sectional data gathered so close to the initiation of a program that reasonably anticipated effects have not had time to occur. This strategy is not adequate for assessment of efforts at institutional change, which is not easy to detect in a snapshot and typically does not happen quickly. Predictions of the time that elapses before the appearance of desired effects should be very different for social programs with institutional change goals than, say, for a crackdown on speeding. A program's achievements may look very different in the long run than in the short run. Organization theory tells us that resistance is an expected initial outcome of efforts to change organizations; whether resistance persists and is successful is a question that needs answering farther from the beginning of the effort.

An all-too-common approach in policy studies is simply to observe what happens after a new program has begun. Unfortunately, because observed "effects" May predate the program, it is impossible to attribute such effects to the program; some understanding of preprogram conditions is necessary.

Design feature: Indicators of program effect and other measures and descriptions will be obtained for the ten-year period 1966-1975 (from before Model Cities to eight years after its initiation, and several years into revenue sharing).

Table 1

Model Cities	Population[1]		Non-Model Cities
San Francisco	715,674		
San Jose	445,779		
Oakland	361,561		
Berkeley	116,716		
		93,058	Hayward
		87,717	Santa Clara
Richmond	79,043		
		70,968	Alameda
		66,922	Daly City
		66,733	Vallejo

	Population below poverty level[2]		
Oakland	12.2%		
Berkeley	10.6		
Richmond	10.6		
San Francisco	9.9		
		8.9%	Alameda
		8.4	Vallejo
		6.5	Hayward
San Jose	6.4		
		5.2	Santa Clara
		5.1	Daly City

	Black population[3]		
Richmond	36.2%		
Oakland	34.5		
Berkeley	23.5		
		16.6%	Vallejo
San Francisco	13.4		
		5.4	Daly City
		2.6	Alameda
San Jose	2.5		
		1.8	Hayward
		.8	Santa Clara

	Population of Spanish Origin[4]		
San Jose	21.9%		
		20.3%	Hayward
		18.7	Daly City
		18.1	Santa Clara
San Francisco	14.2		
Richmond	10.1		
Oakland	9.8		
		9.8	Alameda
		8.9	Vallejo
Berkeley	5.5		

1. U.S. Census Bureau, *General Population Characteristics, 1970, U.S. Summary,* Table 66.
2. U.S. Census Bureau, *General Social and Economic Characteristics, 1970, California,* Table 90.
3. Same as note 1, Table 67.
4. Same, Table 97.

Over-time data will permit the analysis of changes over time as well as of differences between cities. We can expect the two analyses to yield different results because cities change over time in different ways and degrees than they vary one to another (Gray, 1973).

CHOICE OF CITIES

Because of the intensiveness of the empirical work required by our design, including the development of many time series over a ten-year period, our research focuses on ten cities. The actual selection of the ten cities is designed to allow testing for the program effect of Model Cities. Comparison of Model Cities with non-Model Cities permits a strong check of hypotheses about program effect: if an observed effect appears in the non-Model Cities as well as in the Model Cities our confidence in the program-effect hypothesis decreases.

Design feature: Of the ten Bay Area cities chosen for study, five were and five were not in the Model Cities program.

The Model Cities are San Francisco, Oakland, San Jose, Berkeley, and Richmond; the five non-Model Cities are Alameda, Santa Clara, Hayward, Daly City, and Vallejo. From the set of Bay Area cities, the five non-Model Cities were chosen to be as like the Model Cities as possible on key social and economic characteristics: size, poverty level, and relative size of black and Spanish minorities. Nevertheless, as Table 1 shows, the Model Cities are mostly larger and have larger poor populations and larger black populations. All these variables are selection factors for Model Cities, because the problems that Model Cities was intended to deal with are located in cities with these characteristics; furthermore, hypotheses involving these variables compete with the hypothesis of program effect. Nevertheless, the partial matching on selection factors which is part of our design helps reduce the variance of variables that we strongly suspect are related to the dependent variable, the effects on city government and politics. The remaining variance will be handled by two strategies. First, we will trace aspects of city government and politics back to the period prior to Model Cities legislation. This will enable us to ascertain the extent to which minorities in the Model Cities were already on their way to demanding and getting benefits that we might erroneously attribute to the programs. The second strategy involves a combination of statistical analysis and close examination of political action and response which we explain more fully in other places.

FIRST FINDINGS

The exploratory phase of this study focuses on the impact of Model Cities on city governments. We compare the changes in the five Model Cities with the changes in the five non-Model Cities —specifically, changes in personnel and structure.

Mayors have often said that federal programs to improve city government services for the poor and to redress the balance between the advantaged and disadvantaged groups in the city should be part of the city government. Model Cities was an attempt to fulfill these conditions, so we ask how much innovation occurred when the cities *were* given responsibility. Early studies of Model Cities show that assigning Model Cities to city governments did not insure increasing city government responsiveness to disadvantaged groups. Model Cities was grafted onto the city but the graft did not always take. City halls typically wanted to keep Model Cities agencies at a distance (Sundquist, 1969; Washnis, 1974). Model Cities agencies, like community action agencies, often turned out to be foster children, born out of Washington but boarding with city hall. We are asking, what effect do the foster children have on their foster parents?

In particular, have the Model Cities changed more in the direction of responsiveness to the needs of disadvantaged groups than the non-Model Cities? Are they more committed to social programs rather than simply the traditional housekeeping or amenity functions of city governments? Have Model Cities institutionalized a concern with equality more than the non-Model Cities (May, 1973)? Respondents shared this interest in social responsiveness of cities, often referring to cities as "turning the corner" or "getting in tune with the times."

DID MODEL CITIES MAKE A DIFFERENCE IN
CITY EMPLOYMENT OF MINORITIES?

One of the goals of the Model Cities program was reduction of unemployment among residents of the slum and blighted areas that were to become "model neighborhoods" (Harrison, 1972). Cities were encouraged to "develop stable careers in public and private employment," and to "reduce institutional obstacles to public and private employment" (HUD, 1967). We do not have information about employment of model neighborhood residents directly, but we can bring data to bear on the question of city government employment of the racial and ethnic minorities that make up very high proportions of model neighborhood populations. In these five Model Cities, the minorities that are both large and active in Model Cities efforts are the black and the "Spanish" groups, the latter being mainly people of Mexican and Latino origin. (Henceforth in this paper, "minority" means only black plus Spanish, and we confine our attention to these two groups.)

The hypothesis of program effect on city employment of minorities needs to be tested with an eye for the possibility that levels of minority employment are importantly determined by levels of minority population. Therefore, estimates both of minority employment in city government and of the relative size of the black plus Spanish minority in the population are needed, for three points in time: 1966, before Model Cities; 1970, after Model Cities but before the Equal Employment Opportunity Act of 1972; and 1974. With these data, we can examine the relationship between minority employment and minority population in our cities; and we can determine whether the five Model Cities have increased their employment of minorities more rapidly than the five non-Model Cities, taking into account whatever changes in minority population were occurring at the same time.

Obtaining the desired information immediately involves us in a series of difficult puzzles about how to interpret the available data and how to get at least approximate estimates of the figures we need.

Estimating Minority Employment

For all ten cities, recent data are available in ethnic surveys of city employment carried out by the cities for the federal Equal Employment Opportunity Commission (EEOC). For nine cities, figures reflect minority employment on various dates ranging from December 1973 to April 1974; these constitute our 1974 data. For San Francisco, which has not completed its 1974 survey, we extrapolate forward to a 1974 estimate from surveys for 1970 and December 1971. San Francisco and Berkeley also did surveys in 1966 and 1970, Oakland in 1970 but not 1966. None of the other cities did official surveys before 1974, although scattered information is available in some.

Procedures for obtaining data and analyses produced in the ethnic surveys vary somewhat from city to city. Where variations exist, we have, with the assistance of personnel officials, standardized the data so as to include all employees (part-time or full-time) other than those hired for short-term or intermittent employment; to include all departments of city government (and county government in San Francisco, a combined county and city); to include the Model Cities organization; but not to include schools and urban redevelopment agencies. Thus our measure of city employment of minorities includes the high percentages of minorities found in the Model Cities agencies themselves.

Where data for 1966 and 1970 were not available from ethnic surveys, we asked personnel officials with long experience and intimate knowledge of city government to estimate the percentage of black and Spanish employment. There is undoubtedly some error in these estimates; however, in most cases the error is probably small because such small numbers of employees are involved—so small that personnel officials were frequently able to enumerate by name, from memory, almost all their black and Spanish employees in 1966 and 1970. For the non-Model Cities, the range of estimated black plus Spanish employees in 1966 runs from only 5 to about 30.

The Meaning of "Spanish"

Special problems arise about the definition of the category "Spanish"—the term used by both the Bureau of the Census and the EEOC. "Spanish" for present purposes, as applied to population data, means having a Spanish surname and/or Spanish language. "Spanish language" means that Spanish was the language spoken in the person's home in early childhood, or that the person was living at the time of the census in a family "in which the head or wife reported Spanish as the mother tongue." For the 1970 census, only about 4.7 million persons are reported as having Spanish surnames in the five southwestern states; 9.6 million were reported as "persons of Spanish language." From a question asked of the Census Bureau's final five percent sample, it was estimated that more than 9 million persons in these five states considered themselves to be of one or another Latin or Spanish origin (U.S. Census Bureau, 1970: v-vi).

Spanish surname alone substantially underestimates Spanish origin; hence we use the published surname and/or language figures. (Even so, these 1970 census figures were attacked by Mexican American groups as serious underestimates of the Spanish population.)

We were unable to find the comparable figures in publications of the 1960 census, but 1960 data on Spanish surnames were reported. To obtain a rough estimate of the total Spanish surname plus Spanish language in 1960, we increased the published 1960 surname data in the same ratio that the 1970 surname data bear to the 1970 surname plus language data, for each city:

$$\frac{\text{Est. 1960 surname + language}}{\text{1960 surname}} = \frac{\text{1970 surname + language}}{\text{1970 surname}}$$

For ethnic surveys and other estimates of city employment, the definition of "Spanish" is more ambiguous. According to EEOC officials, EEOC instructions for the ethnic surveys leave much discretion to the cities. The operational definition of "Spanish" and the procedure for ascertaining who meets whatever definition is used are left up to the cities. The cities generate the data by what the EEOC refers to as a "self-auditing" process. Clearly there is leeway for measurement error in the figures for city employment of Spanish people.

Interpolating Minority Population Figures

With estimates of black and Spanish employment in 1966, 1970, and 1974, perhaps it would be best if we also had minority population data for the same years, but we do not. One alternative is to interpolate for 1966 and extrapolate the 1960-1970 trend for 1974, but we rejected this: comparison of the 1960 and 1970 figures for minority population shows that quite rapid shifts can occur in a few years' time, and we have no basis for stating that shifts from 1970 to 1974 have occurred in the same direction and rate as from 1960 to 1970. Furthermore, it is not clear that having minority population figures simultaneous with minority employment is appropriate. How soon should we expect increases in minority population to show up in city government employment? If minority employment is related to minority population, is it most closely related to simultaneous or to lagged population figures?

If simultaneous data are not possible, we still need at least some

Table 2. MINORITY (Black plus Spanish) EMPLOYMENT IN CITY GOVERNMENT, 1966-1974, AND POPULATION, 1960-1970, TEN BAY AREA CITIES

City	Per cent minority of total city population				Per cent minority of total city government employment[d]		
	1960[a]	1962[b]	1966[b]	1970[c]	1966	1970	1974
Model Cities							
San Francisco (N)	23.1 (740,316)	24.0	25.8	27.6 (715,674)	19.9 (16,758)	24.5 (19,785)	26.9 (21,065)
San Jose (N)	20.5 (204,196)	21.3	22.9	24.4 (445,779)	2.6 (2,700)	12.1 (2,581)	14.5 (2,796)
Oakland (N)	32.8 (367,548)	35.0	39.7	44.3 (361,561)	9.0 (3,642)	18.8 (3,502)	26.5 (3,683)
Berkeley (N)	27.9 (111,268)	28.1	28.5	29.0 (116,716)	19.9 (915)	25.5 (1,064)	34.6 (1,100)
Richmond (N)	31.3 (71,854)	34.3	40.3	46.3 (79,043)	7.0 (709)	12.0 (852)	28.6 (727)
Non-Model Cities							
Alameda (N)	13.4 (63,855)	13.2	12.8	12.4 (70,968)	0.9 (489)	2.0 (527)	6.2 (645)
Daly City (N)	13.5 (44,791)	15.6	19.9	24.1 (66,922)	4.0 (279)	4.6 (310)	5.4 (401)

Hayward (N)	17.0 (72,700)	18.0	20.0	22.1 (93,058)		5.0 (479)		8.0 (566)		12.5 (731)	
Santa Clara (N)	27.0 (58,880)	25.4	22.2	18.9 (87,717)		4.8 (550)		7.5 (644)		9.6 (697)	
Vallejo (N)	26.4 (60,877)	26.2	25.9	25.5 (66,733)		5.4 (384)		5.4 (426)		8.8 (435)	

a. Sum of percent black and percent Spanish. Percent black from U.S. Bureau of the Census, *Census of Population: 1960, General Population Characteristics, California*, Table 21. Percent Spanish incremented from 1960 Spanish-surname figures, *Census of Population: 1960, Subject Reports, Persons of Spanish Surname*, in the same ratio as 1970 Spanish surname percentages (*Census of Population: 1970, Subject Reports, Persons of Spanish Surname*, Table 19) to 1970 Spanish-language percentages (see note c). Totals from *Census of Population: 1970, General Population Characteristics, U.S. Summary*, Table 66.

b. 1962 and 1966 interpolated from 1960 and 1970.

c. Sum of percent black and percent Spanish. Percent black from *Census of Population: 1970, General Population Characteristics, U.S. Summary*, Table 67. Percent Spanish (surname plus "persons of Spanish language," see text), same, Table 97. All these data are based on the Census Bureau's 15 percent sample.

d. See text for explanation of percentages. Totals from ethnic surveys for 1974 for all cities, and for San Jose and Berkeley in 1966 and 1970. San Francisco in 1966, Oakland in 1970. All other totals from Bureau of the Census, *City Employment in 1970* and *City Employment in 1966*, Table 3, total full-time equivalent employment.

consistent lag between the employment and the population data. The simplest lag is four years, as follows:

> 1970 minority population with 1974 minority employment
> 1966 minority population with 1970 minority employment
> 1962 minority population with 1966 minority employment

The 1970 minority population data for each city are the census figures: percent black plus percent Spanish. The 1966 and 1962 figures are interpolated between the 1970 census figure and the sum of percent black in 1960 and our estimate (above) of percent Spanish.

These various forms of prestidigitation yield the data reported in Table 2. We take the percentage minority for each city as the basic element of analysis. The table shows that minority population increased from 1960 to 1970 in all of these cities except Alameda, Santa Clara, and Vallejo, which registered modest drops. Minority

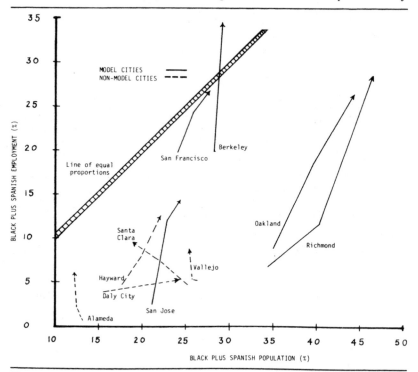

Figure 1: RELATION OF MINORITY EMPLOYMENT IN CITY GOVERNMENT (1966, 1970, 1974) TO MINORITY POPULATION (1962, 1966, 1970).
(Source: Table 2.)

employment in city government increased in all the cities. Figure 1 graphs these movements for each city separately.

Is City Employment of Minorities Increasing Faster in Model Cities than in Non-Model Cities?

A first answer is obtained from Table 3 and Figure 2.

(1) The Model Cities were on the average somewhat higher in minority population in 1962, and their mean percentage minority increased more rapidly than for the non-Model Cities (Table 3). Still, as a glance at Figure 1 shows, there is some overlap between the two sets of cities on this variable, more in 1966 than in 1974 because of declines in percent minority in three of the non-Model Cities.

(2) The Model Cities were on the average substantially higher in minority employment in city government already in 1966 (11.7 to 4.0, about three times higher). Both Model and non-Model Cities more than doubled their mean percent minority employment from 1966 to 1974, and in 1974, the Model Cities were still employing the black and Spanish minorities at about three times the non-Model Cities rate (26.2 to 8.5).

(3) Figure 2 shows that mean minority employment for the five Model Cities increased more rapidly than that for the non-Model Cities.

(4) Because we expect minority employment to be influenced by levels of minority population, statement (3) needs to be qualified by

Table 3. MINORITY (Black plus Spanish) EMPLOYMENT IN CITY GOVERN-
MENT (1966-1974) AND MINORITY POPULATION (1962-1970),
MEAN PERCENTAGES FOR MODEL AND NON-MODEL CITIES

| | Population | | | Difference |
	1962	1966	1970	1962 to 1970
Model Cities	28.5	31.4	34.3	5.8
Non-Model Cities	19.7	20.2	20.6	0.9
	Employment			Difference
	1966	1970	1974	1966 to 1974
Model Cities	11.7	18.6	26.2	14.5
Non-Model Cities	4.0	5.5	8.5	4.5

SOURCE: See Table 2.

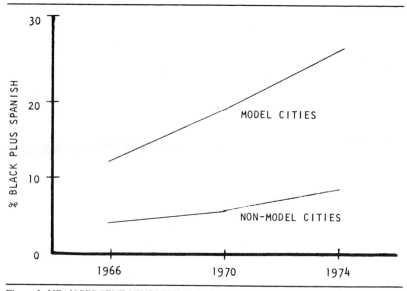

Figure 2: MEAN PERCENT MINORITY EMPLOYMENT IN CITY GOVERNMENT,
1966-1974. (Source: Table 3.)

the relation between them. Minority population is a rough measure of the size of the local pool of minority applicants for city employment. An increase in minority employment from 5 to 15 percent seems a quite different event in a city with 10 percent minority population than in a city which is 40 percent minority. To reflect this difference, we take the ratio of each city's percent minority employment in a given year to its percent minority population in the corresponding year (lagged four years). This measure, times 100 to express it as a percentage, indicates readily how closely minority employment approaches minority population. A score of 100 indicates that minority employment and population are equal. Between 0 and 100, scores show what percentage of the distance to equal proportions the city has covered.

Table 4 and the corresponding Figure 3 show the means of these ratios of minority employment to minority population for Model and non-Model Cities. The Model Cities, on the average, were already much higher on the index than the non-Model Cities. And between 1966 and 1974, the Model Cities increased somewhat more than the non-Model Cities—a mean increase of 37.2 for the former versus 22.9 for the latter, a difference of 14.3. A randomization test against the hypothesis of equal means yields Pr = .15 for a difference this large or larger.

Table 4. MEAN RATIO OF MINORITY EMPLOYMENT (1966-1974) TO
MINORITY POPULATION (1962-1970), MODEL CITIES AND
NON-MODEL CITIES

	Mean ratio X 100			
	$\dfrac{1966}{1962}$	$\dfrac{1970}{1966}$	$\dfrac{1974}{1970}$	Difference 1966 to 1974
Model Cities	42.4	62.9	79.6	37.2
Non-Model Cities	20.0	26.7	42.9	22.9
Difference	22.4	36.2	36.7	14.3

The difference between Model and non-Model Cities is not a
function of the larger size of the three largest Model Cities: for
Berkeley and Richmond, the smallest Model Cities and within the
size range of the non-Model Cities, the mean increase in the minority
employment/population ratio is 45.0, greater than the 37.2 recorded
for all of the Model Cities together.

Is the difference between Model and non-Model Cities a function
of larger minority populations in the Model Cities? We attempt an
answer to this question in the following section.

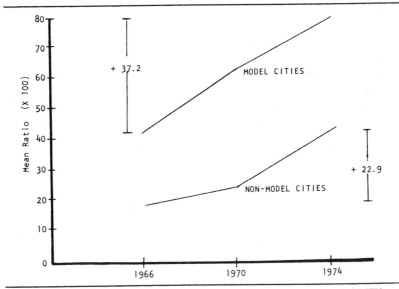

Figure 3: MEAN RATIO OF MINORITY EMPLOYMENT (1966-1974) TO MINORITY
POPULATION (1962-1970). (Source: Table 4.)

Clearly, the Model Cities differ from the non-Model Cities at the outset; and clearly, both groups of cities have increased their mean ratios of minority employment to minority population, the Model Cities perhaps somewhat more rapidly than the non-Model Cities. The Model Cities are clearly higher than the non-Model Cities in all three years, somewhat higher still in 1974 than in 1966. In 1974, the minority employment rate in the Model Cities stands at almost 80 percent of the minority population proportion; in the non-Model Cities, at 43 percent. (If 1966-1974 rates of increase in these means are sustained, the mean for Model Cities will reach 100—equal proportions—in 1979, the non-Model Cities not until 1990.)

The Correlation Between Minority Employment and Minority Population

The analysis above examines the ratios of employment to population over time for Model and non-Model Cities. Here we ask, what is the relationship between employment and population at each point in time, within the two sets of cities? Table 5 presents the correlation coefficients.

Only the .76 for non-Model Cities in 1966 is significantly different than zero ($t = 2.0$). Because of the very small numbers and resulting instability year to year, we cannot place much weight on these figures; nevertheless, perhaps there is a trend such that minority employment in the Model Cities is becoming more closely, and positively, related to minority population, while the reverse is true for the non-Model Cities.

Another way of checking the difference between Model and non-Model Cities is to examine within each group the way in which increases in minority employment are related to increases in minority population. (For employment, "increase" is 1974 minus 1966 percent minority of city employment; for population, 1970 minus 1962 percent minority.) For the Model Cities, this $r = .83$; but for the

Table 5. RELATION OF PERCENT MINORITY EMPLOYMENT TO PERCENT MINORITY POPULATION (Pearson's r)

	1966	1970	1974
Model Cities	-.10	-.26	.33
Non-Model Cities	.76	.63	.23

non-Model Cities, it is r = −.31. The finding supports our speculation that the Model Cities have responded positively (with higher minority employment) to a large and increasing minority population, whereas those non-Model Cities with the largest minority populations have accomplished the least so far.

Thus in a complex way, the difference in gains in minority employment between Model and non-Model Cities is associated with the higher minority populations in the Model Cities. It is not a simple function of higher minority population, however. Instead, we find that we are here registering another difference between the two sets of cities in their responses to high or increasing minority population: the Model Cities turn out again to be the more responsive.

In short, the data on black and Spanish employment lead us to conclude that the five cities in the Model Cities program probably experienced somewhat greater increases in minority employment in city government than the five cities that did not participate in the program; and that this difference is not a function of the larger size or larger minority populations of the Model Cities.

The data do not, of course, establish the Model Cities program as the causal factor, they are merely consistent with that hypothesis.

Factors Accounting for Changes in Minority Employment Patterns

Explanations for the employment patterns described above come from 28 exploratory interviews with personnel, city manager, and finance officers in the ten cities. The interviews were from 20 minutes to 1½ hours in length. The twelve respondents familiar with personnel were asked, "What accounts for the shifts in minority employment?" and were subjected to a series of probes to specify actors, actions, and key events.

All five of the non-Model Cities reported that the most important factor was the passage of the federal Equal Employment Opportunity Act in 1972 (one respondent cited the Emergency Employment Act as equally important). None of the Model Cities respondents gave that answer, probably because the Model Cities became active in equal employment earlier than the non-Model Cities and before 1972. One indication of this timing is that the Model Cities started ethnic surveys earlier than the non-Model Cities: three of the Model Cities started ethnic surveys before 1972 and two in 1972. Only one non-Model City started an ethnic survey in 1972; the rest started after 1972.

To what factors did the Model Cities respondents attribute shifts in minority employment? All the Model Cities respondents cited various kinds of community pressures and four out of five listed these as the most important factors (in Richmond an aggressive personnel director was cited as the most important factor). The community pressures mentioned included coalitions pushing for city employment of minorities, groups bringing law suits and filing complaints, and the nationwide civil rights movement.

Did Model Cities groups contribute to the community pressure? Respondents in three of the five cities (Oakland, San Jose, and Richmond) said yes and mentioned the names of the Model Cities groups. Records confirm that Model Cities groups were active in the pressure and the coalitions (newspaper accounts and Thompson, 1973). We plan to do a new round of interviews to trace the links in these three cities between Model Cities groups and city employment efforts and to search for links in the other two Model Cities. For now, we conclude that Model Cities began putting equal employment issues on the agenda earlier than non-Model Cities, due partly to community pressures, and that the Model Cities groups played a role in creating these pressures.

Employment in city hall has historically been a concomitant of politicization of ethnic groups (Wolfinger, 1974), and the interviews suggest that Model Cities programs have contributed to increasing city employment of minorities.

DID MODEL CITIES MAKE A DIFFERENCE IN THE MINORITY COMPOSITION OF CITY OFFICIALS?

The preceding discussion of city employment of minorities does not distinguish the types of positions held by minorities. Increases in minority employment may all be at the lowest levels. Is Model Cities associated with increases in the number of blacks and Spanish in top administrative positions? We compiled lists of department heads and city managers' staffs in 1966, 1970, and 1974 and asked informants to identify black and Spanish people on the lists.[1] Then we calculated the percent black and Spanish in these top leadership positions in each city for each year and determined the means for percent of minority officials in Model Cities and non-Model Cities.

Table 6 shows that Model Cities differ markedly from non-Model Cities. In 1966 Model Cities and non-Model Cities had approximately the same small percent black and Spanish officials, and officials in

Table 6. MINORITY (Black plus Spanish) OFFICIALS IN CITY
GOVERNMENT (1966-1974)

	Mean per cent		
	1966	1970	1974
Model Cities	1.4	11.9	18.8
Non-Model Cities	2.3	3.3	5.7

Model Cities were actually less representative of the minority composition of their populations than were non-Model Cities officials. But Model Cities increased their percentage of black and Spanish officials much more rapidly than the non-Model Cities; in the eight years, Model Cities increased from 1.4 to 18.8, an increase of 17.4, and non-Model Cities increased only 3.4 percentage points on the average.

The increase in the five Model Cities is partly explained by an examination of the positions held by the new minority officials. Most hold jobs which were directly or indirectly a result of federal funding for social programs, including directors of Model Cities agencies, manpower programs, community action agencies, social planning, community development programs, and intergovernmental assistance. The non-Model Cities have not increased their activities in these areas at the same rate as the Model Cities and show a corresponding lag in the hiring of the minorities which typically staff these activities. Model Cities in 1974 do not differ very much from non-Model Cities in the minority composition of department heads of traditional city departments; of the 30 black or Spanish officials in Model Cities, only six are heads of traditional departments—i.e., a tax collector in San Francisco, a parks and recreation director in Oakland, and four department heads in Berkeley (parks and recreation, library, personnel, and city attorney). Only in Berkeley have minority officials penetrated top positions in the traditional departments; nor can we attribute that development primarily to Model Cities in Berkeley, because the mayor and four other members of the city council are black, and the demand for hiring black officials is insistent and well-organized quite apart from Model Cities.

Thus other federal social programs as well as the Model Cities program have contributed to the more rapid growth in minority composition of officials in the five Model Cities. We are not sure of the role of the Model Cities program itself in this development. One possible linkage runs from participation in the program to perceptions of federal program managers that the Model Cities have greater need for and are better able to utilize federal assistance for social programs and planning (*because* of their participation in Model Cities), to increased federal funds for such programs, to increased minority hiring to staff them.

DID MODEL CITIES MAKE A DIFFERENCE IN STAFFING FOR SOCIAL PLANNING?

Model Cities included provisions to improve the cities' capacities for coordinating federal social grants, and later revisions such as Planned Variations reflected increased emphasis on management programs. Have the Model Cities developed a greater capacity for social planning than non-Model Cities?

Two indicators of social planning capacity were used: the size of the city manager's office and the number of specialized social planning positions in city government. Data were obtained from interviews and city budgets and directories. Changes in the size of city managers' offices did not differ systematically between Model and non-Model Cities.[2]

But Model Cities did differ from non-Model Cities in the increased number of social planning positions. In 1966 both Model Cities and non-Model Cities had similar numbers of general planning jobs with titles such as planners and analysts. By 1974 Model Cities had greatly increased the number of specialized social planning positions with such titles as manpower planner, community development planner, and intergovernmental and management analysts. These structural changes are part of the phenomena described in the preceding section; Model Cities have been most actively involved in federal grant programs and have changed their structures most to cope with federal inputs. Model Cities have increased the number and specialization of social planning positions more than non-Model Cities.

We do not have the information to assess how much Model Cities programs actually contributed to this increase. We think it likely that they were a significant factor because the federal government stressed the importance of social planning capacity in funding Model Cities and funneled other funds such as the 701 planning grants to Model Cities to strengthen their ability to do social planning.

DID MODEL CITIES MAKE A DIFFERENCE IN THE MINORITY COMPOSITION OF CITY COUNCILS?

To answer this question we followed similar procedures to those described in the preceding section on officials. Table 7 shows that Model Cities increased the proportion of minorities on councils and that non-Model Cities did not. In 1966 Model Cities had a higher mean percent of minority city council members, and the difference increased steadily and dramatically in 1970 and 1974. The mean percent of black and Spanish council members actually decreased in the non-Model Cities over the eight-year period.

Our hypothesis is that the political climate in Model Cities is becoming more conducive to the election of black and Spanish city council members. The task now is to see whether Model Cities itself contributed to this changing climate. To do this we will inquire into the coalitions which supported the newly elected minority candidates, the characteristics of the other candidates for the positions, and the voting turnouts in the various districts.

CONCLUSIONS

First findings from a comparison of changes from 1966 to 1974 in the city governments of five Model Cities (San Francisco, San Jose, Oakland, Berkeley, and Richmond) with changes in five non-Model Cities (Alameda, Daly City, Hayward, Santa Clara, and Vallejo) can be summarized as follows:

(1) The five Model Cities have probably increased minority (black plus Spanish) employment in city government faster than the non-Model Cities, and this difference is not a function of the larger size or larger minority population of some of the Model Cities. Indications are that some Model Cities groups played an active role in

Table 7. MINORITY (Black plus Spanish) CITY COUNCIL MEMBERS* (1966-1974)

| | Mean per cent | | |
	1966	1970	1974
Model Cities	15.2	19.2	28.7
Non-Model Cities	5.4	2.9	0.0

*These figures include mayors except in San Francisco.

pressuring their city governments to move forward on minority employment well before the Equal Employment Opportunity Act of 1972.

(2) The employment of black and Spanish people in top administrative positions in the five Model Cities has increased much more rapidly than in the five non-Model Cities. However, the linkage to the Model Cities program is not yet clear. Perhaps some of the difference stems from decisions of federal agencies to place new grants for social programs and social planning more heavily in the Model than in the non-Model Cities, and officials heading these programs are likely to be black or Spanish. Participation in Model Cities may have led to the perception by federal program managers that the participating cities were better able to utilize, and more in need of, federal assistance toward more active social programming.

(3) Probably for the same reasons as in (2), governments in the Model Cities have developed a greater capacity for social planning, in terms of the number of positions in city government with titles such as manpower or community development planner.

(4) In the five Model Cities, black and Spanish representation on city councils nearly doubled over the period 1966 to 1974, but actually declined in the non-Model Cities. More research is required to ascertain to what extent the activities of Model Cities groups have been central to the movement for greater minority representation.

The changes in city governments noted above, taken together, measure potentially important increments in the long struggle of minority ethnic groups to gain access to their governments and an increased share of the benefits. The five Model Cities already differed in some ways from the non-Model Cities in 1966; but the Model Cities have also moved farther toward increased responsiveness to their black and Spanish minorities, in terms of our indicators of employment, representation, and participation.

When we examine the evidence on how these changes have come about, we find some indications that developments stemming from participation in Model Cities have been important influences. Our tentative impressions need to be confirmed by research into the linkages through actions over time between the Model Cities program and alternative causal factors, on the one hand, and observed changes in city government and politics, on the other.

Our work suggests that it is too early to conclude that Model Cities has failed to contribute to changes in city governments toward increased responsiveness to the demands of disadvantaged minorities.

On the other hand, the changes may not be profound or well established enough to survive the withdrawal of federal pressure.

NOTES

1. The lists included Model Cities directors and the principal staff positions, excluding clerical, in the city managers' offices. In San Francisco the mayor's office is taken as the equivalent of the city mangers' offices in the other cities.

2. The size of the city manager's office did not prove to be a good indicator of capacity because the size of the city manager's office was cyclical. City managers' offices were incubators for innovative programs. When new programs are starting they are placed under the city manager's wing; then as they develop and gain support they are reorganized and placed outside of the manager's office to stand on their own as departments or divisions. Because of the cyclical changes in the sizes of city managers' offices taking place in both Model Cities and non-Model Cities, tallies of sizes in 1966, 1970, and 1974 do not tell us about changes in capacity but about stages in organization.

REFERENCES

AIKEN, M., and ALFORD, R. (1970). "Community structure and innovation: The case of public housing." American Political Science Review, 64(September): 843-865.

AUSTIN, D. (1972). "Resident participation: Political mobilization or organizational co-optation?" Public Administration Review (special issue, September): 409-420.

BANFIELD, E. (1974). The Unheavenly City Revisited. Boston: Little, Brown.

BARDACH, G. (1974). "The implementation game: What happens after a bill becomes law." Unpublished manuscript.

GRAY, V. (1973). "The use of time series analysis in the study of public policy." Policy Studies Journal, 2(Winter): 97-102.

GREENSTONE, J. D., and PETERSON, P. (1973). Race and Authority in Urban Politics. New York: Russell Sage Foundation.

HARRISON, B. (1972). "Ghetto employment and the Model Cities program." Paper presented at the Annual Meeting of the American Political Science Association, Washington, D.C., September.

KIRLIN, J., and ERIE, S. (1972). "The study of city governance and public policy making." Public Administration Review, 32(March/April): 173-184.

KRAMER, R. (1969). Participation of the Poor. Englewood Cliffs, N.J.: Prentice-Hall.

LOWI, T. J. (1964). "American business, public policy, case-studies, and political theory." World Politics, 16(July): 677-715.

MARSHALL, D. R. (1971a). "Public participation and the politics of poverty." In P. Orleans and W. R. Ellis, Jr., Race, Change, and Urban Society (Urban Affairs Annual Review, vol. 5). Beverly Hills, Calif.: Sage.

— — — (1971b). The Politics of Participation in Poverty. Berkeley: University of California Press.

MAY, J. V. (1973). "Struggle for authority: A comparison of four social change programs in Oakland, California." Unpublished Ph.D. dissertation, University of California, Berkeley.

PRESSMAN, J., and WILDAVSKY, A. (1973). Implementation. Berkeley: University of California Press.

REIN, M., and RABINOVITZ, F. (1974). "Implementation: A theoretical perspective." Unpublished manuscript.

ROSSI, P., and WILLIAMS, W. (1972). Evaluating Social Programs: Theory, Practice, and Politics. New York: Seminar Press.

SALISBURY, R., and HEINZ, J. (1970). "A theory of policy analysis and some preliminary applications." In I. Sharkansky (ed.), Policy Analysis in Political Science. Chicago: Markham.

SUNDQUIST, J. (1969). Making Federalism Work. Washington, D.C.: Brookings Institution.

THOMPSON, F. (1973). "Bureaucratic response to minority challenge: The case of recruitment." Paper presented at the Annual Meeting of the American Political Science Association.

U.S. Bureau of the Census (1973). Census of Population: 1970, Subject Reports, Persons of Spanish Surname (PC [2]-1D). Washington, D.C.: Government Printing Office.

U.S. Department of Housing and Urban Development (1967). Improving the quality of urban life: A program guide to model neighborhoods in demonstration cities (PG-47). Washington: Author.

WASHNIS, G. (1974). Community Development Strategies: Case Studies. New York: Praeger.

WOLFINGER, R. (1974). The Politics of Progress. Englewood Cliffs, N.J.: Prentice-Hall.

10

THE REDISCOVERY OF FEDERALISM:
THE IMPACT OF FEDERAL CHILD HEALTH
PROGRAMS ON CONNECTICUT STATE HEALTH
POLICY FORMATION AND SERVICE DELIVERY

CHRISTA ALTENSTETTER

Fogarty International Center

JAMES WARNER BJORKMAN

Yale University

The New Deal was a major source of initiative for child health programs in the United States. The vehicle chosen to achieve this federal policy goal was the formula grant, which offered each state funds if certain minimum requirements were met. Much of the New Deal's social legislation was intended to encourage state governments to develop and improve their health-care delivery systems. A main theme of American politics is that the federal government exists in order to provide seed money, redistribute wealth, and create initiatives to which the constituent states will then respond in order to attain self-sufficiency.

American child health policy is expressed in a number of federal laws, the most comprehensive of which is the Social Security Act.

AUTHORS' NOTE: *This is a revised version of a paper originally delivered at the 1974 Annual Meeting of the American Political Science Association, Chicago, August 29-September 2. The research reported is funded by grant number 5-R01-HS-00900 from the National Center for Health Services and Development, D/HEW. We wish to thank Dr. George Silver, Ms. Anne-Marie Foltz, and various Connecticut officials for their advice. Also we wish to thank Barbara Hall, Michael Halle, M. Elisabeth Lorenzi, Barbara Novak, Eric Peterson, Elizabeth Stevens, and Alan Stoga for their assistance in the preparation of the original paper. The errors of fact and interpretations are, of course, our own responsibility.*

Passed in 1935 as part of the New Deal, its provisions include a clear commitment to promote the health and well-being of mothers, infants, and disadvantaged children. The act was repeatedly amended and expanded in the following decades, most notably during the Great Society years.[1] This paper examines how federal initiatives over forty years shaped the provision of child-care services in Connecticut by examining the impact of two Title V programs. Until 1969 the federal administrating agency for them was the Children's Bureau (CB).

The Social Security Act of 1935 authorized annual formula grants to the states in order to extend and improve health services for mothers and children, especially in rural areas. Federal monies were distributed in proportion to each state's number of live births, and each state was required to match its allotment. Each state was also granted a supplemental sum based on its financial need and its proportion of live births but without the requirement of matching funds. The programs supported by these Title V grants included well-child conferences, dental hygiene education, prenatal counseling, public health nursing, licensing, and inspection. For convenience, this package is collectively called Maternal and Child Health (MCH).

Title V also authorized annual formula grants to find children who were crippled or who were suffering from conditions leading to crippling and to provide them with medical, surgical, corrective, and other services. The program supported by these grants is called the Crippled Children's Services (CCS), and each state is entitled to a fixed sum of money annually, with the remaining CCS appropriations being allocated according to the number of crippled children in a state and its relative economic need. The requirement of matching funds resembles that of the MCH program.

Because there are several kinds of impact, studies of intergovernmental policy face difficulties of operational measurement. Other than being identified in the broadest terms, how can political, administrative, fiscal, and service impacts be weighed? And since relationships in a federal system are rarely unidirectional, how can reciprocity be described and assessed? For purposes of exposition, federal impacts on Connecticut will be discussed from three perspectives as if they were direct, indirect, and reciprocal. But we must note that these perspectives are a matter of convenience rather than exhaustive or innovative.

Direct impact compares service outputs of federal child health programs with their stated intentions. The Title V program goals were operationalized as the federal share of state program budgets, the number of children served, and the rural placement of clinics. This comparison of goals and achievements most closely approximates the conventional understanding of an evaluative methodology for policy analysis. The underlying aim was to assess program efficiency by discovering whether explicit goals were achieved and, if so, at what cost per unit.

In addition to stimulating the provision of direct services, federal initiatives also influence a state's administrative capabilities. Such indirect impact is instrumental for it changes the organizational structure in which child health programs operate. Furthermore, federal policy can have an impact on the political system (Lowi, 1973). By their very nature, political inputs almost automatically have reciprocal effects among governmental levels in a federal system. State receptivity and local predispositions toward federal initiatives are potential determinants of change in federal policy.

Three broad interactive areas of inquiry guided our research on child-health policy and served as vantage points for exploring implementation of Title V programs. These foci are governmental relations, program delivery systems, and private interests. The downward flows of federal initiatives were examined in law, appropriations, and administrative regulations. Study of the program delivery system included administrative controls over state health services, the decentralized units which deliver direct services, and the program personnel who operate the programs or are reimbursed after providing health care. And because the provision of health care services remained mainly in the private sector, an array of health-related interest groups at state level was examined for their influence over policy implementation.

DIRECT IMPACT:
FINANCES, HEALTH STATUS, AND SERVICE DELIVERY

Much of the New Deal's social legislation was intended to encourage state governments to raise additional revenues. The question is whether MCH and CCS achieved this goal for child health services. A major, or at least a convenient, indicator of federal impact on state-level programs is the proportion of a state program's budget which is financed by federal expenditures. Fiscal data are intuitively simple measures of policy commitments and presumably are easy to locate in a record-keeping society. But even on such well-established programs as MCH and CCS, comparative fiscal information has been difficult to find and validate. Nonetheless, from 1938 to 1971 the magnitude of the annual federal grants to both programs has increased more than 15-fold in current dollars. Even when inflation is controlled by calculating constant dollars, federal largesse grew fivefold as the annual federal grants to Connecticut's Title V programs steadily increased by modest increments.

As seed money, Title V funds have apparently been successful in stimulating state responses. Table 1 indicates the relative federal share of costs per treated child in Connecticut's Title V programs. Over the decades the federal government has paid for a diminishing share of the costs incurred per child. Unfortunately, the declining federal share is deceptive. Shortly after the MCH and CCS programs began in the mid-1930s, Connecticut learned that special new state appropriations were not needed to obtain federal matching funds. Instead, federal administrators permitted Connecticut to aggregate its state and local expenditures on health affairs and to present their cumulative sum as its matching money (Friedman, 1974: 20).

Table 1. COSTS PER TREATED CHILD OF CONNECTICUT'S TITLE V PROGRAMS[a] (moving averages expressed in constant dollars)

| Year | CCS Program | | | MCH Program | | |
	Total Cost	Federal Share	Federal Percentage	Total Cost	Federal Share	Federal Percentage
1940	$ 97.88	$ 88.33	90	$ 27.46	$ 19.42	71
1945	94.53	59.47	63	29.35	16.40	56
1950	73.37	54.66	74	52.39	26.57	51
1955	107.22	72.59	68	40.56	26.81	66
1960	N.A.	62.00	N.A.	N.A.	77.76	N.A.
1965	128.79	N.A.	N.A.	346.65	146.30	42
1970	209.68	120.05	57	328.06	195.12	59

a. Grants and expenditures on mental retardation programs have been excluded from MCH figures, as have grants and expenditures for special M&I and C&Y projects. Also, grants are recorded only in the year of their initial award; annual figures do not include any carry-overs of unspent funds. Thus, an annual federal expenditure may logically exceed an annual federal grant.

SOURCES: Report of the Comptroller, Connecticut Public Documents, respective years 1936 through 1956; Annual Report of the United States Secretary of the Treasury, respective years 1956 through 1970; "Detailed Expenditures of All Funds," Connecticut Public Documents, respective years 1940 through 1955; and "Quarterly Statement of Recipients and Expenditures of Federal Funds for Health Services" plus and/or SOC," Washington: D/HEW.

The federal formula grants did increase the financial resources available to Connecticut for programming child-health services. And these grants enabled the state to initiate a CCS program, although some efforts in the private sector already existed at Newington Home for Crippled Children. It is not clear, however, that the formula-grant device increased the state's willingness, much less its ability, to raise additional resouces for maternal and child health programs. Indeed, annual program budgets have been repeatedly juggled through supplemental budgets, and "matching" is an administrative rather than a fiscal enterprise. Federal administration of health formula grants has encouraged, or at least allowed, Connecticut to contravene federal regulations. Despite the annual rigmarole of requiring federal approval of state health plans, federal criteria for obtaining state matching funds have not been enforced.

The goal of Title V is to improve child health, and we sought evidence of change in the health status of Connecticut children. Health care specialists were consulted about indicators which would connect federal dollars with improved health status. One promising suggestion was the rate of infant deaths per thousand live births. Such rates had been declining in towns with federally financed projects, but close inspection of the data revealed the equivocal nature of the presumed causal link. The infant mortality rate had declined throughout the state, and, while that measure of child health status is malleable in the short run (Etzioni, 1971: 12), it is also subject to contamination by multiple factors. Consequently, no unambiguous link between federal initiative and child health could be demonstrated. For want of anything better, criteria for service delivery became the relative number of children served and the urban/rural locations of program clinics.

The federal MCH dollars which became available in FY 1936 found a state-financed package of MCH programs already underway in Connecticut. Although one of the few states not to participate in the 1923-1929 federal Shephard-Towner Act, Connecticut's Bureau of Maternal and Child Hygiene had developed state cosponsored Well-Child Conferences (WCCs) and the Summer Round-Ups (SRUs) on preschool children. Of course, these programs would not be expected to reach all Connecticut children since private medical practice provided and continues to provide screening services for many of them. However, we anticipated that a substantial proportion of Connecticut's child population under five would be examined at state cosponsored clinics.

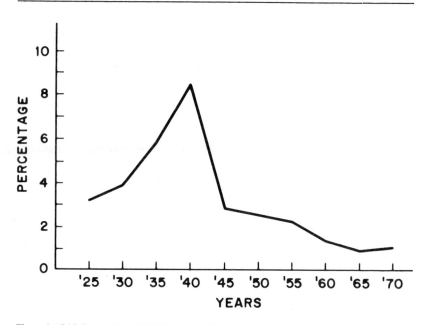

Through 1946 the number of children treated by Connecticut's MCH Program include those seen at the preschool Summer Round-ups. Thereafter, the SRUs ended, and only children seen at state cosponsored Well-Child Conferences are recorded.

SOURCES: Connecticut State Department of Health Annual Report, respective years 1923 through 1946; Annual Administrative Report to the Governor, respective years 1947 through 1972; and "MCH Health Services Provided or Paid for by State or Local Official Public Health Agencies," respective years from 1946 through 1970.

Figure 1: PERCENTAGE OF CONNECTICUT CHILDREN DIRECTLY EXAMINED AT STATE COSPONSORED MCH PROGRAMS

Figure 1 depicts the percentage of Connecticut's population under five examined by state WCCs and SRUs. The percentage increased steadily until World War II, when the federal Emergency Maternal and Infant Care program (1943-1949) came into effect. Thereafter, the percentage began to decline until by 1970 only one percent of Connecticut's children under five were examined.

MCH program goals would seem unaccomplished. Although WCCs did not represent the total package of MCH programs, it was the one program in Connecticut which directly served children. Yet while the actual federal dollars spent for the Connecticut MCH program had doubled between 1936 and 1945, and had more than trippled by 1950, the relative number of children declined. Suggestions have been made that Well-Child Clinics still continue on a local (*not* state cosponsored) basis and function adequately. But if so, the federal MCH monies no longer can be traced to direct child health services, even though the formula-grants continue.

According to average rates of prevalence reported in various medical studies, about seven percent of American children have some crippling defect[2] (Wholey and Silver, 1966: 11-10; Wallace, 1962: 269). The federal initiative under CCS stimulated Connecticut to start a state program for crippled children in 1937. If this medical estimate is correct for Connecticut, its record is unimpressive. The number of children assumed to be suffering from handicapping conditions was obtained by taking 7 percent of the total number of children under 21 in Connecticut for the designated year. From the number of children actually served by the CCS a percentage was then calculated of afflicted children who actually received some care. After three years of operation, 7.1 percent of all children assumed to be suffering from a defect were served by Connecticut's CCS program. The highest percentage ever reached was attained in 1950 when a total of 3,521 children received care, but 92 percent of the presumed target population's needs remained unmet. Since 1950, the percentage of children suffering from a crippling condition who have received care from the federal-state CCS program has steadily declined. Even if Congress intended only to serve poor children, as some scholars argue, the proportion of American children receiving treatment under CCS would still be very small.

The state CCS performance record in Connecticut may be due to general economic reasons. The inclusion of more expensive diseases

Table 2. **APPROXIMATE PERFORMANCE RECORD OF CCS PROGRAM IN CONNECTICUT**

Year	Population Under 21	Number of Handicapped[a]	Number Served by CCS Program[b]	Percentage of the Handicapped Actually Served
1940	371,065	25,975	1,859	7.1
1950	624,901	43,743	3,521	8.0
1960	943,773	66,064	3,642	5.5
1970	1,163,806	81,466	3,220	3.9

a. Estimated at seven percent of Connecticut's children.

b. Figures for children served in 1940 are based on the fiscal year; all other figures are for calendar years.

SOURCES: U.S. Census Bureau, Census of the Population, vol. 1, "Characteristics of the Population—Connecticut"; and Connecticut State Department of Health chapters in the annual Administrative Reports to the Governor, respective years.

under the CCS program necessarily limits the number of children who can be adequately treated. And as Table 1 indicated, the cost per child in constant dollars had doubled since the CCS program began. Also, in the earlier years of program operations, health professionals may have given more free time to CCS clinics than they are willing to provide today.

Rural placement of maternal and child health services was another major federal goal of the legislation in 1935. Federal legislation was intended to improve maternal and child health services in depressed rural areas. Although there has been a secular decline in the number of Connecticut towns covered by state cosponsored Well-Child Clinics, the MCH program originally stressed the provision of services in rural areas. In the early years, the towns in rural counties[3] were considerably more likely to have WCCs than their counterparts in the urban counties, so the federal objective was at first fulfilled. But since the 1940s the number of towns covered by WCCs had declined consistently, especially in rural counties. The only exception is New London County, which is just off center on an urban/rural continuum.

The federal government also expected the new CCS program to find and treat crippled children in rural areas. As a direct result of federal initiatives, Connecticut established several permanent hospi-

Table 3. LOCATIONS OF STATE COSPONSORED MCH WELL-CHILD CONFERENCES IN CONNECTICUT IN PAST THREE DECADES

Counties[a]	Percentages of Towns with Clinics			Total N of Towns
	1940	1959	1971	
Urban Average	47	27	15	
Fairfield	43	26	13	(23)
New Haven	33	30	11	(27)
Hartford	64	25	21	(29)
Rural Average	72	38	20	
Litchfield	73	19	19	(26)
Middlesex	80	40	20	(15)
Tolland	69	62	23	(13)
Windham	87	27	23	(15)
New London	57	52	43	(21)
State Average	61	33	18	(169)

a. The county demographic data are approximate because rural counties have urban centers and urban counties have rural towns. The urban-rural differences are calculated on the basis of town population densities; however, the reported trends remain evident.

SOURCES: Connecticut Health Bulletin, January 1941: 21; Connecticut State Department of Health; and Tyler (1973: 70-75).

Table 4. LOCATION OF CRIPPLED CHILDREN'S SERVICES
          IN CONNECTICUT

Opened	Clinic Site	Town Location	County Service Area
1938	Windham Hospital	Rural (Willimantic)	Rural (Windham)
1938	Backus Hospital	Urban (Norwich)	Rural (New London)
1938	Danbury Hospital	Rural (Danbury)	Urban (Fairfield)
1938	Stamford Hospital	Urban (Stamford)	Urban (Fairfield)
1938	Newington Home for Crippled Children	Rural (Newington)	Urban (Hartford)
1939	Griffin Hospital	Urban (Derby)	Urban (New Haven)
1942	Day/Kimball Hospital	Rural (Putnam)	Rural (Windham)
1943	Torrington Hospital	Urban (Torrington)	Rural (Litchfield)

SOURCES: Connecticut State Register and Manual, 1940; and Levenson, 1966.

tal-based clinics and other temporary clinics for more specialized
screening as needed. One private hospital already specialized in
treating the state's physically handicapped children, and from 1938
through 1943 the Newington Home for Crippled Children served
temporarily as a CCS clinic. Four new hospital-based clinics opened
in Connecticut in 1938, of which two were in rural towns and two in
urban ones. Three of those original five clinics actually served urban
counties, but after 1943 the balance shifted so that the rural counties
had four of the state's seven permanent CCS clinics. Clinic location
was a very important factor in locating, diagnosing, and treating
children with crippling conditions. For instance, in 1939 equal
numbers of children received CCS services in towns with and without
clinics, although towns without clinics had 175,000 more children.
The same finding holds for 1969 data despite the two additional
hospital-based clinics. Apparently outreach efforts were unable to
compensate for the advantaged access of children living in towns
where CCS clinics were located. Consequently, Connecticut only
partially fulfilled the rural-oriented goals of the CCS program.

**INDIRECT IMPACT:
INTERVENING SERVICES, ADMINISTRATION, AND POLITICS**

In order to link federal initiatives with state achievements, the
process of transforming dollars into deeds was examined. Between
fiscal indicators and the target child populations are several different
service outputs which have been partially financed with federal
dollars. Some services under each program were directly relevant to

health care while others were only supplementary. Originally the Children's Bureau emphasized direct medical services, clinical examinations of children, and the establishment of new health clinics; the bureau also allowed state programs to purchase health services from private providers. After 1949, however, regulations began to emphasize such administrative services as developing standards of quality, delivery techniques, and personnel training. MCH and CCS monies could be also increasingly used for overhead expenses such as salaries and travel costs, rent, tenant repairs, and upkeep of space exclusively housing MCH and CCS program units.

The Connecticut MCH program had included both direct and supplementary services from its origin. Because the CB had allowed state programs to develop, strengthen, and improve standards and techniques, to train personnel, and to provide other necessary administrative services, Connecticut's package of MCH services was varied. It included well-child conferences, summer roundups, inspection, licensing, consultations, training programs, and site visits.

CCS delivers health care to Connecticut children through outpatient (clinic, home, or office visits) and inpatient (hospital-based or in convalescent homes) services. Only a small percentage of the children served ever actually received inpatient services. As the range of direct health services became more comprehensive, the number of inpatients declined. From its minimum prewar diagnostic services, the CCS program expanded to include orthopedic, cardiac, nephrotic, audial, and other screening and therapeutic services. In addition, Connecticut CCS also financed advisory, supervisory, and administrative services.

During the forty years of Title V program operations in Connecticut, there has been a shift away from direct health services into nonhealth supplementary services. Neither program contravened federal regulations by using its federal funds for supplemental services because the federal priorities between health and nonhealth services were never clear.

The indirect effects of federal initiatives in health policy were markedly evident on Connecticut's state agencies. Changes also appeared in Connecticut's laws and its pattern of interest groups politics. In particular, federal regulations modified the internal structure of the state's administration. The "single agency" concept, an administrative device widespread in New Deal programs that has survived to the present, required that all federal money be channeled through the State Health Department. The Children's Bureau wanted the state administrating agency to exercise complete control over the state money used for matching purposes. The State Department of Health did not have such authority, so in 1935 the General Assembly authorized the State Health Commissioner to administer all federal health and welfare funds.

The CB also required that states establish separate units for Title V programs before federal funds could be released. In Connecticut a Bureau of Child Hygiene already existed when the Social Security legislation came into effect and therefore met the federal requirement for MCH program administration. A new division of Crippled Children was created in the Bureau of Child Hygiene in the same year. These separate administrative units have survived, with occasional shifts in nomenclature, the four major administrative reorganizations of the Connecticut State Department of Health since the early 1930s.

In addition, the Bureau required the State Health Department to change its administrative procedures. It required first the submission of a state plan of action, which was periodically revised. Federal formula funds could only be released after a state's plan had been approved by federal authorities, and changes in the plan could not be made without explicit approval from Washington. The plans became increasingly detailed (and confused) over the years, partly because new areas of interest in the health field had developed which required additional decisions, partly because experiences had been gained in program administration, and partly because such lessons had become embedded in the federal regulations.

In order to obtain uniform data about health efforts in the American states and about their systems for supervising the actual delivery of services, the federal government also required the state agencies to report both fiscal and service information about child health activities. Periodic reports had to be submitted on standardized federal forms, and altogether six different multicopy reports had to be submitted at regular intervals during each year. Connecticut conformed with these federal prescriptions for administering its Title V programs.

After an audit in 1971, however, HEW sharply criticized Connecticut's State Health Department for late reporting, for using federal funds on services not included in the state plan, and for not disbursing all federal funds. The submissions of some mandatory reports were delayed up to 23 months and, over six years, almost one million dollars or about 10 percent of the annual federal grants had not been spent by the state's Title V agencies. Such charges reflect adversely on Connecticut's administrative capabilities.

The HEW criticisms are, however, partly misdirected. Connecticut's poor performance with Title V funds is inexcusable, but the federal administrators are equally at fault. While the federal government had augmented state resources for child-care services and has stimulated the state bureaucracy's growth in order to meet the multitudinous reporting requirements, it has not been very successful in ensuring administrative efficiency. Federal surveillance of state performance is desultory, and often the federal officials do not understand their own procedures, especially for fiscal accounting.

Federal initiatives in child health had one final impact on the administrative structure of Connecticut. The federal government required states to establish advisory boards composed of representatives from other state executive agencies, private child-care agencies, and medical professional groups. The Congress itself mandated states to furnish proof that they "provide for the cooperation with medical, health, nursing, and welfare groups and organizations, and with any agency in such state charged with administering state laws providing for vocational rehabilitation of physically handicapped children." Connecticut immediately obliged by setting up a series of advisory councils, the most important of which was the General Advisory Committee to the State Health Department. At first, this committee met regularly and appears to have made the decisions about administering the MCH and CCS programs.

The most important professional organizations represented on advisory boards were the Connecticut State Medical Society (CSMS), the Connecticut State Dental Association, the Connecticut Nurses Association, and the Connecticut branch of the American Association of Medical Workers. The first and last groups, respectively, provided the Health Department with a Technical Medical Advisory Committee and a Medical Society Worker Advisory Committee. Because of overlapping membership in separate advisory bodies, the influence of these groups (and particularly of CSMS) was cumulative.

Federal initiatives encouraged professionals (particularly physicians) to become integral parts of programs administration and ensured them privileged access to the health policy process, whereas the public consumers were generally ignored. Over the decades, however, these provider groups became less interested in MCH and CCS program operations, whereas consumer groups became increasingly active (Bjorkman, 1974).

Although federally stimulated changes in state administration in Connecticut required conforming legislation, the General Assembly has had only a marginal role in formulating or even overseeing child-care policy. Control over the state purse would have been the Assembly's most effective weapon but the matching funds required by federal law were provided through the health department's annual block appropriations. Also, matching in-kind as well as in-cash was permitted. Consequently, the Assembly's knowledge of and/or concern about child health programs was limited. Indeed, although children have always numbered over two-fifths of Connecticut's population, less than 1 percent of the legislative bills placed before the legislature in the past 40 years have dealt with child-care issues, and only 3 percent were devoted to health and welfare issues, broadly defined (Bjorkman, 1973a).

Of the legislative proposals which were related to child-health, most have been aimed at special target populations with identifiable characteristics; that is, bills considered those children who are already sick or destitute or abandoned rather than all children in general. Topics such as general child health, maternal health, and school health received little attention whatsoever. However, although crippled children have received some attention, no indisputable causality between these state legislative activities and the federal-state CCS program was established.

The inactivity of Connecticut's General Assembly in health affairs was confirmed by a subsequent study (Bjorkman, 1973b), which concluded that the legislature routinely approved decisions about health care made elsewhere by administrators and state party leaders. Descriptive studies of the individual federal child-care programs further supported our thesis that considerable influence is wielded by the bureaucracy in formulating state health policy (Altenstetter, 1973; Friedman, 1974). A preliminary survey of Connecticut interest groups has also indicated that lobbyists are less active (or at least less visible) in the legislative chambers than in administrative corridors.

Our findings about interest groups in Connecticut's health policy process are provisional, but suggestive. Initially we had expected the Connecticut State Medical Society (CSMS) to dominate the policy area because its members sit on a number of advisory boards, and the federal regulations require these programs to have directors who are physicians. But CSMS seems more interested in fee schedules than in program operations. In any case its membership on these boards is not visibly used, perhaps because the physicians approve of the limited scope of these routinized programs.

Another unexpected impact of federal initiatives is the incentive which they provide a group to organize. Connecticut has several groups that formed at state level to lobby for access to Title V programs. Decisions about diagnostic categories for CCS treatment had been left to the states and usually state health administrators exercised their discretion to include new clients whenever possible. In several cases, however, the costs of providing such additional treatment would have been prohibitive, so the state agency declined to expand its rolls. Interest groups, often composed of parents, then organized to present their claims in the public and legislative arenas. Associations were formed on behalf of those children afflicted with cystic fibrosis, cerebral palsy, and cardiac defects. In 1947, in 1950, and again in 1955, the General Assembly passed legislation to include rheumatic heart disease, cerebral palsy, and cystic fibrosis, respectively, in the state's CCS program. Connecticut's CCS director credits these special legislative enactments to the activities of interested parents' groups.

The accomplishments of the Cystic Fibrosis Association of Connecticut (CFAC) provided the most dramatic illustration. Formed in the early 1950s, much of CFAC's activity now is devoted to raising funds for research and disbursing money for clinical treatment and care. But the group's considerable impact on the state is indicated by Connecticut's being the first state to include cystic fibrosis under the CCS. It is also the only state that aids those over 21 years of age afflicted with cystic fibrosis,[4] and the only American state that appropriates money for both treatment of and research in cystic fibrosis.

Given counsels of self-help, there is some feeling that Connecticut has made more progress in treating (and researching) this once fatal childhood disease than if the federal government had been involved. Indeed, since federal guidelines often only encompass the lowest common denominator of contemporary state-level activities, CFAC fears that concern for cystic fibrosis in Connecticut might regress if the CCS was ordered to become responsible. Such fears account for CFAC's remarkable record of vigilance in opposing efforts to reduce its appropriation or eliminate its line item from the state budget.

Federal initiatives may activate and energize state-level interests, but often the groups are only temporary. Groups formed in Connecticut, for example, which lobbied on behalf of children suffering from kidney disease. During the 1950s, these groups had succeeded in adding nephrosis to the list of diseases covered by the

CCS, only to wither away after attaining their limited end. Their behavior conformed to an emergent pattern that health groups interested in very specialized target populations dissolve after an initial success. Consumer groups have a "hit-and-run" philosophy which leads them to accept limited goods, usually financial assistance, and then leave the public arena.

RECIPROCAL IMPACT: REGULATIONS, LAW, AND GROUPS

In our study of federal influences on state practices in Connecticut, we discovered some irregularities in the sequence of presumed impact. While impact was expected to flow downwards from federal to state level, examples began to appear in which state practices and state groups influenced federal laws and regulations. These findings brought a "rediscovery" of federalism as a reciprocal process (Grodzins, 1966; Friedrich, 1968)—a simple point which is often lost amidst policy studies.

The CCS program illustrates the complex circularity of the policy process. Not only did federal initiatives affect state responses, but also state practices preceded federal action. The regulations of the Children's Bureau occasionally sanctioned informal administrative relationships and state practices, which later became embodied in federal law. For example, Congress did not specify any socioeconomic restrictions in 1935 nor set any upper age limit for CCS services. The only criterion of eligibility was affliction by a crippling disease. But during 1936-1949 many states, including Connecticut, regarded all children under 21 as eligible for CC services. Federal reporting forms implicitly required service data on any one under the age of 21, and eventually in 1949 bureau policies explicitly stated that all children under the age of 21 should be eligible for CCS diagnosis and treatment. Finally, in 1968 Congress made state practices and bureau policies an integral part of the federal law by stating that "a crippled child should be an individual under the age of 21 who has an organic disease, defect, or condition which may hinder the achievement of normal growth and development."

The point here is that impact is not unidirectional from federal to state level. Another example is how Connecticut in 1937 appointed physicians to head its Title V programs and thus institutionalized the participation of medical professionals. By 1939, 35 other states also had appointed MDs as program directors. Not until 12 years later, however, did the federal regulations require this practice of involving medical professionals in program administration.

Reciprocity is not only evident in administrative procedures but also in the amorphous world of interest groups. The Cystic Fibrosis Association of Connecticut illustrates how state-level groups create a national counterpart. CFAC was originally founded in Cheshire (a local town) as the Children's Cystic Fibrosis Association. The organization cultivated its political contacts and in 1955 scored a legislative breakthrough by getting a line-item appropriation for cystic fibrosis in the state budget. At the same time, the Connecticut groups cooperated with its counterparts in Pennsylvania and New York to set up a national organization which was incorporated in 1955. Since these groups set up the National Cystic Fibrosis Research Foundation, state-level chapters have multiplied through the country, and 45 other American states have included cystic fibrosis patients in their CCS programs.

CONCLUSIONS

Connecticut's experience indicates that federal initiatives in social policy produce state-level results, although not always as expected. In the field of child-health—at least as represented by two long-standing programs of the Social Security Act—the federal impact is sometimes obvious, sometimes not. As federal proposals and requirements developed, the MCH and CCS programs produced a series of direct, indirect, and reciprocal impacts.

To recapitulate, Connecticut easily made its organizational changes in direct response to federal requirements. Also Connecticut laws were sometimes amended to conform with federal regulations, although most state statutes and administrative codes did not contradict the spirit of federal intentions. Prior state practices and health-related interest groups influenced the operation of the federal-state child-care programs in such substantive matters as the eligibility criteria, clinic locations, kinds of services, referral policies, quality of care, and professional standards.

The performance record of the two federally assisted but state-run health programs is mixed. Federal grants helped Connecticut to increase its resources for improving the conditions of child-health in the state, even as the federal share of program expenses declined. These trends indicate that the federal goal of encouraging state-level actions in child-health policy was attained because state financial participation in child-health programs did increase, both absolutely and proportionately. On the other hand, the numbers of Connecticut's children served by the MCH and CCS programs has been minimal and the percentage served has actually declined. In direct effects, federal intervention increased money supply but fewer children were served. Furthermore, while these programs conformed initially to the federal requirement of providing rural services, they now serve both urban and rural areas equally well by serving them equally badly.

While the Title V programs have had a poor performance record of direct service inpact in Connecticut, their indirect effects are more marked. Program monies were spent on supplementary functions to establish and enlarge the state bureaucracy. Significant innovations occurred in state administration and, to a lesser degree, in Connecticut's health interest-groups system. It may be inferred that, contrary to the explicit letter of the Congressional law, the real federal goal under Title V was to build up the state's administration. If so, the programs were resoundingly successful. But when federal dollars pay for administrative expenses, they cannot buy tangible services for the target population of children.

The mixed performance record indicated by these direct and indirect impacts leads to a major conclusion for all policy analyses. The federal-state child-health programs of Title V reemphasize that ambiguous goals necessarily hamper efforts to evaluate the impact of social policies and even their implementation. Programs with broad aims have elusive results which make intended effects hard to locate and measure. Initial ambiguities in the federal law leave a great deal of policy-making power to the federal program implementors and their state-level counterparts. For political reasons, of course, neither Congress nor the President can always specify precise objectives, and even programs with explicit intentions can produce unexpected consequences. But most policy analyses presume clarity of purpose, a presumption of dubious value in social policy studies. In most cases, social goals must be further clarified—or even originally specified—by federal administrators. Certainly over the years since 1935, the Children's Bureau did so for the Title V programs.

Another conclusion related to the ambiguity of federal goals is that in practice the Title V formula grants operated like contemporary proposals for health revenue-sharing. Although that term had yet to be invented, federal money was redistributed among the states according to a fixed formula for a single categorical purpose. The purpose of improving child-health was broad and vague, however, without objectively defined measures of potential success. Some instrumental means were prescribed by the federal government, but these were more administrative than substantive. As such, federal requirements provided an insufficient basis for continued federal surveillance of state performance. Consequently, the Title V grants were a prototype of health revenue-sharing, which gives the states discretionary powers over how to spend federal funds.

The third conclusion about state child-health policy is more in the nature of a negative observation, but the federal initiatives did not, in fact, increase the attention paid to the conditions of children's health in Connecticut. At least as measured by legislative activities in the General Assembly, child-health issues are not now and never have been salient. The federal programs may well have obviated Connecticut's need to develop its own comprehensive programs for children. And if, as suggested above, Title V funds are prototypical of revenue-sharing, the future impact of that particular federal program may be dismal as far as the health of children is concerned.

Finally, federal initiatives ensured privileged access by special interest groups in the policy process. The federal initiatives in the Title V programs helped medical professionals, particularly physicians, to become integral parts of program operations. The participation of medical groups was institutionalized through mandatory advisory councils which remain in effect today. Ironically, after federal government directives helped such professional interest groups to dominate the child-health programs, the groups themselves began to lose interest in them. Later, however, consumer groups became more active at state level, and these were *not* directly encouraged by federal program regulations.

Our research into the operation of selected child-health programs in Connecticut suggests a concluding note about measurements in policy analysis. Because of its quantifiable nature, the amount of money spent on government programs is a standard measure of policy outcomes.[5] But that measure is increasingly suspect in the field of intergovernmental relations. The political dynamics of intergovernmental relations may complicate the analysis of policy impacts, but such dynamics set a more realistic context for program operations.

Although financial expenditures may be a good place to start measuring policy impacts, there are two reasons to be wary about relying on them exclusively. First, the government's goals are usually multiple in nature. Congress is justifiably concerned with how federal dollars are used, but congressional intentions often vary widely. Federal appropriations may, for example, be intended to improve the health of children. Alternatively, they may serve to reinforce status quo interests. They may also be used to balance centripetal and centrifugal forces in American federalism. And most perplexingly, federal monies may finance tangible goods and services for a clearly defined target population, while simultaneously they may underwrite programs which are intended to enhance a state's ability to achieve a further goal.

And second, the field of intergovernmental relations explicitly recognizes that the levels of American government interpenetrate in "marbled fashion." Federal, state, and local governments emphasize different goals, have different value orientations and traditions, and involve different mixes of actors (Elazar, 1972; Grodzins, 1966). Therefore, there are wide ranges of motives for and receptivity to federal policy priorities. The fiscalists may artificially assume the autonomy of state systems, but the federal-state nexus does make a difference in the policy implementation process (Vincent Ostrom, 1973). For these reasons, the explanations offered by the models of disjointed incrementalism and bureaucratic politics seem more plausible for policy analysis.

NOTES

1. Special local projects for promoting maternal and child health in low-income areas were authorized in 1963 and 1965. Also in 1965, Title XIX (Medicaid) was added to the SSA. The new title consolidated provisions of Titles I, IV, XIV, and XVI and set the goal of extending services to all people who need help in meeting their medical obligations. The new title established criteria of eligibility so that in addition to persons authorized to receive direct welfare payments (the indigent), all children under 21 who need but cannot afford medical care, all families without fathers (AFDC), and those families who need help with excessive medical bills (the medically indigent) could also receive assistance. Furthermore, in 1968 a special amendment required the states to intensify efforts to screen and treat children with disabling conditions through early case-finding and periodic screening of children (EPSDT).

2. The medical and public health literature does not make us confident that anyone knows the degree of unmet need in the child population for treating the handicapped. American health policy toward handicapped children is truly a case of "limited information" and one should not expect even "satisficing" behavior in the policy process, much less rational calculations. As Wholey and Silver (1966) observe, "except for data from studies of congenital malformation, little hard data exist on the incidence and prevalence of chronic conditions in childhood. Populations examined (and corrections counted) in the major studies are usually not comparable. Neither are definitive data available on the extent of disability caused by chronic illness."

3. Connecticut's towns are appropriate units for comparing service-delivery systems because of their long-standing political importance. Until 1965, representation in the lower house of the General Assembly was based on towns rather than populations. Also, although Connecticut's counties were legally abolished in 1959, they remain useful geographic entities for extra-state comparisons. It is generally understood that Fairfield, New Haven, and Hartford counties are urban, with the remainder being considered rural; only New London county approximates a 50-50 demographic split.

4. Formerly, cystic fibrosis was a lethal childhood disease, but improvements in medical science have now prolonged life expectancy to the point where six Connecticut citizens with CF are over 21. They all qualify for state aid, and, although this aid money is administered by the CCS program, it is not matched by federal funds.

5. The conceptualization of state policy in terms of the amount of dollars allocated to a particular issue area is associated with the work of Thomas Dye and Ira Sharkansky. While conducive to empirical measurement, the policy-dollars approach has come under increasing criticism (Elinor Ostrom, 1973). Also Schaefer and Rakoff (1970: 61) observe that "the Dye model . . . suffers from its oversimplification of complex phenomena, its tendency to substitute ease of measurement for conceptual rigor, and the fact that it has been (and perhaps can only be) applied to the analysis of expenditure policy."

REFERENCES

ALTENSTETTER, C. (1973). "Federal policy goals under the Crippled Children's Program and the responses of the State of Connecticut, 1935-1969." Health Policy Project Working Paper No. 16, Yale University (November).

BJORKMAN, J. W. (1973a). "Legislation and sponsors in Connecticut: 1930-1970." Health Policy Project Working Paper No. 7, Yale University (October).

--- (1973b). "Government and politics in Connecticut: A descriptive essay with special emphasis on the role of the General Assembly in making state health policy." Health Policy Project Working Paper No. 6, Yale University (November).

--- (1974). "Preliminary findings on Connecticut interest groups in the state health policy process." Health Policy Project Working Paper No. 19-2, Yale University (July).

DYE, T. R. (1966). Politics, Economics and Public Policy Outcomes in the American States. Chicago: Rand McNally.

--- (1971). "The measurement of policy impact, conference summary." Pp. 1-8 in T. R. Dye (ed.), The Measurement of Policy Impact. Proceedings of the Conference on Measurement of Policy Impact, Florida State University.

--- (1972). "Policy analysis and political science: Some problems at the interface." Policy Studies Journal, 1(Winter): 103-107.

ELAZAR, D. J. (1972). American Federalism: A View from the States (2nd ed.). New York: Crowell.

ETZIONI, A. (1971). "Policy research." American Sociologist, 6(supplemental issue): 8-12.

FRIEDMAN, D. H. (1974). "Federal policy goals under the maternal and child health legislation and the responses of the State of Connecticut." Health Policy Project Working Paper No. 21, Yale University (May).

FRIEDRICH, C. J. (1968). Trends in Federalism in Theory and Practice. New York: Praeger.

GRODZINS, M. (1966). The American System. (D. J. Elazar, ed.). Chicago: Rand McNally.

LEVENSON, R. (1966). County Government in Connecticut: Its History and Demise. Storrs, Conn.: Institute of Public Service, University of Connecticut.

LOWI, T. J. (1973). "What political scientists don't need to ask about policy analysis." Policy Studies Journal, 2(Autumn): 61-67.

OSTROM, E. (1973). "The need for multiple indicators in measuring the output of public agencies." Policy Studies Journal, 11(Winter): 87-91.

OSTROM, V. (1973). "Can federalism make a difference?" Publius, 3(Fall): 197-237.

SCHAEFER, G. F., and RAKOFF, S. H. (1970). "Politics, policy and political science: Theoretical alternatives." Politics and Society, 1(November): 51-77.

SHARKANSKY, I. (1970a). Policy Analysis in Political Science. Chicago: Markham.

––– (1970b). Regionalism and American Politics. New York: Bobbs-Merrill.

––– (1971). "Systems analysis by McNamara and Easton: A proposal of marriage that should illuminate linkages between public expenditures and service performance." Pp. 148-159 in T. R. Dye (ed.), The Measurement of Policy Impact. Proceedings of the Conference on Measurement of Policy Impact, Florida State University.

TYLER, N. C. (1973). "The well-child conference: A reflection of the nation's policy toward children at the national and state level." Health Policy Project Working Paper No. 15, Yale University (November).

WALLACE, H. M. (1962). Health Services for Mothers and Children. Philadelphia: Saunders.

WHOLEY, J. S., and SILVER, G. A. (1966). "Maternal and child health care programs." Washington, D.C.: Department of Health, Education, and Welfare, Office of the Assistant Secretary for Program Coordination (October).

11

THE ORGANIZATIONAL CONTEXT
OF EVALUATION RESEARCH

BRUCE A. ROCHELEAU

Northern Illinois University

Is evaluation research worthwhile?[1] Under what conditions is evaluation likely to lead to useful change in the operations of organizations? One review of governmental evaluation efforts shows that they have had little impact on programs (Buchanan and Wholey, 1972). Another study concludes that organizational obstacles largely explain the futility of much evaluation (Weiss, 1973). The purpose of this chapter is to use the empirical data drawn from a study of 14 mental health organizations and probe the influence which three organizational elements have on the success of evaluation research. These organizational elements are the informal system, concern with organizational survival, and organizational authority.[2]

The informal system is used here to refer to an organization's unprogrammed elements such as informal groups, beliefs, and norms. These elements often contribute to resistance to innovation, especially when the innovation is viewed as threatening by organizational personnel (Thompson, 1969). The introduction of formal evaluation may be perceived by organizational members as a threat and encroachment on aspects of their organization previously dominated

AUTHOR'S NOTE: *An earlier version of this chapter was presented at the 1974 Annual Meeting of the American Political Science Association.*

by informal and subjective judgments such as beliefs about the quality of agency programs and the effectiveness of individual members.

Based on the analysis above, the following issues are examined with empirical data:

(1) Does resistance to evaluation arise from the informal system elements? If so, how important is hindrance from these elements in comparison with other obstacles to evaluation?

(2) Do organizational personnel resist more strongly evaluations which focus on individuals than those which center on programs and whole organizations?

Finally, we outline some ways in which the informal system "works on" the evaluator.

Concern with organizational survival is frequently cited as a goal of the highest priority for organizational members (Selznick, 1947). Indeed, it is a maxim that organizations seek to continue their existence even after the original reasons for establishing them no longer remain (Sills, 1957). An evaluation may reflect unfavorably on an organization and thus threaten its survival. Consequently, the following questions are studied:

(1) What do organizational members see as being the major functions of evaluation research? How do they perceive evaluation to be related to organizational survival?

(2) What impetus leads organizations to undertake evaluations voluntarily?

In addition, we analyze the kinds of tasks to which evaluators devote most of their time.

Evaluators may need substantial authority to overcome anxiety and resistance. Authority is defined here as the "ability to evoke compliance" (Presthus, 1960). However, there are several potential sources of authority including the following: (1) authority of position based on a person's place in the formal hierarchy; (2) authority of competence resulting from an individual's education, experience, and talent; (3) authority of person drawn from the individual's ability to develop effective interpersonal relationships in the organization (Peabody, 1964). This relationship between evaluation and authority gives rise to the following problems which are studied here:

(1) What resources do evaluators and other organizational members regard as being most important in helping the evaluator to establish an effective evaluation program?

(2) What types of authority do evaluators rely on in practice?

We also analyze the consequences, both intended and unintended, of using each kind of authority.

METHODS

This research was carried out on 14 mental health organizations in Florida. Five of these organizations had full-time evaluation staffs, and several of the other organizations were carrying out evaluation research of their own or planning to hire evaluators. The author employed three major methods of data collection to study these organizations: participant observation, interviews, and question-naires.

The participant observation consisted of five months of obser-vation of a community mental health center which had a full-time evaluation staff. This writer was also a participant observer at meetings of a consortium of mental health organizations which had been formed in Florida to study and foster evaluation research.

The interviews were conducted with three different groups of personnel in the 14 organizations: directors, evaluators, and clini-cians.[3] The interviews were semistructured in nature and totaled 35 with 47 different individuals. With two exceptions, the interviews were taped.

The questionnaire was constructed in order to explore the attitudes of organizational personnel toward the issues discussed above. They were sent to all directors and evaluators in the 14 organizations.[4] Questionnaires were also distributed to four clinicians in each organization.[5] The total number of responses to the questionnaire was 63 of the original 84 sent.

The combination of the questionnaires with interviews and participant observation provides a good overview of the organiza-tional context of evaluation research. Generalizations supported by data gathered through a variety of methods are more likely to be valid than those supported by a single technique (Webb et al., 1966). Qualitative research such as participant observation is especially useful when the subject of the research involves a conceptlike evaluation which is likely to evoke response bias (Becker, 1970). Few persons are likely to admit openly to being "against evaluation."

FINDINGS

THE INFORMAL SYSTEM

To assess the importance of the informal system as a hindrance to evaluation, the author constructed a list of potential obstacles to evaluation. One obstacle was anxiety about evaluation which is likely to occur when the informal system is threatened (see Table 1). The evaluators, clinicians, and directors were asked to rank this and four other obstacles to evaluation in their order of importance. An index measuring the importance of each obstacle was formed by summing the rankings of the members of each of the three groups surveyed.

Table 1 shows that anxiety was not ranked as the most important obstacle by any group. Rather the lack of resources to carry out an evaluation was perceived to be the major barrier. Although the nature of the data warrants caution in drawing conclusions, clinicians, evaluators, and directors consider anxiety to be only the third, fourth, and third (tie) most important obstacle respectively.

Organizational members may prefer general evaluations which focus on units such as programs to evaluations which center on individuals because the former are less threatening. In order to study this issue, severl questionnaire items were constructed to compare the degree of favorableness of clinicians, directors, and evaluators toward evaluations with a general and individual focus (see the Appendix for a list of the specific items). The responses of the three groups were then classified and averaged to form indices of support for these two types of evaluation (see Tables 2 and 3).

The data in Tables 2 and 3 indicate that organizational members

Table 1. OBSTACLES TO EVALUATION

Ranking of Obstacles to Evaluation	Clinicians	Directors	Evaluators
1. Lack of reliability	134	49	27
2. Anxiety as to use	107	38	27
3. Unnecessary	82	34	24
4. Lack of evaluative skills	103	43	23
5. Lack of resources to execute	139	55	39

Scoring: Points were assigned as follows: five points to an obstacle rated as most important by a respondent; four for the next most important, etc.

Table 2. VIEWS ON GENERAL EVALUATIONS (in percentages)

	Clinicians	Directors	Evaluators
Strongly favorable	41.6	41.3	66.7
Favorable	49.0	45.2	33.3
Undecided	8.4	6.3	0.0
Unfavorable	1.0	7.5	0.0
Strongly unfavorable	0.0	0.0	0.0
	100.0	100.3[a]	100.0

a. Sum of percentage figures is unequal to 100 due to rounding.

do favor evaluations with a broader focus to evaluations aimed at individual performances. Table 2 shows that over 40 percent of the clinicians and directors are strongly favorable toward the less threatening evaluations, while Table 3 shows that less than 15 percent are strongly favorable to evaluations aimed at individuals. Organizational members strongly support evaluations for such purposes as providing feedback to organizational members, evaluating the output of programs, or evaluating the quality of whole organizations. They are much less favorable to evaluations used for functions like rating personnel and deciding promotions or terminations.

Nevertheless, a surprisingly large percentage of clinicians favor evaluations for even the most threatening of uses. The basis of such support may lie in the fact that some clinicians feel that they have been mistreated by the current subjective and informal mode of evaluation of individuals in these organizations. Said one evaluator who encountered such a case with a program head who invited the evaluators to evaluate his program:

> I don't know why, but several times [name of a clinician who headed a program] was put down. People in the organization were saying that he simply wasn't doing anything worthwhile. So, he said, "All right, I want to be evaluated. Come over and evaluate us." It was like, "We're open to anything."

Table 3. VIEWS ON INDIVIDUAL EVALUATIONS (in percentages)

	Clinicians	Directors	Evaluators
Strongly favorable	7.9	12.5	8.3
Favorable	32.9	26.6	19.4
Undecided	19.1	29.7	25.0
Unfavorable	35.5	23.5	36.1
Strongly unfavorable	4.6	7.8	11.1
	100.0	100.1[a]	99.9[a]

a. Sum of percentage figures is unequal to 100 due to rounding.

Generally, then, the responses of the clinicians may be expressed in the following decision criterion: support evaluations that do not threaten your own position and that offer you positive rewards.

The responses of the evaluators are more surprising. They demonstrate almost total support for evaluations which deal with the overall organization. However, like the clinicians and directors, they show little evidence of a desire to evaluate individual performances (as indicated by the data in Table 3). Their responses are surprising, because if evaluators could use formal evaluation to judge individual performances, they would immediately become very powerful figures in the organizations.

Yet, interviews and participant observation demonstrate that evaluators prefer much less threatening evaluations. They anticipate great anxiety, fear, and general resistance to any attempt on their part to use formal evaluation to evaluate individual performances. The author asked one evaluator if he distinguished between the evaluation of programs and the evaluation of individuals. The evaluator replied:

> Yes, program evaluation is the basic unit here. We will take a program like the outpatient clinic . . . measuring the success of the individual therapists is possible using similar methodologies. But I don't think I would take the analysis down that way unless somebody asked me.

The evaluator was then asked what advantages he saw in program evaluation over the evaluation of individual therapists. He replied:

> Well, it is less threatening.

Another evaluator supported his preference for program evaluation with similar reasoning:

> Well, my personal preference is for program evaluation, but, unfortunately, if a program flops, it is pretty obvious that somebody is at fault there. I would rather not have to get down to evaluating specific people. I think that is why I have encountered so little resistance—because I have made it clear that I would not be evaluating people, at least for the time being, if at all.

At a meeting attended by evaluators and state officials bent on encouraging evaluation, there was a discussion of the issue of whether to go slowly in the implementation of evaluation by avoiding threatening evaluations or to begin with a program that included evaluation of individual performances:

[State official] I can't imagine pressure being put on the therapist. I think that you will find that most anxiety is a problem before evaluation is implemented—if it isn't used to club them.

[Evaluator No. 1] I found the same thing: resistance before the implementation of evaluation.

[Evaluator No. 2] But I was placed on a probationary period for my first few months at [name of a mental health center], and I don't see why evaluation can't be used to evaluate the staff.

[State official] It is a good idea. But it is a problem of not threatening or frightening people too much. You have to use tact. If it is done in a cooperative way. . . .

In short, these evaluators appear to be using a foot-in-the-door technique of introducing evaluation (Freedman, 1966). The influence of the informal-system elements on evaluation is more indirect than direct—the evaluators anticipating resistance beforehand and modifying their behavior accordingly. It should be noted, however, that all groups were agreed that the performance of the individual clinician is a key to the success of the programs and to the overall quality of service provided by the organization. Thus, the informal-system elements tended to limit the nature of the evaluations carried out, although more through the indirect means of anticipated reactions of evaluators rather than by overt resistance.

EVALUATION AND ORGANIZATIONAL SURVIVAL

Evaluation can perform several functions for an organization and its members (Suchman, 1972). Based on a search of evaluation literature, a list of nine potential functions of evaluation was constructed, and the three groups were asked to rank these functions as to their relative importance.[6] Table 4 shows that the one function that is most clearly associated with organizational survival —namely, "providing justification for the funding of the mental health organization"—is rated low in importance. The clinicians, directors, and evaluators rank this function of evaluation as being only seventh, seventh, and sixth in importance respectively.

The data in Table 4 reveal that feedback and evaluation of the quality of programs are ranked as the two most important functions of evaluation by all three groups. Clinicians and directors chose "evaluating the quality of programs" as first in importance, while the evaluators preferred "feedback for clinicians." Consequently, the data in Table 4 suggest that the functions regarded as most important

Table 4. THE FUNCTIONS OF EVALUATION

	Clinicians	Directors	Evaluators
1. Feedback	257	104	68
2. Staff performance	156	50	22
3. Program quality	273	109	67
4. Community accountability	216	84	56
5. Clientele accountability	189	67	45
6. Organization efficiency	238	100	52
7. Funding justification	176	64	46
8. Resource allocation	182	78	52
9. Regulate behavior	80	27	11

Scoring: Points were assigned as follows: nine points to the most important function as rated by the respondent, eight to the next most important, etc.

by members of these organizations are related to program improvement rather than personal or organizational goals of survival. This low rating assigned to the funding of the organization is particularly impressive in view of the situation of the mental health organizations. In the late 1960s and early 1970s, they had become quite worried about their funding. Adequate funding of programs and even survival of the entire organization became active matters of concern for their personnel (Holden, 1973).

However, interview and participant observation data indicate quite a different perspective concerning the uses of evaluation. They revealed that the concern of organizational members with their funding situation influenced their attitudes toward investing in a formal evaluation staff. One director describes how he considered hiring an evaluator but decided against doing so because it would not be "cost effective":

> This cost is difficult to justify. We originally had a full-time research and evaluation person written into our grant. We costed it out, and the amount of service did not justify the dollars cost. I didn't see how we could do it. We went the route of being primarily service-oriented, trusing that somehow we were doing some good.

Another director noted that he had also considered employing an evaluation staff. However, decreases in federal funding of the mental health center had led to a scarcity of resources so that priority was given to the clinical programs:

> I think that we need somebody in the organization who has the education, background, and experience in research and evaluation, but now we have gotten to the point in our grant that we see clinical needs as more

important—this was our last discussion concerning this matter—that we may not pursue this [hiring an evaluator] any further. We have so many clinical needs. Why should we flounder around, especially since nobody else seems to be doing anything much? So why should we go head over heels?

In short, most organizational directors see evaluation as an "extra service" with lower priority than the "direct" services. All of the organizations, even the five who had invested in a full-time research and evaluation staff, agreed that the costs of evaluation were significant.

What, then, are the positive inducements which led some organizations to invest in evaluation and others to consider doing so? While there is no doubt that many organizational members are sincerely interested in obtaining feedback from evaluation to improve the efficiency and effectiveness of their programs, nevertheless, there was substantial evidence that the actual causes of interest in evaluation were more directly related to the problems of organizational survival and security. First, the impetus to undertake evaluation was basically the result of the increasing demands of outside funding sources for proof or evidence of effectiveness from the organizations they were supporting. This theme of undertaking evaluation in response to outside pressures was repeated again and again in interviews conducted by the author:

[Evaluator] Well, of course, I think that there is pressure from the government. You know that they want to know that the money they are spending is doing some good.

[Director] Really, the main impetus for evaluation has been outside forces. The board of the center, for one, wants to know what we are doing, and NIMH [National Institute of Mental Health] is asking us to be more accountable. Anyone who is receiving government funds knows that there is obviously a big push for accountability and a little more than that, not just to account for hours, but whether you are really doing something. This is the impetus as I see it.

[NIMH official] We don't know what the future holds. With revenue sharing, the county commissioners and the cities are going to get at some of the dollars. This calls for an additional emphasis to do something in evaluation efforts—to sell them to the community.

[State official] Evaluation and cost effectiveness are what the mental health boards are talking about. These boards want to talk about evaluation in a different sense from what evaluators are usually thinking of—that is, "How do we justify the money being used to the community?"

Participant observation and interview data below show that organizations investing in evaluation saw at least four potential ways in which hiring evaluators and undertaking formal evaluation could contribute to the survival and security of their organizations: (1) evaluation as a defensive strategy in anticipation of future requirements for evaluation and accountability by funding agencies and other bodies to whom they are accountable, (2) evaluation as a means of providing justification of the worth of the mental health services to the community, (3) evaluation as a method of securing grants and other resources for the organization and individuals within it, and (4) the use of the evaluation staff to carry out "nonevaluative" activities necessary or useful to the organization's survival.

Many organizational leaders think that by undertaking evaluation voluntarily they will get a head start on what they perceive to be an inevitable movement toward a requirement for evaluation of all social service programs. Thus, when the author asked an evaluator why the director of the organization had hired him, the evaluator replied:

> Well, as he [the director] expressed it to me, it was a case of doing
> something that was going to come anyway and that he would rather have
> our center in the forefront of the movement.

Another director said he saw a chance to get greater input and control over the forms of evaluation likely to be imposed later:

> The community is doing it [evaluation]. It is saying, "Do I want my
> United Fund dollar to go here?" or "Do I want my tax dollar going here?"
> So, whether you think it is being done fairly or not, it is being done. And
> if somebody else is going to do it, you might as well do it yourself, coming
> up with some kinds of guidelines to feed back to them. If we don't do it,
> somebody else will do it for us.

Several directors were using their evaluation staffs to carry out evaluations which they expected to justify the money already being spent on the organization and, if possible, to provide justification for asking for even more funds. For example, some of the evaluation staff were directing most of their efforts to carrying out needs assessment surveys which were likely to show high rates of incidence of mental illness and thus provide "hard" data in support of their requests for funds. Other evaluators were involved in attempting to calculate the dollars-and-cents equivalent of mental health services or provide data to show that the organization was not getting its fair share of public funds.

Many of the evaluation programs either were receiving or expected to receive funding support from the state and federal governments. The author asked one evaluator if the amount of money a mental health center invested in evaluation could be used as an index of an organization's interest in evaluation. He replied:

> Not necessarily. If somebody could give us a grant, and the center may not have any particular interest or investment in evaluation, but if somebody gave us a grant to do it, then I think it would create interest in the field.

In addition to grants that directly supported the evaluation programs, the evaluators were also involved in writing the evaluation sections of grants for other programs. For example, if an organization wishes to get a grant for special alcholism or children's programs, it now usually has to include an evaluation section within the grant proposal.

Some of the evaluation staffs observed in these organizations spent much of their time on activities other than evaluation, such as general administration. Several clinicians noted that the evaluators were mainly involved in working on problems of billing patients or gathering data to report to the citizens' board which oversees the operations of the center rather than research and evaluation:

> [Clinician No. 1] I have seen the department responsible for evaluation as being involved almost entirely in administrative functions, and it has not been really able to begin research.

> [Clinician No. 2] I would like to see them [the evaluation staff] give us programmatic suggestions. In the first year, they seemed to be caught up in gathering data and reporting to the board.

Evaluators themselves perceived an expectation on the part of the directors that they were to focus on nonevaluative activities:

> [Evaluator No. 1] Well, [name of the director] has his own agenda, and in his agenda anything that I can do to take weight off of his shoulders in terms of administrative duties, especially his relationship with the state and board and the like, is of primary value to him.

> [Evaluator No. 2] I was the logical person to get him [the director of the center] that information. There were other people but they had so many other things to do, or they didn't really know how to get this kind of information. And so it just kind of fell to us to get it.

In summary, the impetus behind hiring evaluators and carrying out formal evaluation appeared to be aimed most directly at supporting the survival and security of the organization rather than at providing feedback or evaluating the quality of programs. The discrepancy between their preferences on the questionnaires and the actual uses to which evaluation was put appears in large part due to a form of what has been called "Gresham's Law of Planning" (Simon, 1960). This law states that programmed activities are likely to drive out nonprogrammed activities. The activities most closely associated with survival (e.g., billing patients, meeting deadlines set by funding agencies and regulatory bodies) tend to be programmed into the daily schedule of the organization and have a higher priority than other activities such as critical self-evaluation.

EVALUATION AND ORGANIZATIONAL AUTHORITY

As noted earlier, evaluators may rely on several sources of organizational authority including their formal position, functional competence, and interpersonal relationship skills. A questionnaire item was developed to obtain some idea of which resources organizational personnel consider to be most important in order for an evaluator to achieve responsiveness to his evaluation.

Directors clinicians, and evaluators agree that the evaluator's technical competence is the most important resource (see Table 5). However, competence can cover several types of abilities, education, and experience. For example, knowledge of the decision-making structure of an organization and experience in operating programs can be as important components of an evaluator's competence as knowledge of research design and specific evaluative techniques. Several clinicians argued that they would prefer an evaluator who had a clinical background and experience in the programs of the

Table 5. THE RESOURCES OF AN EVALUATOR

	Clinicians	Directors	Evaluators
1. Role and powers	101	36	27
2. Friendships and staff relationships	101	36	24
3. Staff respect	152	63	37
4. Support from superiors	111	56	30
5. "Nonevaluative" contributions[a]	80	34	16

Scoring: Points were assigned as follows: five points to the most important resource as rated by the respondent, four to the next most important, etc.

a. Refers to such activities as data collection, grant writing, and administration.

organization. Perception of competence and objective competence are not necessarily the same. Some evaluators felt that most organizational members do not have the knowledge to judge statistical skills. As one evaluator noted:

> Well, the problem is that a lot of clinicians—and also the nonclinical people who hire you—don't really understand a sophisticated data analysis. So, if you give them a report that is in terms of the number of people handled and the percentages of clients who say, "Gee, that was really peachy," that is something that is readily intelligible to them. And they can go to their board . . . and say, "Look, isn't this nice? Everyone thinks we are so wonderful. We handled so many patients." . . . I bet that when I start feeding variables in and do something like a discriminant analysis that there are not more than one or two people over there who would know about that.

Most evaluators have a "mix" of different types of competence. Choosing an evaluator often involves making trade-offs between competence based on experience and knowledge in a substantive area and competence based on methodological expertise. Operational personnel in organizations appear often to favor an evaluator who shares their own perspective as closely as possible. Several clinicians indicated that they would like the evaluator to "come and live with their program" so that he could see the particular problems which they faced in their work.

Table 5 indicates that the evaluator's formal power is ranked as being less important a resource than his personal relationship to the head of the organization. This fact is not surprising because the study showed that the director was the key individual responsible for deciding whether the organization invested in evaluation (Rocheleau, 1974). However, the importance assigned to personal relationships can be especially important because of the problem of turnover. An earlier study found a surprisingly high turnover in the evaluation staffs (Weiss, 1973). In the organizations studied here, there was not only a high turnover in the evaluators but also in other leadership positions including that of director. Given the high degree of mobility of both evaluators and other leadership personnel in many organizations, it makes it especially difficult for a continuous and effective evaluation program to be established. The important personal relationships between the evaluator and other organizational leaders have to be reestablished frequently.

Table 5 reveals that all three groups rate the evaluator's relationships with the clinical staff and his performance of support activities to be less important than the evaluator's competence and relationship with the head of the organization. Yet, interviews and participant observation show that evaluators gave much attention to the former part of their job. It has already been pointed out that evaluators emphasized that they undertake only nonthreatening evaluations. Indeed, some evaluators see it as a prime requisite of their job to establish to the rest of the staff that they are "good guys." As one evaluator put it:

> You have probably heard in the past that they have experienced problems in research and evaluation and couldn't get the staff to do this and that. The thing that I think has enabled us to get past that is to do a study that is in no way threatening to the staff. They could care less. When they saw that I was a fairly decent guy, that I wasn't out to be a threat to them, they would say, "Maybe he has got someting to offer us."

Another facet of the evaluator's role is the fact that his contribution to the organization is less concrete than that of operational personnel. Both evaluators and other staff members remarked on seeing an important difference between clinicians who "produce" something immediately of value to the organization and evaluators whose product and worth take longer to develop and are less easily defined and measured. An awareness of this point is evident in the following comments by a director and evaluator:

> [Director] Research takes some time before production comes forth but this isn't true of clinicians. When we hire one, usually the first day or two they have seen a couple of patients and have produced something.

> [Evaluator] I am a member of tne planning staff [of the mental health organization], and, as director of research and evaluation, I am supposed to be there at the meetings. I want to be there, but I won't go until I have something to take with me. I look at [name of a clinician who is outpatient director] and he provides a service—sits down and talks, writes out an admission form, progress report, and he has done something. I am attempting to develop a credibility, doing small kinds of projects for the outpatient.

Thus evaluators attempt to contribute something of immediate value to the organization in order to both justify their position and improve their relationships with clinical personnel. They perform data collection and data description activities for clinicians heading various service programs. While performing such duties may indeed develop good interpersonal relationships with the other staff, it also deflects the evaluator from undertaking more analytical and critical evaluative tasks. An evaluator noted:

> What happened was that when I started, I got myself overloaded with a lot of descriptive stuff and didn't get into any actual evaluation for several months because of it. As a result, a lot of people kept asking me—they got the impression that that [data collection] is what I am supposed to do—so they kept asking me to do all of this such as compiling the ages of people in the programs. Not that it is not interesting and important, but it doesn't tell you all that much about how your programs are doing. I was using that initially to provide public relations and a service but I ended up constantly having to provide the service.

In summary, the inside evaluator is performing in a difficult role. He needs several sources of authority—one will not suffice. While competence in the area of evaluation is important, he also needs to develop good interpersonal relationships with the head of the organization and key program personnel. Developing such relationships is an exchange process in which authority is accumulated at the expense of deflecting him from critical or negative evaluation.

CONCLUSION

Organizations have an important effect on the nature and outcome of the evaluations carried out within them. In this chapter, we have examined three among several organizational elements that influence the course of evaluative research: the natural system, the organizational concern with survival, and the nature of organizational authority.

The evaluators under study were highly conscious of the organizational context in which they worked. The natural system elements had little direct effect on the outcome of evaluations in the form of overt resistance. But the evaluators had done everything possible to avoid creating any anxiety and resistance among operational personnel.

The organization's concern with survival plays a curious, almost schizophrenic role, in affecting the evaluation effort. On the one hand, organizations with funding difficulties view evaluation as an "extra" activity and are reluctant to invest in it. However, forces in the environment of these organizations have been creating conditions in which there are positive inducements to undertake evaluation from the point of view of contributing to organizational survival, which we have outlined. Ironically, the personnel of the organization would prefer to use evaluation for much more "idealistic" purposes than merely contributing to the organization's security. Nevertheless, it appears that there occurs a natural tendency to sacrifice lofty notions to the more mundane but compelling demands of everyday organizational behavior.

Much of the evaluator's authority seems to depend on his personal relationships with the head of the organization and other important leaders. Because of the high mobility and turnover not only in the position of evaluator but in other leadership positions, it appears difficult for there to be a stable and enduring organizational evaluation program. Moreover, these internal evaluators placed a high priority on obtaining the trust and respect of operational personnel. Their pursuit of good relationships often leads them to spend their time in activities and pursuits quite different from those they had originally planned.

Can organizational obstacles to evaluation research be overcome? Is evaluation worth doing? An unsatisfactory but nevertheless honest answer appears to be "it all depends" (Sherman, 1966). It depends on the skills, both technical and interpersonal, of the evaluators. It is also contingent on the character of the evaluation program, the nature of the organization and its leadership, and the organization's technology, among other factors. It is necessary to be cautious about the impact that evaluation research is likely to have. Carrying out a successful and useful evaluation appears to be a highly difficult and tenuous activity with no assurance that the results will justify the cost of the evaluation.

APPENDIX

The index of the degree of favorableness to evaluations with a general focus was calculated based on responses to the following five questions:

(1) Evaluation can and should be used to furnish feedback for the clinical staff.

      Strongly Agree   _____
      Agree   _____
      Undecided   _____
      Disagree   _____
      Strongly Disagree _____

(An identical series of five responses was repeated after each item in the questionnaire.)

(2) Evaluation can and should be used to determine whether or not the overall organization is performing well.

(3) Evaluation can and should be used to determine the impact of the organization's programs on the community.

(4) Evaluation can and should be used to determine which service programs, if any, are performing poorly.

(5) Evaluation can and should be used to determine whether individual mental health programs are successful or not.

The index of the degree of favorableness to evaluations with an individual focus was calculated based on the responses to the following four questions:

(1) Evaluation can and should be used to determine whether or not individual clinical staff members are performing their jobs well.

(2) Evaluation is neither valid nor reliable enough to be used to determine who is doing a good job.

(3) Evaluation is currently neither valid nor reliable enough to be used to determine who should be promoted within the organization.

(4) Evaluation can and should be used to determine who should be fired from their jobs.

NOTES

1. Evaluation and evaluation research are used here to refer to formal scientific evaluation. By scientific evaluation, we refer to evaluations which use the tools of science and thus are able to be repeated by someone other than the original evaluator. A totally subjective evaluation is the "property" of the person making the judgment.

2. There are many other organizational elements which also influence evaluation research, such as organizational leadership and technology. The author has studied their influence on evaluation research elsewhere (Rocheleau, 1974).

3. The assignment of the respondents to the three groups was based on a questionnaire item asking them to define their jobs.

4. The reason for there being 16 directors for the 14 organizations is that a director of one center resigned and was replaced by another during the course of the study. Another center had two directors—one for clinical and one for administrative matters.

5. The questionnaires were distributed nonrandomly to the clinicians.

6. Many of these functions overlap. For example, the evaluation of the quality of programs would yield feedback to the clinicians involved in the programs. Nevertheless, the responses indicate which uses the groups would prefer to see emphasized.

REFERENCES

BECKER, H. S. (1970). Sociological Work: Method and Substance. Chicago: Aldine.

BUCHANAN, G., and WHOLEY, J. S. (1972). "Federal level evaluation." Evaluation, 1(Fall): 17-22.

FREEDMAN, J. L. (1966). "Compliance without pressure: The foot-in-the-door technique." Journal of Personality and Social Psychology, 4(August): 196-202.

HOLDEN, C. (1973). "Mental health: NIMH reeling over proposed budget cuts." Science, 185(April 20): 284-285.

PEABODY, R. L. (1964). Organizational Authority. New York: Atherton.

PRESTHUS, R. (1960). "Authority in organizations." Public Administration Review, 20(Spring): 86-91.

ROCHELEAU, B. A. (1974). "Evaluation and organizations: The case of community mental health centers." Unpublished Ph.D. dissertation, University of Florida.

SELZNICK, P. (1949). TVA and Grassroots. Berkeley: University of California Press.
SHERMAN, H. (1966). It All Depends: A Pragmatic Approach to Organization. University: University of Alabama Press.
SILLS, D. (1957). The Volunteers. New York: Free Press.
SIMON, H. A. (1960). The New Science of Management Decision. New York: Harper & Row.
SUCHMAN, E. A. (1972). "Action for what? A critique of evaluative research." Pp. 52-84 in C. H. Weiss (ed.), Evaluating Action Programs: Readings in Social Action and Education. Boston: Allyn & Bacon.
THOMPSON, V. A. (1969). Bureaucracy and Innovation. University: University of Alabama Press.
WEBB, E. J.; CAMPBELL, D. T.; SCHWARTZ, R. D.; and SECHREST, L. (1966). Unobtrusive Measures: Nonreactive Research in the Social Sciences. Chicago: Rand McNally.
WEISS, C. H. (1973). "Between the cup and the lip . . ." Evaluation, 1(2): 49-55.

12

FOLLOW-UPS, LETDOWNS, AND SLEEPERS:
THE TIME DIMENSION IN POLICY EVALUATION

LESTER M. SALAMON

Duke University

In recent years, policy evaluation has come to be the new "philosopher's stone" for the solution of public problems, just as "coordination" was before it.[1] The American public, so the argument goes, has grown disenchanted with government for the very good reason that government has not performed. Programs are created but then stagnate as careerist ambitions frustrate original goals and then block efforts to hold the programs up to any test of performance. "The great questions of government," Daniel Patrick Moynihan thus informs us (1969: 145), have to do with not "what *will* work, but what *does* work." What is "urgently" needed, Peter Drucker concurs (1969: 16), is an ongoing process of evaluation that will first insist on "the clear definition of the results a policy is expected to produce" and then provide a "ruthless examination of results against these expectations." If programs were thus regularly and systematically evaluated and the results of the evaluation fed back into program design, so the argument goes, overall performance

AUTHOR'S NOTE: *Portions of this article are adapted from a paper delivered at the 1974 American Political Science Association Convention entitled "The Time Dimension in Policy Evaluation: The Case of the New Deal Land Reform Experiments." Under the same title this paper is being published as No. 04-039 of the Sage Professional Papers in American Politics.*

would improve and governmental programs would finally begin to "work." For some enthusiasts, in fact, evaluation almost comes to be more important than the programs themselves. "At this point," former HEW Secretary Robert Finch thus told the House Education and Labor Committee in 1969, "evaluation is probably more important than the addition of new laws to an already extensive list of educational statutes."

Appealing though this argument is, however, it fails to acknowledge the serious difficulties that impede and frustrate evaluative research. As a team of Urban Institute researchers recently concluded (Wholey et al., 1970: 5), "the art and techniques of evaluation are indeed underdeveloped." This is so, moreover, not simply because of inattention, but also because of a variety of inherent dilemmas built into the whole process of evaluation that collectively interact to make evaluative studies, in the words of one practitioner, "one of the more difficult ventures in the social sciences" (Mann, 1965: 177).[2] The simple prescription to subject programs to a "ruthless examination of results against expectations" turns out, therefore, to be an immensely complicated assignment.

Perhaps nothing illustrates this better than the problem of coping with the time dimension in evaluative research. Virtually every student of policy evaluation has acknowledged that the real impact of governmental programs may not appear until after a considerable period of time. In his pioneering evaluation of the Volunteer Work Camps in 1952, for example, Henry Riecken noted (1952: 22) that "all experience with action programs indicates that their real effects cannot be gauged without considering the long-run forces that may support, negate, or even reverse the immediate effects." Nor have more recent writers forgotten the point.[3] Yet, when it comes to actual practice, these warnings too often come to nought. Constrained by limited budgets, pressured by anxious administrators, and eager to produce results in time to influence program contents, evaluators rarely have the luxury of assessing program impacts over a sufficiently long period of time. In much of the policy evaluation work, in fact, "long term" has been functionally redefined as "six months to a year," and systematic, experimental evaluations covering more than a year or two are extremely rare.[4]

While this widespread neglect of the time dimension in actual evaluative research is understandable given the pressures on evaluators, however, it is also potentially dangerous, for it can lead to the systematic neglect of important program impacts and thus leave the public and policy makers alike the captives of far more limited—and frequently negative—early program consequences. The Great Society programs of the 1960s may be suffering today from just such a premature rush to judgment. (See, for example, Moynihan, 1969; Banfield, 1969; for a critique of evaluations of OEO on these grounds, see Rossi, 1973.) In fact, much of the current malaise about governmental nonperformance—at least among the literati—may really be a product of this critical shortcoming in existing evaluative research. Alice Rivlin (1970: 86), for example, points to "the lack of information on the same individuals over time" as a prime reason for our general inability to establish significant relationships between governmental activities and the improvement of health, education, and social services. Gary Orfield reaches a similar conclusion from a review of studies evaluating the impact of school integration. Notes Orfield (1973: 4):

> The most basic problem about the existing research . . . is its narrow focus on the short-term impact of desegregation on cognitive achievement. If desegregation really brings about basic change in the educational process, it would appear in the educational program and in the attitudes of teachers, principals, and students in individual schools. Such basic change would not likely come suddenly, or while the controversy was still raging.

What makes this situation especially serious, moreover, is that the impact of this widespread failure to account for the time dimension in evaluative research may not be neutral. Rather, it may systematically bias the results in favor of some types of programs and against others. Indeed, it may discredit public initiatives wholesale. To the extent this occurs, the policy evaluation function will have been transformed into an inherently conservative one—not just, as Peter Rossi has noted (1970: 80-81), because "all that can be evaluated is what has been tried," but also because too narrow a time frame or too little sensitivity to the incipient stages of social change can make immensely promising programs appear to be ineffective duds.

Despite the importance of the time dimension in evaluative research, however, the subject has so far received little more than passing mention. The purpose of this article is to remedy this, at least in part, by examining the "time dimension" problem more closely and thus sensitizing evaluators more effectively to its implications. To do so, we first explore some general theoretical notions about the impact of time on social action efforts and about the consequences this has for evaluative research. Against this backdrop we then review the results of a recent longitudinal evaluation undertaken by this author that illustrates exceptionally well the importance of the time dimension in evaluative research. Finally, in a concluding section, we offer some suggestions, based on both our theoretical observations and our detailed case study, about how evaluators can best cope with the time dimension problem given the constraints likely to continue to surround their work.

THE TIME DIMENSION IN SOCIAL ACTION PROGRAMS: A THEORETICAL OVERVIEW

Most students of policy evaluation would readily agree that program impacts can decrease, increase, or remain the same with the passage of time. The policy evaluation literature provides little theoretical guidance, however, about which of these results to expect under what circumstances, or about what time perspective is appropriate for what type of program (see, for example, Suchman, 1967: 100-102). If we are to cope with the time dimension problem in evaluative research, therefore, two crucial theoretical issues must be addressed early on: first, are there different types of time-related effects that can be distinguished for analytical purposes? and, second, is it possible to relate different types of time-related effects to particular kinds of social action programs?

So far as the first issue is concerned, what limited attention the time dimension has received in the existing evaluation literature has focused almost exclusively on a single type of time-related effect —namely, the "staying power" of program results. The assumption here is that program results will diminish over time and a "letdown" effect appears as participants forget what they have learned. Underlying this assumption, typically, is a kind of medical analogy that conceives of social action intervention as a form of "treatment" designed to cure a group of "clients," but which frequently does so only partially and temporarily. "Follow-up" inquiries are thus necessary to determine how durable the treatment really is or how rapidly, if at all, the effects wear off. Closely related to this is the so-called "Hawthorne effect," i.e., the frequently observed tendency of behavior to change simply as a result of doing something new, regardless of what that something is. Where this occurs, the crucial question again is how durable the behavior change detected is and when, if at all, some kind of reversal will occur.[5]

In addition to these staying-power or letdown effects, however, two other types of time-related impacts can also be distinguished for analytical purposes. The first are what Hyman (1962: 262) calls "latent effects," i.e., effects that are apparent during a program's operation but that *increase* with the passage of time as the program's impact sinks in. The second are what Suchman (1967: 40) calls "sleeper effects," effects which do not even appear during a program's operation but which show up at a later time.

From the point of view of policy evaluation, latent effects and staying power effects present similar problems. Both call for follow-up studies to determine the rate of change in more or less observable program impacts—the former on the assumption that such impacts will wear off or be forgotten, the latter on the assumption that they will sink in and become operational. Since the *rate of change* is what is important, however, the follow-up can be accomplished almost any reasonable time after completion of the treatment—albeit, for reasons we will elaborate below, somewhat more time will probably be necessary to detect latent effects than staying-power effects.

Far different is the situation with regard to sleeper effects. Here program effects are unlikely even to make their appearance for many months or years. Not just the *amount* of impact, but also the *kind* is therefore likely to be sensitive to the passage of time. Evaluators unaware of the likelihood of sleeper effects may consequently disregard whole ranges of program impacts in designing their evaluation instruments and thus thoroughly misjudge program results.[6]

Given the varying implications that these different types of time-related impacts have for evaluative research, it is especially important to determine whether there are theoretical grounds for expecting that particular types of time-related effects will be associated with different types of programs. In his pioneering evaluation of the Volunteer Work Camp program in 1952, Henry Riecken offered one clue that is of considerable assistance in conceptualizing this issue. "Delayed responses" to program initiatives are likely, Riecken suggested (1952: 22), where opportunities are lacking to put program-imparted benefits to work, where the environment confronting a program participant "simply does not provide him with instances in which the change can become evident." What this implies is that the more the exercise of program benefits is dependent on factors external to the participant, the more likely are delayed responses or sleeper effects.

But this dependence of program benefits on external factors is, in turn, a function of the approach to social change embodied in the program and in the model the evaluator brings to the task of assessing that program. Broadly speaking, two such approaches or models can be distinguished for analytical purposes (Coleman, 1972: 61-74). The first identifies changes in the skills, attitudes, or outlook of identifiable program participants as the key to desired program effects. The assumption here is that something about the individual himself is wrong or in need of improvement and that the desired change can be accomplished by operating at the individual level. (For the theoretical bases of this view, see Coleman, 1972: 167-170; Hagen, 1962; McClelland, 1961.) Thus, in the federal antipoverty programs launched in the early 1960s, for example, most of the actual program activity focused not on changes in social structure but on changes in the values and beliefs of the poor. This approach was premised on the so-called poverty cycle or "culture of poverty" theory, which attributed poverty to the allegedly dysfunctional values of the poor. Even though the broader social situation was acknowledged to be the ultimate cause of the poverty, unemployment, poor school performance, and delinquency at which these programs aimed, the prevailing theory viewed the outlook and attitudes of the target population (the poor) as the proximate cause and the one at which intervention should be aimed. As one analyst summarized the theory (Noble, 1970: 451), "dysfunctional societal conditions are thought to act upon affected individuals and groups by producing subjective anomie, alienation, variant value orientations, and an impoverished self-concept, all of which, in turn, incline the individual toward deviant behavior." (See also Merton, 1957; Miller, 1958; Schneiderman, 1964; Banfield, 1969.) The thrust of this theory, as Marris and Rein note (1967: 39), was "to leave the responsibility for their poverty with the poor themselves." Poverty thus comes to be seen not as the result of some fundamental conflict of interest among social groups that is firmly rooted in the prevailing social structure, but rather as the product of the perverse cultural norms of the poor. To quote Marris and Rein again (1967: 40), "the theory . . . seems to assume that the poor must face up to the demands of their society, rather than the other way about."

In contrast to this first type of theory, which finds the locus of necessary changes in the so-called "target population" or "clients," the second type stresses the need for changes in the social *conditions* in which these individuals find themselves. Under this theory,

societal conditions and structures are identified as the obstacles to
desired results, and programs are designed to alter these conditions in
the expectation that individual behavior will respond in due course.
In the context of the poverty program of the 1960s, for example,
this view found expression among the advocates of "maximum
feasible participation" by the poor, who contended that the plight of
the poor was a direct consequence of the vested interests and
superior political power of the nonpoor. "Poverty means not only
lacking money but also lacking power," noted Saul Alinsky (1965:
47), perhaps the best-known advocate of this view. Only by
generating political power, therefore, could the poor alter the
structure of community influence and thus open up opportunities
currently denied them—for example, by breaking the dependence of
the social service agencies on the local middle class. Noted one
adherent to this view (Brooks, 1965: 31):

> A well-conceived community action program is, in a very real sense, *a
> social movement with far-reaching implications for existing patterns of
> community life*. . . . It calls for new voices in the process whereby
> community decisions are made; it proclaims the need for more equitable
> means of allocating community resources. [Italics added]

As the example of the poverty program suggests, no social action
program incorporates either of these two approaches to the complete
exclusion of the other. Yet, it seems reasonable to expect that to the
extent that a program primarily reflects the first approach outlined
above and concentrates on imparting certain values or skills to
particular individuals in a target population, either latent or staying
power effects are most likely. The former should occur where the
program seeks to alter its clients' personality or values, since such
impacts take time to become integrated into an individual's
preexisting personality structure, even though traces may become
evident at once. The latter, or staying power effects, should occur
where the program seeks to provide particular skills or information,
since skills and information are even more easily forgotten than
learned.

By contrast, programs that embody more of the second theory
outlined above and that focus primarily on changing the external
social and political conditions confronting program participants are
more likely to have significant sleeper effects calling for special
attention to the time dimension by evaluators. This is so for at least
two reasons. In the first place, general social arrangements are

complex organisms inherently resistant to major change. Even if change were welcomed, therefore, it would take time to work its way through the system. In the second place, however, social change is frequently not welcomed. Those in positions of greatest power and status in a system are likely to resist innovations that seriously disturb the status quo. In Everett M. Rogers' terms, such elites serve as "gatekeepers" in controlling the flow of innovations in a system. While they may accommodate themselves to "functioning innovations," which do not threaten the system's social structure, they are likely to resist restructuring innovations (Rogers, 1973: 79; see also Arensberg and Niehoff, 1964: 98-100). To the extent that such elites are interested in, and capable of, performing this role, therefore, planned social change will be unlikely. For such changes to take place under these circumstances, they must take place inadvertently through the introduction of ostensibly "functioning innovations" that have second generation "restructuring" results, a not uncommon occurrence.[7] For the advocate of planned efforts to produce substantive changes in social conditions, the task is therefore to disguise his intentions in otherwise benign-looking program activities while confidently awaiting the day when the true restructuring effects of these activities become manifest. This was the case, for example, with the "maximum feasible participation" provision that many observers credit with whatever structural changes were produced by the poverty program (Marris and Rein, 1973: 259-261; Vanecko, 1970; Kramer, 1968). This provision would never have been adopted, Moynihan (1969: 79-95) assures us, had it been clear what the advocates had in mind by it.

Programs embodying this "time bomb" theory of social change can produce negative sleeper effects as well as positive ones, of course. If the time bomb explodes too early or, in some circumstances, too vigorously, it can trigger a backlash that more than cancels out its positive contributions.[8] Indeed, it is this characteristic that makes such programs so exceptionally difficult to evaluate fairly in the time frame normally available; for, to be effective in the face of powerful opposition, the effects of such programs should not become apparent until they are irreversible, i.e., until they can survive the destruction of the program that initially produced them. Beyond that, such effects are unlikely to be reflected prominently in the stated objectives of the program. Evaluators who, following approved procedure, take their cues about program goals primarily from these stated objectives and design their instruments for measuring program results accordingly may consequently miss some of the most important program payoffs.

In short, there is a whole range of social action initiatives the real effects of which are likely to be significantly delayed. Unless evaluators devise ways to tap these sleeper effects or "delayed responses," this whole range of initiatives may be systematically and improperly discredited. At a minimum, this requires sensitizing evaluators more effectively to the likelihood of such delayed effects for certain kinds of programs and to the form that such effects can be expected to take. Beyond that, it requires that in the design of evaluations and in the theoretical literature more attention be paid to suggesting how program activities will affect the broader social structure, both immediately and over time.

LONGITUDINAL EVALUATION: A DEMONSTRATION[9]

Perhaps the best way to illustrate these points and to underline the importance of the time dimension in evaluative research is through a concrete example. For this purpose, the New Deal's "resettlement program" is an ideal choice. Under this program, which began in 1934 and extended until 1943, the federal government, through the Resettlement Administration (RA), the Farm Security Administration (FSA), and two other New Deal agencies, purchased approximately 1,865,000 acres of land in almost 200 locales across the country and established a series of supervised farming and/or industrial communities. Of these 200 projects, 141 were primarily agricultural and were designed to equip sharecroppers and tenants with the technical and managerial skills necessary for successful operation as farmowners and then to sell the land to these farmers on long-term low-interest mortgages.[10] In the South, where most of these farm projects were concentrated, this social action initiative represented nothing less than an experiment in land reform, as large plantations were reorganized as cooperative farms or, more commonly, broken up into family farm units complete with improved housing and necessary livestock and equipment. Moreover, at least 13 of these community projects were reserved for blacks, thus redeeming, albeit on a meager scale, the Reconstruction dream of "forty acres and a mule" by distributing some 92,000 acres of land on quite favorable terms to about 1,150 black tenant families. An additional 1,117 black farm families participated in 19 other "scattered farm" projects in the South that yielded an additional 70,000 to 80,000 acres of land to formerly landless black share-croppers. Despite its pitifully small size in comparison to the scope of the problem it was addressing, here was a bold experiment in social reform, a fascinating alternative to the public relief mode of assistance to the poor.

Most important for our purposes, the resettlement program seems to be just the kind of undertaking that our theory suggests is likely to generate significant sleeper effects and, therefore, to call for special attention to the "time dimension" by evaluators. By providing access to decent agricultural land on generous terms, the resettlement program was, after all, working directly on the prevailing rural social structure by releasing the depressed tenant class from the enforced passivity of the sharecrop system. This was especially important for blacks, moreover, since access to land-ownership was typically not available from any other source, yet land was the key to whatever independence and autonomy blacks could hope to attain in the rural South.

If the resettlement program produced any long-term effects, however, they were never charted. To the contrary, like many social action programs, the resettlement program quickly encountered stiff opposition. Indeed, as the most radical initiative of the New Deal relief effort, resettlement served as the lightning rod for antagonism to the New Deal generally. "Of all the programs of the FSA," notes the author of the most thorough study of this phase of the New Deal, "the resettlement projects attracted the most uniform verdict of failure" (Baldwin, 1968: 215). Critics complained bitterly about the alleged "socialistic" and "communitarian" character of the projects and their presumed excessive costs. Especially irksome was the handful of projects run as "collective farms," though more general congressional hostility was also aroused by the tendency of FSA officials to grant government loans to down-and-out tenants unable to meet traditional credit standards. Once the President's attention turned toward preparations for war in the early 1940s, therefore, congressional critics got their chance. In 1943, the House Agriculture Committee created a select committee to investigate the program and, with the aid of the House Appropriations Committee, managed to bring it to a halt. By late 1945, therefore, all but 232,000 acres of the usable farm land incorporated in the various projects had been sold, most of it as individual farming units (House Appropriations Committee, 1946: 1390). Within another 15 months, the New Deal's land reform experiments had come to an end, and the Farm Security Administration soon after reorganized as the Farmer's Home Administration with a far different mission in life.

Despite the vigor of the attack, however, the case against the resettlement program was not based on any solid body of evaluative research. And it was certainly not based on any evaluation that took account of the long-term implications and impacts of the experiments, as academic critics at the time readily conceded.[11] Like other New Deal programs, experimental and nonexperimental alike, all we really know about the resettlement program was that it existed.[12] Whether it was more or less costly than traditional relief, whether it produced benefits that justified its costs, and whether its long-term effects differed from its apparent short-term impacts were all questions that had hardly been raised, let alone systematically answered, when the outpouring of congressional hostility reached its crescendo in 1943 and forced the abandonment of the program by the federal government. "At some future date," reported a Harvard economist to War Food Administrator Chester C. Davis at the time, "it will be highly desirable to have a review and analysis made of this whole undertaking to see what was really accomplished and what lessons can be derived from the experiments" (cited in Baldwin, 1968: 216). Yet, 25 years later, historian Sydney Baldwin was still bewailing the absence of any systematic evaluation of the important resettlement experience. Noted Baldwin (1968: 216):

> Since men are not guinea pigs and society is not a laboratory, students of politics and public administration are generally denied the benefit of controlled experimentation. Yet, the resettlement administration did offer a *unique experimental opportunity whose lessons have not yet, a generation later, been fully evaluated, let alone applied.* [Italics added]

In an effort to remedy this situation, we undertook a detailed evaluation of the resettlement program in 1973-1974, focusing especially on the black sharecroppers who constituted the program's most needy and disadvantaged participants. As with any policy evaluation, this involved three basic steps: first, clarifying the goals of the program and the criteria by which success should be gauged; second, devising ways to translate these goals and criteria into measurable form and measuring the results; and, third, comparing the progress of program participants to that of a suitable control group in order to differentiate effects due to the program from those due to extraneous causes. Because the 30-year evaluation period made these tasks even more difficult than normally, it may be useful to review briefly how we coped with them before presenting the results.

EVALUATION DESIGN

Defining Success: Program Goals

Like most public programs, the resettlement experiment began its life burdened by a host of official and unofficial goals and expectations. This common problem was intensified in its case, however, by the fact that Congress had never explicitly authorized the program. Rather, the resettlement program operated under the somewhat doubtful authority of the loosely worded Federal Emergency Relief Act of 1933 and secured its funds out of general relief monies, largely at administrative discretion. The program was, therefore, very much an administrative creation, which facilitated experimentation but complicates evaluation.

From the outset, in fact, three distinct images of what the resettlement experiment was to accomplish vied for official attention. The first was that of Resettlement Administration head Rexford Tugwell and his imaginative assistants, who saw the resettlement program as the entering wedge of a broad-gauged agricultural and social policy designed to retire hundreds of thousands of acres of submarginal land and resettle the displaced "fatigued farmers" on newly organized farm or farm-and-factory communities organized around essentially cooperative principles. The program was thus to serve the twin goals of eliminating agricultural overproduction and instilling a new cooperative ethic in the countryside (Tugwell, 1936, 1937; Conkin, 1959: 102, 160, 202).

Such schemes fell on deaf ears in Congress, however, which condoned the resettlement program only as a means to reverse the alarming trend toward farm tenancy among the traditional family farmer class. Not cooperative farm communities or even significant social reform through the elevation of the *chronic* tenant class, but, rather, as Senator Bankhead (Democrat, Alabama) put it, "the restoration of that small yeoman class which has been the backbone of every great civilization" (quoted in Conkin, 1959: 87) was thus the purpose Congress seems to have had in mind.

The third image, espoused by such RA/FSA officials as Assistant Administrator Will Alexander, a long-time Southern moderate, essentially accepted the Congressional view that creating viable family farms was the goal of the program, but went beyond this in two ways: first, by stressing the importance of involving the submerged rural tenantry in the program, and, second, by recognizing that for this class land acquisition meant not only economic viability but also independence, security, a degree of freedom, and the opportunity to develop the pride of ownership and to gain a greater measure of control over one's destiny. The goal of resettlement for Alexander and his supporters, therefore, was not just the creation of family farms, but the conversion of down-and-out, chronic tenants into "self-reliant individuals" (Alexander, 1936: 536; see also C. B. Baldwin testimony, House Agriculture Committee, 1943: 7).

Given the narrowness of the congressionally defined goal and the constraints that limited funds and scope placed in the way of achieving the macroagricultural and social-policy goals envisioned by Tugwell, this moderate image seemed the most reasonable one to use in evaluating the impact of the resettlement program on its black participants. Accordingly, we undertook to determine the extent to which the resettlement program helped create a cadre of "self-reliant individuals" among its black participants.

Measuring Success: Program Impact Measures

To go from broad definitions of program objectives to measurable criteria for gauging success in achieving those objectives, a body of theory is necessary.[13] Fortunately, this is available for the resettlement program in the rich sociological and anthropological literature on post-Civil War Southern society (Davis et al., 1941; Dollard, 1957; Powdermaker, 1943; Myrdal, 1944; Moody, 1968; Raper, 1936; Woofter, 1930). What this literature makes clear is that landownership for blacks meant an opportunity to break the pervasive chain of dependence that kept them in total subservience and that sustained the prevailing two-caste system at the core of Southern social life. To the extent that the resettlement program worked as this theory would suggest, therefore, this should be evident in three kinds of indicators: first, the success of the recipients in holding on to their land; second, improved well-being, especially in psychological and social terms; and third, greater civic involvement and political participation, including involvement in early civil rights activities. (On this latter point see U.S. Civil Rights

Commission, 1968, and Salamon and Van Evera, 1973). In addition, the recent literature stressing the importance of "class culture" in perpetuating poverty suggested a fourth indicator: the degree of "future orientation" (see, for example, Banfield, 1969).

To measure these four dimensions of program impact, three different methods were used. First, a detailed search of county land records for eight of the thirteen known all-black resettlement projects was undertaken to trace what happened to each parcel of land conveyed to blacks under the project. The fact that the major benefit imparted by this program was title to land thus eased the evaluation task, since land leaves behind a permanent documentary record in the form of local deed and mortgage files. Following these title searches, face-to-face interviews were conducted with a sample of 178 project participants still in control of their land during the summer of 1974; the purpose of the interviews was to try to measure income, economic status, net worth, extent of civic participation, future orientation, and general outlook on life. Finally, we tapped a unique body of medical and general economic data collected from the black population in one of the project counties by a community-controlled health research project in collaboration with a University of Illinois research team.

Controlling for Non-Program Impacts: The Attribution Problem

Probably the most difficult task in any evaluation is to differentiate program-related impacts from impacts due to extraneous factors. Ideally, this is done by simultaneously collecting information on an experimental group and a control group that mirrors it. For an evaluation of a program now thirty years old, however, such ideal experimental conditions were impossible to attain. Consequently, we were forced to rely on next-best improvisations. In particular, we employed two sets of control groups against which to compare FSA participants. The first consisted of black landowners generally in the states where resettlement projects were located. Through Census of Agriculture data, it is possible to determine how black landowners fared as a group during the 30-year evaluation period and thus to determine whether the better land, technical assistance, and community context that the resettlement program made available to black participants affected their success in retaining their land. The second control group consisted of a sample of tenant farmers now living in the project counties. These tenants serve as a proxy for the group from which the resettlement program participants were themselves drawn—i.e., the tenants living in the project counties *in the mid-1930s*. In fact, by using the *current* tenants, we probably *underestimate* program impacts, since the tenants who remained in these counties as of 1974 tended to be the more successful tenants, many of whom also served as equipment operators on their landlords' farms or held other off-farm jobs. By comparing the experiences of the FSA landlords to those of these tenants, therefore, we can gain what is probably a conservative estimate of the impact that the resettlement program had on its participants. Accordingly, we interviewed a sample of 100 tenants in the project counties, using a slightly modified version of the project-participant interview instrument.[14]

RESULTS

What emerges from these various sources of data is a rather dramatic demonstration of the importance of the time dimension in evaluative research. So far as land retention is concerned, for example, 283 of the 556 black families that secured land in the eight resettlement projects examined here still held this land 30 years later. Altogether, about 17,000 of the 41,000 acres of project land still remained in the hands of the original participants after 30 years. This is roughly proportional to the decline in the number of black landowners and in the acreage of black-owned land recorded by the Census of Agriculture for the five states in which these eight projects were located. However, the Census figures cover only the period up to 1969, five years earlier than our land search figures. More importantly, they record the ownership of blacks as a group, rather than of particular individuals. The appropriate comparison, therefore, is not between the Census figures and the original program participants, but between the Census figures and the extent of black retention of former project land regardless of whether the land is still in the hands of an original participant or another black who acquired the land from an original participant. This is important since many of the original participants have now reached retirement age or have died. The loss of land by these original participants should, therefore, not be taken as a sign of program failure if new black owners have taken over. When this comparison is made, the results are striking. As Table 1 notes, while the total number of black landowners in the states where our eight projects were located declined by 59 percent

Table 1. CHANGES IN BLACK LANDOWNERSHIP IN EIGHT FORMER
RESETTLEMENT PROJECTS AND IN STATES WHERE THEY
ARE LOCATED

	Number		Percent	Acres		Percent
	1945/1943	1969/1974	Change	1945/1943	1969/1974	Change
All Black Land-owners in Ala., Ark., La., Miss., N.C.	73,880	30,002	−59.4	4,584,829	2,073,897	−54.6
Black Landowners on land encom-passed in 8 former black resettle-ment projects	556	573	+ 3.1	41,247	29,968	−27.3

NOTE: The 1945 and 1969 dates are from the agricultural censuses and apply to the figures
for all landowners. The 1943 and 1974 dates apply to the FSA landowners–1943 being the
year most titles were transferred and 1974 being the year when our title searches were
conducted.

between 1945 and 1969, the number of blacks who own resettlement project land actually increased by 3.1 percent, even after
adjusting for divisions among heirs. Similarly, while the total
black-owned acreage in these states declined by 55 percent, the total
black-owned acreage on former project lands declined by a substantially smaller 27 percent, or half as much. In other words, the
resettlement program seems to have succeeded in creating a series of
small rural islands effectively given over to black ownership on a
long-term basis. In the process, it seems to have contributed to an
absolute increase in the number of black landowners that contrasts
sharply with the substantial decline in these landowners throughout
the South.

To what extent, however, did this contribute to the creation of a
cadre of "self-reliant individuals?" Our "well-being" and "civic
participation" measures provide an important part of the answer. So
far as the former is concerned, the results are somewhat mixed. The
project landowners interviewed do not seem to be more prosperous
than the tenants, at least in terms of reported annual incomes (see
Table 2). However, since the project participants were considerably
older than the tenants and therefore more commonly retired, current
income figures may be a poor index of well-being. Indeed, when we
look at measures of net worth as reflected in ownership of particular
assets, it is clear that the landowners have been considerably more
successful than the tenants in acquiring the critical accouterments of

Table 2. ANNUAL FAMILY INCOME REPORTED BY SAMPLE OF
FSA PARTICIPANTS AND BLACK TENANT FARMERS

Family Income	FSA Participants n = 173	Tenants n = 82
Under $2,000	45.7%	41.5%
$2,000-$5,000	38.7	37.8
Over $5,000	15.5	20.7
TOTAL	99.9%	100.0%

a modest, middle-class life-style, at least by rural standards—a home,
a car, a refrigerator, an automatic washing machine, and a television
set (see Table 3). Moreover, when we look beyond the physical and
monetary manifestations of well-being at the emotional and psychological ones, additional evidence of the long-run impact of the
resettlement experience on participant well-being is apparent. For
example, data generated by the Health Research Project in Holmes
County, Mississipppi, indicates that the resettlement project participants in that county are in better nutritional health and have
lower levels of hypertension than blacks generally in the county,
particularly those owning no land (Shimkin, 1974). Our interview
data seem to confirm this. Tenant interview responses reflect a
significantly greater sense of pessimism and timidity than was
apparent in FSA-participant responses. For example, 49 percent of
the tenants registered agreement with the statement, "These days, a
person can't really trust anyone but himself," compared to only 31
percent of the FSA landowners. By the same token, despite the
prevailing norms favoring political participation, close to a third of
the tenants expressed disinterest in participation and a sense of

Table 3. OWNERSHIP OF VARIOUS ASSETS BY FSA PARTICIPANTS
AND BLACK TENANTS

	Percent of Total Who Own Recorded Asset	
	FSA Participants n = 178	Tenants n = 93
Tractor	46.1	29.0
Truck	40.3	32.3
Car	70.2	59.1
Refrigerator	97.2	93.5
Washing machine	82.0	53.8
Telephone	88.8	53.8
Television set	96.6	82.8
Cattle (5 head or more)	21.1	8.6

complete powerlessness, compared to only 12 percent of the FSA landowners. Finally, when asked if people ever come to them for help with their problems, only 30 percent of the tenants could answer yes, and only 4 percent could provide examples of the help they provided. By contrast, about half of the FSA participants indicated they had been of assistance to others; and most could cite examples.

Finally, there is some evidence in our data that these manifestations of well-being carried over to project participants' children, permitting them to adjust more successfully than the tenants' children to the tensions and problems of migration. Of the 597 FSA-participants' children over 18 years old and in the labor force, for example, 42 percent are in white collar occupations. By contrast, only 25 percent of the comparable group of tenant children hold such jobs (see Table 4).

Even more dramatic evidence of the impact the resettlement program had on the black tenants who participated is apparent in our civic participation indicators. In the first place, despite the prohibitions against even vicarious involvement in the world of politics through the news media (Silver, 1963), FSA participants turn out to be considerably more in touch than the current tenants with the world outside their farms through formal channels of communication like newspapers and journals. Beyond that, they are much more intimately involved in the organizational lives of their communities than are the tenants, playing important leadership roles in local church and fraternal organizations (see Table 5). When the civil rights movement came along, therefore, the FSA landowners emerged as crucial local contacts, precisely as the theory predicted. As Table 6 reveals, the FSA landowners outdistanced the tenants on virtually every indicator of civil rights movement involvement, and the disparities between the two groups was greater the more dangerous the activity. Not only were the FSA-landowners involved in the civil

Table 4. OCCUPATIONS OF CHILDREN OF FSA PARTICIPANTS
         AND BLACK TENANTS

Occupation	FSA Participants n = 597*	Black Tenants n = 261*
Professional, technical, managerial	28.6%	17.2%
Other white collar	13.2	7.3
Blue collar, labor, unemployed	58.1	75.5
TOTAL	99.9%	100.0%

*Includes only children 18 years old and over who are in the labor force.

Table 5. INVOLVEMENT OF BLACK FSA PARTICIPANTS AND TENANTS
IN LOCAL ORGANIZATIONAL LIFE

Type of Involvement	Resettlement Participants n = 178	Tenants n = 93
Officer or deacon in church	59.0%	23.7%
Membership in at least one club or social organization	68.0	32.3
Officer in club	26.3	5.4
Membership in farm cooperative	43.5	8.6

rights struggle more extensively than the tenants, but also they were involved earlier. For example, close to 60 percent of the FSA landowners challenged the local prohibitions on black voting during the critical period prior to passage of the 1965 Voting Rights Act, compared to only 18.5 percent of the tenants.

What emerges from these data, therefore, is rather strong support for the view that the New Deal land reform experiments had a significant sleeper effect in creating an important, black, landed middle class independent and confident enough to shoulder the burden of challenging the two-caste system once conditions became ripe. Freed from the dependency of the sharecrop system and invested with the prestige customarily accorded the landowner in rural society, the FSA landowners emerged as central pillars of local black organizational life, limited though it was. When the civil rights movement appeared, moreover, they were available to give it local roots and nurture it through the critical incubation period prior to formal federal involvement. The resettlement program thus seems to have had a substantial impact on the level of civic participation of its beneficiaries. However, this impact, anticipated in the implicit goals of the agency, at least as conceptualized by some of its personnel,

Table 6. EXTENT OF INVOLVEMENT OF FSA PROJECT LANDOWNERS
AND BLACK TENANTS IN VARIOUS CIVIL RIGHTS ACTIVITIES
RANKED BY DEGREE OF "DANGEROUSNESS"

Activity	FSA Project Landowners n = 177	Tenants n = 91
Attended civil rights organization meetings	73.4%	39.6%
Joined a civil rights organization	49.2	19.8
Worked on Voter Registration	24.9	6.6
Signed a petition protesting actions by local whites	25.4	2.2
Ran for political office	19.2	7.7
Had an outside civil rights worker living in home	12.4	1.1

was nevertheless dormant throughout much of the early postprogram period, emerging only after more than a decade had elapsed.

One final potential resettlement program impact that deserves scrutiny has to do with the effect of the experiment on the participants' orientation toward time. Banfield (1958; 1969: 45-66) and others have argued that the poor are chronically afflicted by a preoccupation with the present that makes them unwilling to resist present gratifications and thus unable to increase future benefits —especially the benefits of escaping from poverty. The land reform experiments of the New Deal, by contrast, were premised on the conviction that whatever present-orientation might be exhibited by the poor was more a consequence of the situation in which the poor found themselves than it was a consequence of some deep-seated and irreversible cultural trait. Take a sharecropper schooled in the principles of dependence and give him access to land, went the theory, and the result will be a citizen as thrifty, responsible, and "future-oriented" as any middle-class burgher, so long as enough time is allowed to elapse for the curative effects of opportunity and responsibility to do their work.

When we test these alternative theories against the evidence generated by our questionnaires, some curious findings emerge. In the first place, the tenants and FSA landowners seem to have strikingly similar orientations toward time. Both groups seem doubtful, on balance, about the proposition that it is better to "live pretty much for today," and both are overwhelmingly in agreement that "blacks do have a chance to make something for themselves in the South." At least so far as avowed values are concened, therefore, there does not seem to be any class culture at work here at all.

When we look behind these avowals at actual behavior, however, some significant differences appear. For example, some 43 percent of the FSA landowners indicated they had purchased an encyclopedia, compared to only 29 percent of the tenants. This is significant since, in the rural South, the encyclopedia salesman is a kind of "litmus paper" of class culture, testing the extent to which families are willing to sacrifice their hard-earned money for the future education of their children. By the same token, the landowner children turn out to have a clear edge over the tenant children in terms of amount of education received, even when we restrict our attention to children over 18. About 55 percent of the landowner children completed high school, compared to about 40 percent of the tenant children. Whether this is a product of variations in cultural predispositions or lack of opportunity is difficult to say. However, *both* owners and tenants expressed the same high degree of confidence in education and indicated the same level of effort to encourage their children to remain in school, at least through high school. The greater success of the landowners in this respect may consequently not reflect any difference in values or attitudes on their part, but rather the greater freedom and more substantial resources that control over their own land gave the landowners to put these common values into practice. To the extent that this is true, it seems reasonable to credit the New Deal land reforms with a real contribution not only to the original generation of blacks who secured land under them but to their children as well.

SUMMARY: BENEFITS VS. COST

The New Deal land reform experiments that were vilified and challenged as wasteful expenditures of the taxpayers' money thus appear, from the perspective of 30 years, as quite impressive social action undertakings. To be sure, the projects provided no overall cure for the problems of agricultural overproduction and thus can hardly be defended as central elements in a national agricultural policy. But as elements of an enlightened welfare policy aimed at alleviating the problems of chronic rural poverty, they have much to recommend them. At least for the blacks who participated, the resettlement program had a substantial, long-term, positive impact, creating a permanent cadre of black middle-class landowners in possession of decent agricultural land and thus able to escape some of the chronic poverty and the debilitating dependence so common to black sharecroppers in the South. Partially insulated from the pressures of economic dependence, these farmowners functioned as strategic links in the spread of democracy in the South during the 1960s and stand as examples of the utility of equity-based or self-help approaches to the problems of the poor. The one serious drawback was that by restricting its recipients to 80- to 100-acre plots, the program failed to provide them with the wherewithal to take a very active part in the mammoth technological changes that have swept Southern agriculture in the past two decades. Yet it has left behind a base upon which larger scale, black, land-based enterprises could be built.

These benefits are all the more impressive, furthermore, when viewed in relation to the costs of the program. Based on figures for six of the eight projects examined here, the total costs of the resettlement program was an average of $2,273 per family over the five-year period that the experiment was in operation, including the cost of construction of community facilities, many of which were ultimately deeded to local governments. If we deduct these community facility costs, since they are not directly related to the development of the farming units, the overall cost of the program comes to the grand total of $460 per family. Here, certainly, is social reform on the cheap. Even if we ignore the savings to the public in terms of foregone welfare costs, the resettlement program thus seems to have been well worth its cost once the true long-term benefits are considered. A social action program generally judged to have been a failure within a half decade of its founding thus appears, now that the long-term impact is visible, to have been a fascinating—if small scale—success.

CONCLUSIONS: COPING WITH THE TIME DIMENSION

The lesson that this example of longitudinal policy evaluation holds for policy evaluators generally should be clear. Unless we take seriously our own exhortations to acknowledge the importance of the time dimension in evaluative research, our work is likely to be seriously flawed conceptually even if rigorously sound methodologically. More than that, there is a danger that policy evaluators will become handmaidens of conservative powers-that-be, since the neglect of the time dimension can systematically bias results against programs that pose the most serious threat to the status quo.

What, then, can be done? Given the pressures they are under and the methodological dilemmas they face, how can policy evaluators escape this fate? Indeed, what type of time frame is appropriate for which programs? One year? Three years? Ten years?

Given the existing state of the art and the benign neglect to which the time dimension problem has been treated, the most we can offer here are some more or less arbitrary rules of thumb. In particular, based on our earlier discussion, it seems clear that the time frame needed depends on the character of the program and the corresponding time-related effect anticipated. For example, we argued that programs aimed at imparting particular skills or information will encounter the time dimension problem most commonly in the form of what we called "staying power" or "letdown" effects. At issue in such programs is the "half-life" of program-imparted benefits, the rate at which they wear off over time. To assess this kind of effect, a follow-up after eight months to a year is probably sufficient in order to determine the rate of change.

A slightly different situation applies with regard to programs involving efforts to inculcate new values or otherwise alter personality characteristics. Such programs, we suggested, are most likely to experience the time dimension problem in the form of "latent effects"—i.e., effects which are barely visible by the termination of the program, but which grow in strength as the program experience is absorbed and integrated into the individual's personality. To be sure, the opposite can also happen, especially via the Hawthorne effect. Under such circumstances, program impacts apparent at the termination of the program treatment would diminish over time, much as in the case of the staying power effects. To tap the possibility of latent effects in such programs, however, a time frame of at least two years is probably necessary.

For programs like the FSA's resettlement program, finally, which seek to alter prevailing social relations and structures of power, the situation is different again. Here the time dimension problem is likely to take the form of "sleeper effects," effects which are invisible while the program is in operation, but which surface later on. Clearly, to tap such effects, the evaluation time frame must be quite long—probably on the order of five years, at a minimum. Evaluators with a good grasp of the relevant social theory may, however, pick up some of these effects as early as three years after completion of the program.

Table 7 summarizes these rough rules of thumb concerning the time frame appropriate for different forms of social action program evaluations. To verify and substantiate these suggestions, however, it will be necessary to experiment far more extensively than has yet been done with measurements of different types of program impacts at different points in time.

Since few social action programs fall exclusively into only one of

Table 7. RECOMMENDED TIME FRAMES FOR EVALUATION OF
VARIOUS TYPES OF SOCIAL ACTION PROGRAMS

Focus of Program	Type of Time-Related Impact Anticipated	Recommended Time Frame
Improving skills	"Staying-power effects"	8 months-1 year
Changing values or personality	"Latent effects"	2 years
Alteration of social structure	"Sleeper effects"	3-5 years

the categories outlined in Table 7 and since evaluations stretching over even three years are not very likely, it seems clear that even the rough rules of thumb offered here will provide little solace to beleaguered evaluators. Accordingly, two further observations seem appropriate. The first is a call to modesty on the part of policy evaluators. In recent years, policy evaluation has come to be a catchword in national political debate as conservative opposition and liberal disaffection have combined to challenge the effectiveness of public initiatives. Though little of this challenge is based on systematic evaluative research, the general climate that it has produced will likely elevate the role of evaluation in the policy process. Unless evaluators remain alert to the profound dilemma that the time dimension creates in their work, however, the result will be to transform a promising tool of scientific inquiry into a pseudo-scientific ideological weapon. Evaluators must take special pains to acknowledge, therefore, how limited an array of potential program impacts they have been able to capture, given the restricted time span available for their research.

The second point that emerges from this discussion and that deserves emphasis is the need for greater attention to theory in evaluative research. Too often, evaluators proceed as if the task of evaluation were the purely mechanical one of measuring the extent to which a program has achieved its narrowly defined, avowed objectives, with little attention to the reasonableness of the link between program activities and expected effects. Such a mechanical approach is almost guaranteed to yield imperfect and incomplete results, even with the best of methodologies. What is needed in addition is a deeper theoretical sense that can alert evaluators to the full range of ramifications likely to flow from a program's activities and that can clarify the relationships between the program and the broader social environment. Theory is necessary, in other words, (1) to indicate what real world effects that reflect program objectives might reasonably be expected to flow from program activities, (2) to rescue evaluators from exclusive preoccupation with avowed program objectives to the neglect of implicit or unintended ones, and (3) to force evaluators to take account of what Harold Shepard (1970: 92) called "the broader reality frameworks" of social action efforts. Careful attention to methodology, in other words, is not enough. Methodology only helps choose the means for measuring impact. It is theory's function to determine which impacts to measure in the first place. A clear theoretical sense can, therefore, help alert an evaluator to the ways in which the time dimension will affect the validity of his findings and, in some cases, equip him to spot latent or sleeper effects in their incipient stages.

Social change is a complex process, frequently moving in strange ways, and by fits and starts, to work its effects. Evaluations of social action programs designed to promote such change must be equally resourceful, explicitly acknowledging the discontinuous nature of social processes and the likelihood that significant program impacts may be intentionally delayed. In this way the time dimension may come to be an ally rather than an adversary in policy research.

NOTES

1. Harold Seidman (1969: 164) called the "quest for coordination" that was particularly evident in the 1960s the "twentieth century equivalent of the medieval search for the philosopher's stone." (The "philosopher's stone" was, of course, the instrument medieval alchemists claimed would, if found, provide the key to the universe and solve all the problems of mankind.)

2. These dilemmas are so serious that some researchers doubt that evaluative research can ever be undertaken with anything approaching the objectivity and precision required (see, for example, Mann, 1965: 210). Others acknowledge the difficulties but are more sanguine about devising ways to cope with them (see, for example, Suchman, 1967; Wholey, 1970; Evans, 1972).

3. According to Cain and Hollister (1972: 127), "the outcomes we wish to measure from many social action programs occur months or years after the participants have completed the program." By the same token, Alice Rivlin (1971: 117) has stressed that "many of the really interesting effects of social action show up only after a period of years." (See also Suchman, 1967: 40; Wholey et al., 1970: 96; Hyman, 1962: 262; Brooks, 1965: 38-39.)

4. One survey of evaluations of federal manpower programs, for example, found only a handful that did not obtain their data at only one point in time (Glennan, 1972: 202). The well-known and elaborate Coleman report, which evaluated the impact of educational investments on student performance, likewise obtained its data at a single point in time. (For a critique of this report on these grounds, see Rivlin, 1971: 74). The well-known Westinghouse-Ohio State evaluation of the Head Start Program undertook to measure impacts over three years, but it did so by looking at *different students* in three different grades at one point in time, rather than following a given group of students for three years (see Williams and Evans, 1972: 254-259). (For other examples see Borus, 1964; Orfield, 1973).

5. The term "Hawthorne effect" originated in a study of determinants of worker productivity made at the Hawthorne Works of the Western Electric Company in Chicago in the late 1920s. As it turned out, output increased whenever management paid any attention to the workers, no matter what the nature of the attention. For example, increased output could be achieved by *either* increasing lighting or decreasing it. *Anything* new produced results. *International Encyclopedia of the Social Sciences*, 7(1968): 241.

6. Examples of this danger are abundant in evaluations of OEO programs. For example, the Westinghouse-Ohio State evaluation of Head Start was severely criticized by OEO staffers during the design phase because of its preoccupation with the educational

aspects of Head Start and its neglect of the health, nutritional, and community involvement goals (Williams and Evans, 1972). So, too, Marris and Rein (1967: 197) fault an early evaluation of the Boston poverty program on similar grounds, noting that the evaluators took a too narrow definition of the program's goals: "It does not take account of the institutional changes which the project hoped to stimulate, nor its general influence upon the poorer neighborhoods of Boston."

7. Rogers (1973: 80), for example, notes how the introduction of chemical fertilizer in Columbia increased agricultural efficiency so much that it prompted expanded rural migration to the urban slums and increased the power of liberal political parties. (See also Nie, 1969: 361-378.)

8. This is what Moynihan (1970: xiii-iv) claims happened with the OEO program: "A program was launched that was not understood and not explained, and this brought about social losses that need not have occurred." (For a contrary view, see Piven, 1971.)

9. The evaluation study reported here is adapted from a longer version being published in the Sage Professional Papers in American Politics series (see Salamon, forthcoming). Funding for this study was made available by the Office of Minority Business Enterprise of the U.S. Department of Commerce, to which I want to express my appreciation. Thanks are also due to Robert Sullivan, Marsha Darling, Romus Broadway, Albert Broussard, Alphine Jefferson, Joseph Carens, and David Perry for invaluable assistance in gathering the data.

10. Of these 141 agricultural projects, 59 were "community projects" involving sizeable tracts of land that were operated as community entities, and 82 were "scattered farm projects" involving numerous, noncontiguous smaller tracts of land. The remaining 60-odd projects were either subsistence homesteads that provided 5- to 10-acre plots of land or defense relocation projects begun in the 1940s. Because the resettlement project grouped together a host of undertakings launched by several different agencies, these numbers are necessarily rather rough. They are based on material available in the following sources: House Appropriations Committee, 1946: 1390; Conkin, 1959; Holley, 1972: 53-65; Baldwin, 1968: 111-113, 214-217, 336-339; Sterner, 1943: 307-309, 423-424; House Agriculture Committee, 1943: 1124-1131.

11. In one of the few academic evaluations of the resettlement experience, for example, the author took pains to stress that "not enough time has elapsed to permit a mature judging of the results" (Wehrwein, 1937: 190; Salter, 1937: 208-210).

12. On the absence of evaluative research on the New Deal social welfare programs generally see Rossi, 1972: 12-13; Moynihan, 1969: 167.

13. On the absence of this theoretical sense in most evaluations, see Kiesler, 1973: 340.

14. The tenant sample was compiled with the aid of a random number table applied to the lists of tenant farmers available in the local offices of the U.S. Department of Agriculture's Agricultural Stabilization and Conservation Service. The number of tenants in the sample from each county was designed to make it proportional to the number of resettlement project participants interviewed in that county, thus guaranteeing some symmetry in the experimental and control group samples.

REFERENCES

ALEXANDER, W. (1936). "Rural resettlement." Southern Review, 1.

ALINSKY, S. (1965). "The war on poverty: Political pornography." Journal of Social Issues, 21: 40-48.

ARENSBERG, C. M., and NIEHOFF, A. H. (1964). Introducing Social Change. Chicago: Aldine.

BALDWIN, S. (1968). Poverty and Politics: The Rise and Decline of the Farm Security Administration. Chapel Hill: University of North Carolina Press.

BANFIELD, E. (1958). The Moral Basis of a Backward Society. New York: Free Press.

——— (1969). The Unheavenly City. Boston: Little, Brown.

BORUS, M. E. (1964). "A benefit-cost analysis of the economic effectiveness of retraining the unemployed." Yale Economic Essays, 4(Fall).

BROOKS, M. P. (1965). "The community action program as a setting for applied research." Journal of Social Issues, 21(January): 29-41.

CAIN, G. G., and HOLLISTER, R. G. (1972). "The methodology of evaluating social action programs." In P. Rossi and W. Williams (eds.), The Methodology of Evaluating Social Action Programs. New York: Academic.

COLEMAN, J. S. (1973). "Conflicting theories of social change." Pp. 61-74 in G. Zaltman (ed.), Processes and Phenomena of Social Change. New York: John Wiley.

CONKIN, P. (1959). Tomorrow a New World: The New Deal Community Program. Ithaca: Cornell University Press.

DAVIS, A.; GARDNER, B. B.; and GARNDER, M. R. (1941). Deep South: A Social-Anthropological Study of Caste and Class. Chicago: University of Chicago Press.

DOLLARD, J. (1957). Caste and Class in Southerntown (3rd ed.). Garden City, N.Y.: Doubleday.

DRUCKER, P. (1969). "The sickness of government." Public Interest, (Winter): 3-10.

GLENNAN, T. K., Jr. (1972). "Evaluating federal manpower programs: Notes and observations." Pp. 187-220 in P. H. Rossi and W. Williams (eds.), Evaluating Social Programs. New York: Seminar.

HAGEN, E. (1972). On the Theory of Social Change. Homewood, Ill.: Dorsey.

HOLLEY, D. (1972). "The Negro in the New Deal Resettlement Program." New South, 27(Winter): 53-65.

HYMAN, H. H.; WRIGHT, C. R.; and HOPKINS, T. K. (1962). Applications of Methods of Evaluation: Four Studies of the Encampment for Citizenship. Berkeley: University of California Press.

JOHNSON, C. S.; EMBREE, E.; and ALEXANDER, W. (1936). The Collapse of Cotton Tenancy. Chapel Hill: University of North Carolina Press.

KIESLER, C. A. (1973). "Evaluating social change programs." In G. Zaltman (ed.), Phenomena of Social Change. New York: John Wiley.

KRAMER, R. M. (1969). Participation of the Poor: Comparative Community Case Studies in the War on Poverty. Englewood Cliffs, N.J.: Prentice-Hall.

MANN, J. (1965). Changing Human Behavior. New York: Scribner's.

MARRIS, P., and REIN, M. (1967). Dilemmas of Social Reform. Chicago: Aldine.

——— (1973). Dilemmas of Social Reform: Poverty and Community Action in the United States (2nd ed.). Chicago: Aldine.

McCLELLAND, D. M. (1961). The Achieving Society. Princeton, N.J.: Van Nostrand.

MERTON, R. K. (1957). "Social structure and anomie: Continuities." In Social Theory and Social Structure. Glencoe, Ill.: Free Press.

MILLER, W. B. (1958). "Lower class culture as a generating milieu of gang delinquency." Journal of Social Issues, 14: 5-19.

MOODY, A. (1957). Coming of Age in Mississippi. New York: Dial.

MOYNIHAN, D. P. (1969). Maximum Feasible Misunderstanding. New York: Basic Books.

MYRDAL, G. (1944). An American Dilemma: The Negro Problem and Modern Democracy. New York: Harper & Row.

NIE, N. (1969). "Social structure and political participation: Developmental relationships." American Political Science Review, 63: 361-378.

NOBLE, J. H., Jr. (1970). "The uncertainty of evaluative research as a guide to social policy." Pp. 451-459 in L. A. Zurcher and C. M. Bonjean (eds.), Planned Social Intervention. Scranton, Pa.: Chandler.

ORFIELD, G. (1973). "School integration and its academic critics: Busing studies—their validity and political uses." Civil Rights Digest (Summer): 2-10.

PIVEN, F. F. (1971). "Federal interventions in the cities: The new urban programs as a political strategy." In E. D. Smigel (ed.), Handbook on the Study of Social Problems. Chicago: Rand McNally.

POWDERMAKER, H. (1969). After Freedom: A Cultural Study in the Deep South. New York: Russell and Russell.

RIECKEN, H. W. (1952). The Volunteer Work Camp: A Psychological Evaluation. Reading, Mass.: Addison-Wesley.

RIVLIN, A. (1971). Systematic Thinking for Social Action. Washington, D.C.: Brookings Institution.

ROGERS, E. M. (1973). "Social structure and social change." Pp. 75-88 in G. Zaltman (ed.), Processes and Phenomena of Social Change. New York: John Wiley.

ROSSI, P. (1970). "No good idea goes unpunished: Moynihan's misunderstandings and the proper role of social science in policy making." In L. Zurcher and C. M. Bonjean (eds.), Planned Social Intervention: An Interdisciplinary Anthology. Scranton, Pa.: Chandler.

ROSSI, P., and WILLIAMS, W. (eds., 1972). Evaluating Social Programs. New York: Academic Press.

SALAMON, L. M., and VAN EVERA, S. (1973). "Fear, apathy, and discrimination: A test of three explanations of political participation." American Political Science Review, 67(December): 1288-1306.

SALAMON, L. M. (forthcoming). The Time Dimension in Policy Evaluation: The Case of the New Deal Land Reform Experiments.

SCHNEIDERMAN, L. (1964). "Value orientation preferences of chronic relief recipients." Social Work, 9(July): 13-18.

SEIDMAN, H. (1970). Politics, Position, and Power: The Dynamics of Federal Organization. New York: Oxford University Press.

SHEPPARD, H. L. (1970). "Some broader reality frameworks for anti-poverty intervention." Pp. 92-98 in L. A. Zurcher and C. M. Bonjean (eds.), Planned Social Intervention: An Interdisciplinary Anthology. Scranton, Pa.: Chandler.

SILVER, J. (1963). Mississippi: The Closed Society. New York: Harcourt Brace Jovanovich.

STERNER, R. (1943). The Negro's Share: A Study of Income, Consumption, Housing and Public Assistance. New York: Harper.

SUCHMAN, E. A. (1967). Evaluative Research: Principles and Practices in Public Service and Social Action Programs. New York: Russell Sage Foundation.

TUGWELL, R. (1936). "Changing acres." Current History, 44(September).

––– (1937). "Cooperation and resettlement." Current History, 45(February).

U.S. Civil Rights Commission (1968). Political Participation. Washington, D.C.: Government Printing Office.

U.S. Congress, House Agriculture Committee, Select Committee to Investigate the FSA (1943). Report (78th Cong., 1st sess.).

U.S. Congress, House Appropriations Committee (1946). Hearings on the Agriculture Department Appropriation Bill for 1947 (79th Cong., 2nd sess.).

VANECKO, J. J. (1970). "Community mobilization and institutional change: The influence of the community action program in large cities." In L. J. Zurcher and C. M. Bonjean (eds.), Planned Social Intervention: An Interdisciplinary Anthology. Scranton, Pa.: Chandler.

WEHRWEIN, G. S. (1937). "Appraisal of resettlement." Journal of Farm Economics, 19.

WHOLEY, J.; SCANLON, J. W.; DUFFY, H. D.; FUKUMOTO, J. S.; and VOGT, L. M. (1970). Federal Evaluation Policy: Analyzing the Effects of Public Programs. Washington, D.C.: Urban Institute.

WILLIAMS, W., and EVANS, J. (1972). "The politics of evaluation." In P. Rossi and W. Williams (eds.), Evaluating Social Programs. New York: Academic Press.

WOOFTER, J. J., Jr. (1930). Black Yeomanry: Life on St. Helena Island. New York: Holt.

ZALTMAN, G. (ed., 1973). Processes and Phenomena of Social Change. New York: John Wiley.

ZURCHER, L. A. (1970). "Functional marginality: Dynamics of poverty intervention organization." Pp. 289-299 in L. A. Zurcher and C. M. Bonjean (eds.), Planned Social Intervention. Scranton, Pa.: Chandler.

ABOUT THE CONTRIBUTORS

CHRISTA ALTENSTETTER is presently Visiting Research Professor at the Fogarty International Center of the National Institute of Health. She was educated as a political scientist in both the United States and Europe. Her work involves research on comparative health care systems.

BRUCE P. BALL is Assistant Professor of Government and Coordinator of the Master of Public Administration (MPA) program at Angelo State University in San Angelo, Texas. Dr. Ball received his Ph.D. in Government at the University of Arizona. His publications include two staff papers prepared while he was a research associate with the South Dakota Legislative Research Council (*Agencies Administering Health and Welfare Services in South Dakota* and *Funding and Administration of Higher Education Facilities in South Dakota*). As Director of Metropolitan Region Studies at the University of Wisconsin, River Falls, he published "Urbanization in St. Croix and Paire Counties" and *The Undergraduate Internships Technique: An Essay on Program Development.*

JAMES WARNER BJORKMAN received a B.A. from the University of Minnesota in 1966 and a Ph.D. from Yale in 1976. He has held fellowships granted by the Woodrow Wilson Foundation, the Falk Foundation, the National Science Foundation, and the Foreign Area Fellowship Program. A political scientist with specialties in comparative administration and public policy, he has conducted research in Lebanon, India, and the United States and has published articles on development administration, foreign affairs, American food policy, and professionalism. At present he is a research staff scientist at the Yale School of Medicine.

RUFUS P. BROWNING teaches data analysis, public administration, and public policy at San Francisco State University, where he chairs the Department of Political Science. Previously he has published work on computer simulation, budgetary decision making, motivation, and bargaining, contributing most recently to the *Handbook of Political Psychology.*

CHARLES N. BROWNSTEIN is a program manager at the National Science Foundation and is responsible for applied policy research projects in advanced applications of new telecommunications technology, social effects of television, and other areas related to telecommunications policy. He was previously a member of the Government Department at Lehigh University, specializing in policy evaluation and political communications teaching and research. He received a B.A. in English and an M.A. in Political Science from Temple University and a Ph.D. in Government from Florida State University.

SHELDON EDNER is Assistant Professor of Political Science at Eastern Michigan University. Dr. Edner received his Ph.D. at the University of California, Riverside. From 1973 to 1974 he was associated with the Ohio Environmental Protection Agency, Division of Intergovernmental Administration.

CHARLES O. JONES is Maurice Falk Professor of Politics at the University of Pittsburgh. He was written articles and books on Congress, political parties, and public policy. His most recent work is *Clean Air: The Policies and Politics of Pollution Control* (1975). Professor Jones was recently selected as the next managing editor of the *American Political Science Review.*

SARAH F. LIEBSCHUTZ is a Research Associate at the Brookings Institution, where she is associated with the institution's general revenue sharing and community development block grant programs. She is currently on leave as Assistant Professor of Political Science at SUNY, Brockport. Since enactment of the State and Local Fiscal Assistance Act of 1972, she has monitored for Brookings the uses of general revenue sharing in the Rochester SMSA. Her publications include articles in the political socialization and urban policy fields. She received her Ph.D. from the University of Rochester.

DALE ROGERS MARSHALL is Associate Professor of Political Science at the University of California, Davis. She received her Ph.D.

from UCLA and has also taught urban politics and public administration at UC, Berkeley, and at UCLA. She is the author of many articles and *The Politics of Participation in Poverty: A Case Study of the Board of the Economic and Youth Opportunities Agency of Greater Los Angeles;* and with J. Bollens she coauthored *Guide to Participation: Field Work, Role Playing Cases, and Other Forms.*

STUART S. NAGEL is Professor of Political Science at the University of Illinois and a member of the Illinois bar. He is the coordinator of the *Policy Studies Journal* and the secretary-treasurer of the Policy Studies Organization and has been Series Editor of the Sage Yearbooks in Politics and Public Policy since its inception. He is the author or editor of *Policy Studies and the Social Sciences, Policy Studies in America and Elsewhere, Improving the Legal Process, Effects of Alternatives, Environmental Politics, The Rights of the Accused: In Law and Action,* and *The Legal Process from a Behavioral Perspective.* He has been an attorney to the Office of Economic Opportunity, Lawyers Constitutional Defense Committee in Mississippi, National Labor Relations Board, and the U.S. Senate Subcommittee on Administrative Practice and Procedure.

RICHARD P. NATHAN is Director, Brookings Institution study of general revenue sharing, and Secretary-Treasurer, Manpower Demonstration Research Corporation. He is presently Visiting Professor at the University of Virginia. Dr. Nathan received his Ph.D. in Political Economy and Government from Harvard University in 1966. He is the author of several articles and books, including *Monitoring Revenue Sharing* with A. D. Manvel and S. E. Calkins and *The Plot That Failed: Nixon and the Administrative Presidency.* From 1971 to 1972, Dr. Nathan was Deputy Under Secretary, HEW.

DAVID O. PORTER is Associate Professor of Administration and Political Science at the University of California, Riverside, and a Research Fellow (1975-1977) at the International Institute of Management, Berlin. He was a NASPAA Public Administration Fellow in 1972-1973 and has written several articles and a monograph on fiscal federalism and grants-in-aid.

BRUCE A. ROCHELEAU is Assistant Professor of Political Science at Northern Illinois University. He received his Ph.D. from the University of Florida in 1972. He is currently a consultant to the

Illinois Department of Mental Health. Dr. Rocheleau has written several papers on public policy and analysis of the aged and evaluation research. Other works include books on evaluation research (*The Technology and Impact of Evaluation* and *Without Tears or Bombast: A Guide to Program Evaluation*).

LESTER M. SALAMON is Associate Professor of Political Science and Policy Sciences at Duke University. He received his Ph.D. from Harvard University. Specializing in the politics of social and economic change, urban politics, and policy analysis, he has written articles for the *American Political Science Review*, the *Journal of Politics*, and *World Politics*. Other recent works include books on congressional housing and banking policy and on modernization in the American South.

ROBERT D. THOMAS is Associate Professor of Political Science at Florida Atlantic University. He served as a NASPAA public administration fellow with the U.S. Environmental Protection Agency in 1973. His publications are in the fields of state and local government, intergovernmental relations, and public administration.

CARL E. VAN HORN is a Research Associate at the Mershon Center of The Ohio State University. He received his Ph.D. from Ohio State in 1976. He is the author of articles on policy analysis and Congress, and his current research includes a study of the implementation of the Comprehensive Employment and Training Act (CETA).

DONALD S. VAN METER is Associate Professor of Political Science at The Ohio State University. He received a Ph.D. from the University of Wisconsin in 1972. He is the author of a number of articles on policy analysis and political methodology that have appeared in such journals as *Administration and Society*, *Political Methodology*, *Sage Professional Papers in American Politics*, and *Policy Studies Journal*. He is also the coauthor of *Policy and Politics in American Governments*.